The Best Quick Breads

BETH HENSPERGER

AUTHOR OF *THE BREAD BIBLE*, A JAMES BEARD AWARD WINNER

The Best Quick Breads

150 Recipes for Muffins, Scones, Shortcakes, Gingerbreads, Cornbreads, Coffeecakes, *and More*

The Harvard Common Press

Boston, Massachusetts

The Harvard Common Press
535 Albany Street
Boston, Massachusetts 02118

Some of the recipes in this book are revised and updated versions of recipes that appeared in Beth Hensperger's *The Art of Quick Breads* (now out of print).

Printed in the United States of America

Printed on acid-free paper

Library of Congress Cataloging-in-Publication Data

Hensperger, Beth.
    [Art of quick breads]
    The best quick breads : 150 recipes for muffins, scones, shortcakes, gingerbreads, cornbreads, coffeecakes, and more / Beth Hensperger.
        p. cm.
    Originally published under title: The art of quick breads. San Francisco : Chronicle Books, 1994.
        ISBN 1-55832-171-3 (pbk. : alk. paper)
        1. Bread. I. Title.

TX769.H427 2000
641.8'15—dc21   00-036962

Special bulk-order discounts are available on this and other Harvard Common Press books. Companies and organizations may purchase books for premiums or resale, or may arrange a custom edition, by contacting the Marketing Director at the address above.

10   9   8   7   6   5   4   3   2   1

For my mother

Contents

Inspiration in the Kitchen

Good quick breads are made from good recipes. This book contributes traditional-style recipes that bake to perfection and have an exceptionally pleasing taste. Breads of all types are blessed with the mystical ability to satisfy much more than mere physical hunger, and for a small amount of effort in the kitchen, they offer the reward of great eating pleasure. Quick breads in particular offer something that modern bakers value: ease of preparation. They are leavened not with the time-consuming demands of yeast, but with baking powder and soda, which respond immediately to moisture and the heat of the oven. All quick breads are so easy, they can be baked fresh for every meal.

Quick loaves (or tea breads), cornbreads, gingerbreads, pancakes, waffles, crêpes, popovers, and coffee cakes are "batter" breads, easy to spot because they do not hold their own shapes and are baked in molds of varying shapes and sizes. In most recipes of this type, liquid and dry ingredients will be in equal proportion. In contrast, biscuits, scones, soda breads, shortcakes, and cobbler toppings are known as "quick dough" breads, with a dough that is stiff enough to be hand-shaped and baked on flat pans. They have a higher percentage of dry ingredients to liquid than the batter breads.

Quick breads are very much like cakes in that they demand precise combinations of liquid, leavening, flour, fat, and flavorings. All the components are important and create a balanced chemical equation, making the home baker an alchemist of sorts. Professional bakers look at these components in a bit more scientific light: The liquids (water, milk, buttermilk, eggs, honey, syrups) moisten and lengthen storage time; dry ingredients (flour, dry milk) give the quick bread its body, bind all the ingredients together, and absorb and retain moisture; the tenderizers (fats, sugar, egg yolks, chocolate, sour cream, yogurt) give a soft, delicate texture; leaveners (baking powder, baking soda, eggs) are added to provide volume and lightness; and, finally, the flavorings (chocolate, eggs, butter, citrus, coffee, nuts, salt, extracts) dictate and enhance the overall taste of the bread. Old-fashioned quick breads may be served at any time of the day: toasted for breakfast, alongside egg dishes for brunch, with crisp fruit or vegetable salads, as a sandwich with a variety of spreads or meats, sliced and served hot for a snack, or for tea parties with fresh fruit or a bit of cheese. Most freeze beautifully and are thus ready to be thawed and served at any time.

Quick breads are economical as well as easy to mix and bake. Once you master the basic techniques, you will be able to produce a staggering variety of batter or dough breads. Many of the recipes can be prepared with a few quick steps and are ready for the oven in under 15 minutes. Except for a few large-sized loaves and coffee cakes, all recipes bake in under 1 hour.

Although all the recipes are written to provide the necessary information to produce a wonderful baked good, the end section titled "Notes from the Kitchen" gives extra helpful tips on techniques, ingredients, and basic recipes, equipment, and extraordinary mail-order resources. Use it as a reference guide when baking all types of quick breads for information as diverse as where to mail-order pure maple or cane syrups and how to make coconut milk, to techniques for adapting your recipes with light baking ingredients. Although quick breads can be deceptively plain looking, whether free-form or molded, they are deliciously rich, moist-textured, and uncomplicated in flavor. The simple batters offer the perfect vehicle for showcasing seasonal ingredients. This genre of baking is a wondrous combination of improvisation, inspiration, and nostalgia—a simple pleasure for both experienced and beginning bakers.

Loaves

Quick Loaves

Quick loaves rely exclusively on the power of chemical leaveners to make their batters light and fluffy. Before the invention of the baking powder mixture by a German inventor in the late 1800s, loaves were compact and dense, usually raised with yeast, naturally fermented starters, beer, or eggs. Early Americans used saleratus (an early form of bicarbonate of soda converted from sea salt), hartshorn (the ground antler of a male deer, the chief source of ammonia), cream of tartar, and pearlash (ashes from wood, seaweed, pea, or bean stalks) for leavening home quick breads, each with its own pronounced flavor. All of these forms of leavening were at times scarce and often unreliable, producing baked goods of inconsistent quality.

Because of the capricious nature of these leavenings, early cookbooks advised bakers to keep the oven shut during baking, to avoid drafts, to dissolve leavenings in water to prevent black spots, to beat batters laboriously by hand for long periods, and never to let a finished batter stand, as it would lose its slightly raised texture very quickly. Adding to the baker's difficulties was the fact that these loaves were often baked in wood cookstoves, known for their quick, intense, and uneven heat. Although some of these directions might still be included in a modern recipe, most are leftovers from another era, made unnecessary by today's reliable leaveners and consistent ingredients.

Modern baking powders are double acting, which means that they begin to rise as soon as the leavening is moistened in the batter and then again during the baking process. Most of the carbon dioxide produced gets released in the oven, making a stable batter that bakes into a high, light bread. With double-acting baking powders, batters can rest overnight in the refrigerator and still bake into an excellent loaf. Aluminum sulfate, a common ingredient in commercial baking powder, can be tasted in quick breads by some people, so I recommend a nonaluminum baking powder sold under the commercial name of Rumford. For more information on leavenings and how to make your own single-acting baking powder, which makes a tender and flavorful baked good, see Notes from the Kitchen, page 325.

The modern quick loaf is a purely American product, with a taste and texture between a yeasted bread and a sweet cake. A large assortment of breads can be made by a simple variation in ingredients. They are delicious with added seasonal fresh or dried fruits or accented with luscious liqueurs, chunks of mellow nuts, creamy cheeses, aromatic herbs, and pungent exotic spices.

One of the most important techniques in baking quick loaves is beating the wet ingredients with a whisk or electric mixer to aerate and expand their total volume. The mixture will double, becoming thick and creamy at the same time. The dry ingredients are mixed separately, with all the leavenings evenly distributed. All intense beating is done while these two mixtures are separate. The dry and the wet ingredients are then mixed together with a quick and light hand (never beat them unless you are specifically directed to do so) to avoid activating the gluten in the flour. Most batters are immediately scraped or poured into greased pans to bake in a preheated moderate oven. Breads made with baking powder improve in texture and flavor by rising for 15 to 20 minutes at room temperature before going into the oven.

Recipes need to be followed exactly, with the mixing done in the manner outlined in each recipe. The proper oven temperature is important for "oven spring," the final expanding of

the batter when it comes in contact with heat. Bake quick loaves on the middle shelf with at least two inches of space between each pan to allow the heat to circulate. When baking on two shelves, make sure the pans are staggered for even baking. A quick loaf is finished baking when the top looks and feels firm and dry; when the edges pull away from the sides of the pan slightly; when the top of the loaf is evenly browned; and when a cake tester inserted into the center comes out dry. If the center is still gooey, continue to bake the loaf for another 5 to 8 minutes. When the bread is done, immediately turn it out of its hot pan onto a rack and then turn it right side up to cool, allowing air to circulate around it. Loaves that are more cakelike in texture can stand for 15 minutes to firm up slightly before being turned out of their pans.

Quick loaves are easier to slice if they are allowed to cool completely, and their flavors and textures are best after the loaves stand overnight. Always use a good serrated knife for even slicing. Loaves store well at room temperature unless they contain chunks of cheese or other dairy products that can spoil easily, in which case they should be refrigerated. Whether stored at room temperature or in the refrigerator, the loaves should be tightly wrapped in plastic. Properly stored, quick loaves will retain good flavor and texture for up to one week. Quick loaves also keep perfectly for up to 3 months in the freezer, wrapped in freezer bags or in plastic wrap and then foil. Often it is nice to make double quantities so you can enjoy some later. Let the wrapped loaves thaw to room temperature before serving.

These loaves are never frosted in the traditional manner of more elaborate cakes, although they are sometimes drizzled with a thin sugar glaze or shiny coating of a sweet counterpoint flavor. For a pretty finish, try dusting the loaves with a mist of sifted plain powdered sugar or your own homemade Blossom- and Leaf-Scented Sugar (page 327). Serve tea loaves plain or with butter or cream cheese spreads, alongside fruit or vegetable salads. They also make excellent sandwiches filled with seafood, meat, or poultry. Savory loaves are good with light meals and are wonderful toasted.

Batter breads can be made in a variety of appealing fluted molds, as well as rectangular loaves, because the batter is too liquid to retain its own shape and takes the shape of the pan it bakes in. Unique alternatives to the traditional rectangular loaf shapes are mini-Bundt or tube pans (small patterned ring molds), charlotte molds, and half-loaf pans, reminiscent of the ridged, half-moon European *rehrücken* loaf pan or guttered mold. Using the correct pan size and filling it only one-half to two-thirds full is important to allow the batter to climb as it rises and to dome attractively. A recipe containing 2 cups of flour will bake perfectly into a rectangular 8- or 9-inch loaf or fill a 6-cup mini-Bundt pan, a pan of 12 muffins, an 8-inch charlotte mold, or three 5- or 6-inch loaf pans. Just remember, if the batter is divided among pans smaller than the size given in the recipe, the bread will require less time to bake.

Troubleshooting Quick Loaves

Soggy Texture with a Sunken Middle:
—Too much liquid in proportion to the dry ingredients in the recipe
—Too little total leavening or leavenings not potent
—Batter left too long before baking

Crack along the Center of the Top Surface:
—Characteristic of a good quick loaf, indicating expansion during baking

—To eliminate the crack, let the batter rise slightly at room temperature for 20 minutes before baking

Coarse, Crumbly Texture:
—Too much fat in proportion to the other ingredients in the recipe
—Too much leavening

Greasy with Crisp Edges:
—Too much fat in proportion to the other ingredients

Thick, Porous, and Overly Browned Crust:
—Too much sugar in proportion to the other ingredients
—Oven temperature too high

Tough-Textured:
—Batter overhandled during the mixing
—Oven temperature too high

Bitter or Soapy Aftertaste:
—Too much baking powder or baking soda

Hungarian Sour Cream Poundcake

Like so many quick-bread bakers, I have a passion for poundcakes. Of course they are dense and rich—they're meant to be. Here is my favorite version, an old Hungarian family recipe made in a Bundt pan, rather than in a loaf shape. Display your beautiful creation at your next family brunch by serving it on a pedestal cake plate. Poundcakes are never iced, but crushed fresh berries are a nice accompaniment, and Brandied Fruit (recipe follows) is a real treat. Use left-overs as a base for trifles, to create the ricotta-filled Italian cassata layer cake, or grind the crumbs to use as a filling for baked apples and peaches. Day-old poundcake is also great gently toasted in thick slices and spread with jam for breakfast. Store this cake at room temperature for up to 5 days wrapped airtight, refrigerate it for 1 to 2 weeks, or freeze it for up to 3 months.

Makes one 10-inch Bundt cake

1 cup (2 sticks) unsalted butter, at room
  temperature
2¾ cups sugar
6 large eggs
3 cups unbleached all-purpose flour
½ teaspoon salt

¼ teaspoon baking powder
¼ teaspoon baking soda
1¼ cups sour cream
2½ teaspoons vanilla extract
Brandied Fruit (optional), following

1 · Preheat the oven to 350°F (325°F if you are using a dark-cast pan). Grease and flour a 12-cup Bundt pan. In a large mixing bowl with an electric mixer, cream the butter and sugar until light and fluffy, 3 minutes. Add the eggs, one at a time, beating well after each addition.

2 · In a small bowl, combine the flour, salt, baking powder, and baking soda. With the mixer running on low speed, add the flour mixture to the butter mixture in three batches, alternating with the sour cream, adding the vanilla with one of the sour cream additions. Beat until well blended and very fluffy.

3 · With a large spatula, scrape the batter into the prepared pan. Bake in the center of the oven until the top is golden brown and crusty and a cake tester inserted into the center comes out clean, about 75 minutes. Let the cake cool in the pan for 10 minutes before turning it out of the pan and setting

it upright on a rack to cool completely. To serve, slice the poundcake into wedges. Use a slotted spoon to top each slice with some of the Brandied Fruit, if desired, and add some of the syrup, if you wish.

Brandied Fruit

Makes 1 quart brandied fruit

3 to 4 cups pitted or unpitted sweet cherries (with the stems still attached if you wish) or halved and pitted fresh plums, about 2 pounds
2 cups sugar
8 whole cloves
4-inch cinnamon stick, broken
2-inch piece vanilla bean
1¼ cups water
Cherry Marnier or Kirschwasser or brandy or *eau de vie* (pear or quince are favorites)

1 · Place the fruit in a clean wide-mouth glass quart jar (I use the springtop style and run it through the dishwasher first). The fruit will almost fill the jar.

2 · Combine the sugar, spices, vanilla bean, and water in a small saucepan. Bring to a boil to dissolve the sugar. Boil 1 minute without stirring. Remove from the heat and let cool for 10 minutes. Pour the spiced sugar syrup, with the whole spices, into the jar over the fruit and top off with brandy (I use brandy or *eau de vie* for the plums and Cherry Marnier or Kirschwasser for the cherries) just to cover. Let cool completely, cover, and refrigerate for 3 days to 1 week before serving. Brandied fruit will keep in the refrigerator for 3 months, with the flavor becoming stronger as the fruit sits.

Chocolate and Brown Sugar Poundcake

I enjoy plain sour cream poundcake so much that I devised a chocolate version. The idea to glaze it and serve it with a creamy whipped topping and strawberries came from Gourmet *magazine. What a hit!*

Makes one 10-inch Bundt cake

1 cup plus 2 tablespoons (2¼ sticks)
  unsalted butter, at room temperature
1⅔ cups granulated sugar
½ cup packed light brown sugar
½ cup packed dark brown sugar
5 large eggs
2½ cups unbleached all-purpose flour
¾ cup unsweetened Dutch-process cocoa
  powder
½ teaspoon salt
½ teaspoon baking powder
½ teaspoon baking soda

1 cup (8 ounces) sour cream
1 tablespoon vanilla extract

Chocolate Glaze
3½ ounces bittersweet chocolate, chopped
2 tablespoons unsalted butter
1 tablespoon Kahlua

Brown Sugar Whipped Cream, following
2 pints fresh strawberries, washed and cut
  in half, for serving

1 · Grease and flour a 12-cup Bundt pan. In a large mixing bowl with an electric mixer, cream the butter and sugars until light and fluffy, 4 minutes. Add the eggs, one at a time, beating well after each addition.

2 · In a small bowl, combine the flour, cocoa, salt, baking powder, and baking soda. On low speed, add the flour mixture to the butter mixture in three batches, alternating with the sour cream, adding the vanilla with one of the sour cream additions. Beat until well blended and very fluffy.

3 · With a large spatula, scrape the batter into the prepared pan. Place the pan in a cold oven. Set the oven to 350°F (325°F if you are using a dark-cast pan). Bake in the center of the oven until the top is golden brown and crusty and a cake tester inserted into the center comes out clean, about 75

minutes. Let the cake cool in the pan for 10 minutes before turning it out of the pan and setting it upright on a rack to cool.

4 · To make the glaze: Melt the chocolate, butter, and Kahlua together in the top of a double boiler over simmering water. Stir with a whisk until smooth. Scrape the mixture into a pastry bag fitted with a small plain tip (#3) or place in a heavy-duty plastic freezer bag and snip off one corner to make a small ⅛-inch hole. Pipe the glaze back and forth over the top of the warm cake, letting the excess drip down the sides. The glaze will firm as the cake cools. Serve slices of poundcake with Brown Sugar Whipped Cream and fresh strawberries.

Brown Sugar Whipped Cream

Makes 2½ cups whipped cream

½ cup cold heavy cream
2 tablespoons packed dark brown sugar, or
  to taste
½ teaspoon vanilla extract
1½ cups sour cream

In a chilled mixing bowl with an electric mixer, whip the heavy cream, brown sugar, and vanilla until very thick. Beat the sour cream with a whisk until smooth and thinned out a bit; then fold it into the whipped cream. (This topping can be made a day ahead and refrigerated, tightly covered.)

Lemon–Poppy Seed Bread

The aromatic poppy seed is a favorite crunchy addition to quick breads. In specialty stores you may find Dutch blue poppy seeds, the highest in quality and very sweet. Store poppy seeds in the freezer to prevent rancidity because, like nuts, they have a high oil content. Lemon–Poppy Seed Bread is completely addictive, so you may want to double the recipe.

Makes one 9-by-5-inch loaf

3 tablespoons fresh poppy seeds
½ cup milk
5 tablespoons unsalted butter, at room
  temperature
1 cup sugar
2 large eggs
1½ cups unbleached all-purpose flour

1 teaspoon baking powder
Grated zest of 2 lemons
¼ teaspoon salt

Lemon Syrup
¼ cup sugar
¼ cup fresh lemon juice

1 · In a small bowl, combine the poppy seeds and milk. Let stand for 1 hour to macerate and meld flavors.

2 · Preheat the oven to 325°F. Grease a 9-by-5-inch loaf pan or spray it with cooking spray. Using an electric mixer, cream the butter and sugar. Add the eggs one at a time, beating well after each addition. Combine the flour, baking powder, lemon zest, and salt in a small bowl. Add the dry ingredients to the creamed mixture in three equal portions, alternating with the poppy seed milk. Beat just until smooth.

3 · Pour the batter into the prepared loaf pan and bake in the center of the oven until golden brown and a cake tester inserted into the center of the loaf comes out clean, about 55 to 65 minutes. Place the loaf, still in its pan, on a rack to cool.

4 · About 10 minutes before the bread is finished baking, make the Lemon Syrup: Combine the sugar and lemon juice in a small saucepan. Place over low heat just until the sugar dissolves.

5 · Pierce the hot loaf about a dozen times to the bottom with a bamboo skewer, toothpick, or metal cake tester. Immediately pour the hot Lemon Syrup over the loaf. Cool for 30 minutes before turning it out of the pan onto a rack, then turning it right side up to cool completely. Wrap tightly in plastic wrap and let stand at room temperature overnight before serving.

VARIATION:

Lemon–Poppy Seed Bread with Saffron

Add ⅛ teaspoon powdered saffron to the milk in Step 1. Continue to mix the batter, bake, and glaze as instructed.

Cranberry-Orange Tea Bread

Cranberries, called sassamanesh *by northeastern Native Americans, range in color from a lusty, deep pink to a deep crimson, appearing in time to announce the arrival of the fall harvest. The cranberry is, surprisingly, a member of the rhododendron and heather families. In combination with other ingredients, sweetened and cooked, the fruit is a boon to creative cooks because of its delightfully tangy flavor. Cranberries can be frozen in bags and used un-thawed, any time of year, in recipes calling for fresh cranberries. Serve this bread thinly sliced, with sweet butter or whipped cream cheese.*

Makes one 8-by-4-inch loaf

1½ cups whole fresh cranberries
1 cup sugar
2 cups unbleached all-purpose flour
1 tablespoon baking powder
½ teaspoon fresh-ground nutmeg
¼ teaspoon ground ginger
¼ teaspoon salt

Grated zest of 2 oranges
½ cup walnuts, chopped
¾ cup orange juice
2 large eggs
1 teaspoon vanilla extract
4 tablespoons (½ stick) unsalted butter, melted

1 · Preheat the oven to 350°F. Grease and flour an 8-by-4-inch loaf pan or spray it with cooking spray. Combine the cranberries and sugar in the workbowl of a food processor fitted with the steel blade. Pulse to coarsely grind. Set aside.

2 · In a large bowl, combine the flour, baking powder, spices, and salt. Add the orange zest and walnuts. Toss to blend.

3 · In a small bowl, combine the orange juice and eggs. Beat with a whisk until frothy. Add the vanilla extract and cranberry mixture and stir to combine. Pour over the dry ingredients and drizzle with the melted butter. Stir with a large spatula just until the batter is moistened and the cranberries are evenly distributed.

4 · Pour the batter into the prepared loaf pan. Bake in the center of the oven for 45 to 50 minutes, or until a cake tester inserted into the center comes out

clean. The top of the loaf should be crusty and golden. Turn the loaf out of the pan onto a rack, then turn it right side up to cool completely. Wrap tightly in plastic wrap and let stand at room temperature overnight before serving.

Pear Bread with Vanilla and Ginger

Vanilla is the strong-scented, dried pod of a tropical orchid native to Mexico, Madagascar, Tahiti, Java, and the Seychelles. It was introduced to Europe via Spain after the Mexican conquest. Ginger, a sturdy East Indian perennial whose root is spicy-hot, took the opposite route from Spain to the West Indies, where some of the finest ginger is cultivated today. The ginger used here blends with ambrosial fresh pears, giving this bread a remarkable perfumed aroma and a variety of textures, with the ginger melting into pockets of sweetness throughout the loaf. Use red or green Bartlett, Winter Nelis, d'Anjou, Bosc, Seckel, or firm Comice pear varieties.

Makes one 9-by-5-inch loaf

½ cup (1 stick) unsalted butter, at room temperature
1 cup sugar
2 large eggs
1½ teaspoons vanilla extract
2 cups unbleached all-purpose flour
1 teaspoon baking powder
½ teaspoon baking soda

Pinch of salt
Grated zest of 1 lemon
⅓ cup finely chopped crystallized ginger
¼ cup buttermilk
1½ cups peeled, cored, and coarsely chopped fresh pears (about 2 to 3 whole pears)

1 · Preheat the oven to 350°F. Grease a 9-by-5-inch loaf pan or spray it with cooking spray. In a large bowl, cream the butter and sugar with an electric mixer or by hand. Add the eggs one at a time, beating well after each addition. Add the vanilla extract and beat just until combined.

2 · Combine the flour, baking powder, baking soda, salt, lemon zest, and crystallized ginger in a small bowl. Add the dry ingredients to the creamed mixture, alternating with the buttermilk, in three equal portions. Beat just until smooth. Fold in the pears gently, just until evenly distributed.

3 · Scrape the batter into the prepared loaf pan and bake in the center of the oven until golden brown and a cake tester inserted into the center of the loaf comes out clean, about 55 to 65 minutes. Turn the loaf out of the pan onto a rack, then turn it right side up to cool completely before slicing.

Fresh Orange–Oatmeal Bread

Individual loaves of this moist, orange-spiked bread are excellent served warm accompanied by a Ricotta Cheese Heart (following) and steaming cups of Darjeeling tea.

Makes eight 4-by-2½-inch loaves

1 cup rolled oats
1 cup buttermilk
2 medium navel oranges or 4 Fairchild
  tangerines
3 tablespoons orange liqueur

Brown Sugar Streusel
½ cup packed light brown sugar
⅓ cup unbleached all-purpose flour
4 tablespoons (½ stick) cold unsalted butter,
  cut into 8 pieces

½ cup packed light brown sugar
2 tablespoons granulated sugar
3 tablespoons vegetable oil
2 large eggs
1⅔ cups unbleached all-purpose flour
2 teaspoons baking powder
1 teaspoon baking soda
¼ teaspoon salt
Ricotta Cheese Hearts (optional), following

1 · In a bowl, combine the oats and buttermilk. Cover and refrigerate for 1 hour.

2 · Meanwhile, grate the zest from the oranges or tangerines and reserve. With a small sharp knife, cut off the remaining outer white membranes. Cut or pull apart the oranges or tangerines into sections and coarsely chop, taking care not to lose too much of the juice. Place the chopped sections in a small bowl and add the zest and orange liqueur. Set aside at room temperature to macerate as you continue.

3 · While the fruit macerates, make the Brown Sugar Streusel: Combine the brown sugar and the flour in a small bowl. Work in the cold pieces of butter with your fingers, a fork, or a pastry blender until coarse crumbs are formed. This can also be done with an electric mixer or food processor, if desired. Set aside.

4 · Preheat the oven to 350°F. Grease eight 4-by-2½-inch mini-loaf pans or spray them with cooking spray.

5 · Add the sugars, oil, and eggs to the cold oat-buttermilk mixture. Beat with a whisk until combined. Stir in the macerated oranges or tangerines and all the juices. In a mixing bowl, combine the flour, baking powder, baking soda, and salt. Add the wet ingredients and stir with a large spatula just until combined. The batter will be lumpy.

6 · Scrape the batter into the eight prepared mini-loaf pans until just level with the top of the pan. Sprinkle each loaf with a few tablespoons of the Brown Sugar Streusel. Bake in the center of the oven for about 30 to 35 minutes. When done, the tops of the loaves will be firm to the touch, the loaves will pull away from the sides of the pans, and a cake tester inserted into the center of each loaf will come out clean. Let the loaves stand in the pans for 5 minutes at room temperature before turning them out of the pans onto a rack, then turning them right side up to cool. Serve sliced, along with a honey-drizzled Ricotta Cheese Heart for each whole loaf, if desired.

Ricotta Cheese Hearts

You will need 6 individual coeur à la crème molds to make these cheese hearts; the cheese is also wonderful served from one large bowl for spreading.

Makes 6 small hearts (about 1 cup cheese mixture)

1 cup whole-milk or lowfat ricotta cheese
3 tablespoons plain yogurt
1 tablespoon sugar or honey (optional)
½ teaspoon vanilla extract or liqueur flavoring, such as Grand Marnier, as desired

⅓ cup regular or spiced honey for drizzling, if desired
6 sprigs lemon balm, pineapple sage, or other edible sweet herb, for garnish

1 · Combine the ricotta, yogurt, 1 tablespoon of sugar or honey, if you are using it, and vanilla in a food processor or small bowl. Pulse no more than half a dozen times in the food processor, or use a wooden spoon, and blend until just smooth and fluffy.

2 · Divide the cheese among 6 individual *coeur à la crème* porcelain molds lined with 2 layers of rinsed cheesecloth. Fold the cheesecloth over the cheese and press gently. Place the molds on a tray to catch the drips, and cover with plastic wrap. Refrigerate overnight. The cheese can also be scraped into a serving bowl, covered, and refrigerated.

3 · To serve: Unmold the individual hearts. Fold back the cheesecloth and gently turn each heart out onto a small plate. Peel off the cheesecloth and discard. If you are using the ⅓ cup honey for drizzling, heat the honey until it is warm, and drizzle a tablespoon over each heart, or over the cheese in the single serving bowl. Top with a sprig of lemon balm or pineapple sage.

Papaya–Macadamia Nut Bread

A fragile fruit, the papaya is imported to produce markets from lands below the Tropic of Cancer: Hawaii, Florida, the Bahamas, and Latin America. Check for ripe fruit by feel (there should be a bit of give), rather than by smell or sight. Pureed fresh papaya has a luxurious texture and perfumed flavor that enhances baked goods, such as this quick bread. One large papaya yields about 1 cup puree.

Makes one 9-by-5-inch loaf

1 large ripe papaya
½ cup sugar
3 cups unbleached all-purpose flour
1 tablespoon baking powder
1 teaspoon salt
½ cup chopped raw, unsalted macadamia nuts

Grated zest of 1 orange
2 large eggs
1 cup milk or canned or fresh coconut milk (page 334)
1 teaspoon vanilla extract
3 tablespoons unsalted butter, melted

1 · Peel and seed the papaya. Mash well with a fork or puree the pulp in a blender or food processor. You should have 1 cup. With a whisk, combine the pulp with the sugar in a small bowl. Let stand for 10 minutes.

2 · Meanwhile, preheat the oven to 350°F. Grease a 9-by-5-inch loaf pan or spray with cooking spray.

3 · Combine the flour, baking powder, salt, nuts, and orange zest in a medium bowl. Add the eggs, milk, vanilla, and butter to the papaya pulp. Stir to combine. Make a well in the dry ingredients and pour in the papaya mixture. Stir just to combine. The batter will be a bit lumpy.

4 · Pour the batter into the prepared loaf pan and bake in the center of the oven until the top is firm to the touch and a cake tester inserted into the center comes out clean, about 50 to 60 minutes. Turn the loaf out of the pan onto a rack, then turn it right side up to cool completely. Wrap in plastic wrap and let stand at room temperature until serving.

*D*ried Apricot–Pecan Bread

Dried Apricot–Pecan Bread is incredibly delicious served plain in thin slices or spread with sweet butter to accompany tea or coffee. I also serve it often for picnics and holidays, sandwiching paper-thin slices of smoked turkey and Black Forest ham between two slices. An equal amount of orange brandy may be substituted for the orange juice, if you prefer a more sophisticated loaf. The combination of dried fruit and rich nuts is one of the most complementary of culinary pairings.

Makes two 7¼-by-3½-inch loaves

1½ cups dried apricot halves
1 cup boiling water
3 tablespoons unsalted butter
1 cup sugar
2 cups unbleached all-purpose flour
1½ teaspoons baking soda

½ teaspoon salt
½ cup whole wheat flour
1 cup (4 ounces) chopped pecans
2 large eggs
½ cup orange juice

1 · Grease and flour two 7¼-by-3½-inch loaf pans. Coarsely chop the apricots by hand or in a food processor. Place in a large bowl and add the boiling water, butter, and sugar. Mix well and set aside to cool to lukewarm.

2 · Combine the unbleached flour, baking soda, and salt. Add to the apricot mixture and stir to combine. Add the whole wheat flour, pecans, eggs, and orange juice. Beat well to make a batter that is evenly combined but slightly lumpy. Do not overmix.

3 · Pour the batter into the prepared loaf pans. Preheat the oven to 350°F. Let the loaves rest at room temperature for 15 minutes before placing them in the center of the oven to bake for 55 to 60 minutes. When done, the tops will be firm to the touch, the loaves will pull away from the sides of the pan, and a cake tester inserted into the center of each loaf will come out clean. Remove the loaves from the pans onto a rack, then turn them right side up to cool completely. Wrap tightly in plastic wrap and chill overnight or for up to 5 days before serving.

Amaretto Nut Bread

Amaretto Nut Bread is my basic all-purpose nut loaf. It has a firm texture that makes it slice perfectly, a moist crumb, and a flavorful, buttery essence of nuts that infuses the bread during baking. The addition of almond-flavored liqueur gives the loaf a subtle quality that complements the nuts rather than overpowering them. I tend to make nut breads most during the cool fall and winter months, and stash lots of loaves in the freezer for unexpected visitors and for gifts. As with all quick loaves, wrap this loaf tightly in plastic wrap and let it rest overnight before slicing, to develop flavor and texture.

Makes one 9-by-5-inch loaf or three 6-by-3-inch loaves

2 cups unbleached all-purpose flour
2½ teaspoons baking powder
½ teaspoon baking soda
½ teaspoon salt
1½ teaspoons ground mace or nutmeg
1¼ cups (6 ounces) chopped walnuts,
   pecans, hazelnuts, or any combination

¼ cup vegetable oil
1 cup packed light brown sugar
2 large eggs
1½ teaspoons vanilla extract
1½ cups sour cream
½ cup amaretto

1 · Preheat the oven to 350°F. Grease and flour one 9-by-5-inch loaf pan or three 6-by-3-inch loaf pans. Combine the flour, baking powder, baking soda, salt, and mace or nutmeg in a medium bowl. Add the nuts and stir until evenly distributed.

2 · In another bowl, with a whisk, or in the bowl of an electric mixer, beat together the oil and brown sugar until fluffy and light colored. Add the eggs and vanilla extract.

3 · Add the flour mixture to the creamed mixture in three equal portions, alternating with the sour cream, adding the amaretto with one of the sour cream additions. Beat until smooth after each addition. The batter will be thin.

4 · Pour the batter into the prepared loaf pan or pans. Bake in the center of the oven for 40 to 45 minutes (28 to 32 minutes for the smaller loaves),

until the top is firm, the loaf pulls away from the sides of the pan, and a cake tester inserted into the center comes out clean. Cool the bread in the pan for 10 minutes. Turn the loaf out of the pan onto a rack, then turn right side up to cool completely. Wrap tightly in plastic wrap and chill overnight or for up to 3 days before serving.

Cream Sherry–Pumpkin Bread

Pumpkins are the fruit of a large herbaceous plant with long, vinelike shoots and curling ten-drils. They have a silky, bright orange pulp that adds a delicate flavor and moisture to quick breads. Use a fresh Sugar Pie pumpkin or other winter squash, such as a large Blue Hubbard, for the best flavor when making your own puree (page 351), although commercially canned pumpkin is also an excellent alternative.

Makes three 8-by-4-inch loaves

2 cups granulated sugar

1¼ cups packed light brown sugar

3⅔ cups pureed fresh pumpkin or one 29-ounce can pumpkin puree

4 large eggs

1 cup nut oil, such as walnut or almond or sunflower seed oil

4⅔ cups unbleached all-purpose flour

1 tablespoon baking soda

1½ teaspoons ground cinnamon

1½ teaspoons ground cloves

1½ teaspoons ground coriander

1 teaspoon salt

½ cup cream sherry

1 · Preheat the oven to 350°F. Grease three 8-by-4-inch loaf pans or spray them with cooking spray. In a large bowl, combine the sugars, pumpkin, eggs, and nut oil. Beat with a large whisk or a heavy-duty electric mixer until smooth, about 1 minute.

2 · In another bowl, combine the flour, baking soda, spices, and salt. With a large spatula, combine the wet and dry mixtures and beat until smooth. Stir in the cream sherry. Vigorously beat until thoroughly blended, about 1 to 2 minutes. The batter will be thick and fluffy.

3 · Scrape the batter into the three prepared loaf pans, filling each no more than three-quarters full. Bake immediately in the center of the oven for 65 to 75 minutes, or until a cake tester inserted into the center of each loaf comes out clean. The top of the loaves will be crusty, and there will be a long crack down the center. Let stand for 5 minutes in the pans before turning the loaves out of the pans onto a rack, then turning them right side up to

cool completely. Wrap tightly in plastic wrap and let sit at room temperature overnight or for up to 4 days before serving.

VARIATION:

Indian Pumpkin Bread

Substitute 1⅛ cups fine-grind yellow, white, or blue cornmeal for an equal amount of unbleached flour in Step 2 when making the batter. Continue to mix and bake as instructed.

Brandy-Glazed Zucchini Bread

Zucchini was the first vegetable I ever tasted that was used like a fruit in baking, making a moist, sweet bread. The smooth, cylindrical fruits of this annual herbaceous plant make a distinguished loaf flecked with green and white. You choose whether to add chopped walnuts or macerated golden raisins (see page 347) to this loaf. Glazed with a good brandy or cognac, this loaf can be served as a dessert or as a tea bread.

Makes one 9-by-5-inch loaf or three 6-by-3-inch loaves

¾ cup vegetable oil
1½ cups sugar
3 large eggs
1 teaspoon vanilla extract
2 cups grated raw zucchini
2 cups unbleached all-purpose flour
1½ teaspoons baking soda
1 teaspoon baking powder
1 teaspoon ground cinnamon

1 teaspoon ground cloves
¼ teaspoon salt
1 cup (4 ounces) chopped walnuts, or
     drained, plumped golden raisins

Brandy Glaze
¼ cup sugar
¼ cup brandy or cognac

1 · Preheat the oven to 350°F. Grease and flour one 9-by-5-inch loaf pan or three 6-by-3-inch loaf pans. In a medium bowl, combine the oil and sugar. Beat hard with a whisk or electric mixer until light colored and creamy, about 1 minute. Add the eggs and vanilla extract and beat again until well combined. Fold in the grated zucchini and stir until evenly distributed.

2 · Combine the unbleached flour, baking soda, baking powder, spices, salt, and walnuts or raisins. Add to the zucchini-egg mixture and stir to combine. Beat just until the batter is evenly combined and creamy in consistency.

3 · Scrape the batter into the prepared loaf pan or pans. Bake in the center of the oven for about 65 to 75 minutes for the large loaf or 40 to 50 minutes for the small loaves. When done, the top of the loaf will be firm to the touch, the loaf will pull away from the sides of the pan, and a cake tester inserted

into the center will come out clean. Remove from the oven and place the loaf, still in its pan, on a rack. Let stand for 5 minutes at room temperature.

4 · While the loaf stands, prepare the Brandy Glaze: Combine the sugar and brandy in a small saucepan. Place over low heat just until the sugar dissolves. Set aside. Pierce the hot loaf to the bottom about a dozen times with a bamboo skewer, toothpick, or metal cake tester. Immediately pour the warm Brandy Glaze over the loaf. Cool for 30 minutes in the pan before turning the loaf out of the pan onto a rack, then turning it right side up to cool completely. Wrap tightly in plastic wrap and chill overnight before serving.

Sour Cream Herb Bread

This is a quick loaf to showcase fresh herbs, so don't substitute dried herbs here. Chives can re-place the watercress for a spicier bread. You should pat the watercress and fresh herbs dry or they will clump in the batter. Be sure to slice this loaf with a serrated knife, since the crumb is deli-cate when the bread is fresh. Serve this with roasted meats or minestrone soup. This bread is best the day it is made.

Makes one 8½-by-4½-inch loaf

2¼ cups unbleached all-purpose flour
2 teaspoons baking powder
½ teaspoon baking soda
1 teaspoon salt
2 large eggs
2 tablespoons olive oil
½ cup sour cream
1 cup buttermilk

¼ cup loosely packed chopped fresh
  watercress
1 tablespoon chopped fresh basil
1 tablespoon chopped fresh dill
2 teaspoons chopped fresh marjoram
¼ teaspoon dried lemon rind or ½ teaspoon
  fresh lemon zest

1 · Set the oven rack to the lower third position and preheat the oven to 350°F. Grease an 8½-by-4½-inch loaf pan or spray it with cooking spray. In a medium bowl, combine the flour, baking powder, baking soda, and salt. Stir to combine.

2 · In a small bowl with a whisk, combine the eggs, oil, and sour cream; beat until smooth. Add the buttermilk, watercress, herbs, and lemon zest. Make a well in the center of the flour mixture and add the buttermilk-herb mixture. Beat well with a spatula or Danish dough whisk to make a batter that is evenly combined and creamy in consistency, about 25 strokes; do not over-mix. The batter will be thick.

3 · Scrape the batter into the prepared pan. Bake for 50 to 55 minutes. When the loaf is done, the top will be brown and dry with a long crack down the center, the edges will contract slightly from the sides of the pan, and a cake tester inserted into the center through the crack will come out clean. Check

the sides of the loaf for proper browning; if the sides are too pale, bake the loaf for another 5 minutes. Let the loaf rest in the pan for 5 minutes before turning it out of the pan onto a rack, then turning it right side up to cool. To serve, cool the loaf completely and reheat. Store any leftover bread at room temperature, wrapped tightly in plastic wrap.

Savory Black Olive Bread

Olives add a surprisingly moist texture to this savory dinner bread. Use canned California olives here; you want their buttery flavor rather than the strong, salty edge of imported olives. Be sure to slice this loaf with a serrated knife, since the crumb is delicate when the loaf is fresh. Serve with fresh goat cheese for spreading, and with simple pasta dishes or roast chicken. Day-old, it is good toasted in thick slices.

Makes one 8½-by-4½-inch loaf

One 6-ounce can pitted black olives, drained
2½ cups unbleached all-purpose flour
2 tablespoons sugar
1½ tablespoons baking powder
½ teaspoon baking soda
1 teaspoon salt
⅓ cup chopped fresh mint leaves

3 green onions, white part and some of the green part, chopped and dried on paper towels
Grated zest of 1 lemon
⅓ cup walnut oil or olive oil
2 large eggs
⅔ cup buttermilk

1 · Set the oven rack to the lower third position and preheat the oven to 350°F. Spray an 8½-by-4½-inch loaf pan with oil-flour spray like Baker's Joy, or grease and lightly flour it. Drain the olives and place on a few layers of paper toweling for 5 minutes to drain further; pat dry. Coarsely chop the olives. If you use a food processor, use only 3 or 4 pulses; you want large chunks, and some whole olives are okay.

2 · In a medium bowl, combine the flour, sugar, baking powder, baking soda, and salt. Stir to combine. Add the mint, green onions, lemon zest, and olives, tossing to distribute.

3 · In a medium bowl with a whisk, combine the oil and eggs and beat until the eggs are incorporated. Add the buttermilk and beat until creamy, about 20 strokes. Pour the buttermilk mixture into the dry ingredients and, using a spatula, beat with a few strokes. Continue beating until you have a batter

that is evenly combined and creamy in consistency, about 20 strokes; do not overmix. The batter will be thick.

4 · Scrape the batter into the prepared pan. Bake for 60 to 70 minutes. When done, the top of the loaf will be dry and springy to the touch with a long crack down the top, the edges will contract slightly from the sides of the pan, and a cake tester inserted into the center will come out clean. Check the sides of the loaf for proper browning; if they are too pale, bake the loaf for another 5 minutes. Let the loaf rest in the pan for 10 minutes before turning it out of the pan onto a rack, then turning it right side up to cool completely before slicing. To store, wrap tightly in plastic wrap and refrigerate.

*A*vocado Bread with Pecans and Lime Glaze

Avocados are available year-round, and if you live by an avocado tree you will know just how many can be harvested from one tree. The creamy-smooth Hass avocado characteristically has a rough, black leathery skin. Choose one that is ready to eat: It should give a little under the skin when delicately pressed with your thumb. I love this unusual, beautifully colored quick bread with a subtle flavor that would be at home in the tropics. The avocado gives the bread a very smooth texture. Serve it with a fruit, seafood, or poultry salad.

Makes one 9-by-5-inch loaf

1 medium ripe Hass avocado
1 large egg, well beaten
½ cup plain yogurt
1 cup finely chopped pecans
2 cups unbleached all-purpose flour or
  whole wheat pastry flour
¾ cup sugar
1 teaspoon baking powder

½ teaspoon baking soda
Grated zest of 2 limes
½ teaspoon salt

Lime Syrup
¼ cup granulated or turbinado sugar
¼ cup fresh lime juice

1 · Preheat the oven to 350°F. Grease a 9-by-5-inch loaf pan or spray it with cooking spray. Peel and pit the avocado, then puree it in a food processor until just smooth. You should have ½ cup.

2 · In a mixing bowl, combine the beaten egg, avocado, yogurt, and nuts. Beat with a spoon to mix well. Combine the flour, sugar, baking powder, baking soda, lime zest, and salt in a small bowl. Add the dry ingredients to the creamed mixture and stir with a spatula or Danish dough whisk until smooth and just moistened. Do not overmix.

3 · Pour the batter into the prepared loaf pan and bake in the center of the oven until golden brown and a cake tester inserted into the center of the loaf comes out clean, about 45 to 55 minutes. Let the loaf rest in its pan on a rack to cool.

4 · To make the Lime Syrup: Combine the sugar and lime juice in a small saucepan. Place over low heat until the sugar just dissolves. Pierce the hot loaf about a dozen times to the bottom with a bamboo skewer, toothpick, or metal cake tester. Immediately pour the hot syrup over the warm loaf. Let cool for 30 minutes in the pan before turning the loaf out of the pan onto a rack, then turning it right side up to cool completely. Wrap tightly in plastic wrap and let stand at room temperature overnight before serving.

Applesauce Bread

Among my first forays into quick-bread baking, along with banana bread, was the dark-hued applesauce bread. I have always loved rich, moist, spicy loaves, slices of which are good as a sweet with breakfast or tea, or as a savory complement to a salad. Applesauce bread is very old-fashioned. It is hard to find a recipe for it these days, unless you have one handed down in your family or get one from a friend. Here is mine.

Makes three 6-by-3-inch loaves

2 cups unbleached all-purpose flour
1 cup chopped walnuts or pecans
2 teaspoons baking soda
½ teaspoon baking powder
1 teaspoon ground cinnamon
1 teaspoon ground cloves
1 teaspoon ground allspice

½ teaspoon salt
1 large egg
¼ cup packed light brown sugar
¼ cup packed dark brown sugar
1½ cups unsweetened applesauce
½ cup vegetable oil

1 · Set the oven rack to the lower third position and preheat the oven to 325°F. Grease three 6-by-3-inch loaf pans or spray them with cooking spray. In a medium bowl, combine the flour, nuts, baking soda, baking powder, spices, and salt.

2 · In a small bowl with a whisk, combine the egg, sugars, applesauce, and oil; beat until smooth. Make a well in the center of the flour mixture and add the egg mixture. Beat well with a spatula or Danish dough whisk just enough to create a moist batter that is evenly combined and creamy in consistency, about 25 strokes; do not overmix.

3 · Divide the batter evenly among the prepared loaf pans. Bake in the center of the oven for 33 to 38 minutes. When done, the edges will contract slightly from the sides of the pan and a cake tester inserted into the center will come out clean. Let the loaves rest in the pan for 5 minutes before turning them out of the pan onto a rack, then turning them right side up to cool. Store the loaf at room temperature, wrapped tightly in plastic wrap.

Whole Wheat Prune Bread with Orange Cream Cheese

The combination of nutty whole wheat flour and moist dried prunes makes for one of the most popular quick loaves I have in my repertoire. When you serve this loaf, be prepared to give out the recipe; at least one person always asks. The Orange Cream Cheese is a sophisticated, tasty touch.

Makes three 6-by-3-inch loaves

12 ounces moist pitted prunes
1 cup whole wheat flour, divided
¾ cup (3 ounces) chopped pecans
1 cup unbleached all-purpose flour
1 teaspoon baking soda
½ teaspoon baking powder
1 teaspoon ground cinnamon

¼ teaspoon salt
4 tablespoons (½ stick) unsalted butter, at
    room temperature
¾ cup packed light brown sugar
1 large egg
1 cup plus 2 tablespoons buttermilk
Orange Cream Cheese (optional), following

1 · Preheat the oven to 350°F. Grease three 6-by-3-inch loaf pans or spray them with cooking spray. Combine the prunes and ½ cup of the whole wheat flour in the workbowl of a food processor. Pulse to coarsely chop. Remove from the workbowl. Add the pecans to the prune mixture.

2 · In a large bowl, combine the remaining whole wheat flour, unbleached flour, baking soda, cinnamon, baking powder, and salt. Add the prune-nut mixture and toss to blend.

3 · In another bowl, cream the butter and brown sugar until fluffy with a wooden spoon or an electric mixer. Add the egg and beat until well combined. Add the flour mixture and the buttermilk alternately to the creamed mixture in 3 equal portions. Beat just until smooth and evenly combined. The batter will be thick.

4 · Scrape the batter into three prepared loaf pans and bake in the center of the oven for 40 to 45 minutes, or until a cake tester inserted into the center of the loaves comes out clean. Let the loaves cool in the pans for 10 minutes

before turning them out of the pans onto a rack, then turning them right side up to cool completely. Wrap tightly in plastic wrap and let stand at room temperature or refrigerate overnight before slicing. Serve with Orange Cream Cheese, if desired.

Orange Cream Cheese

Makes about 1½ cups cream cheese

6 ounces cream cheese
3 tablespoons sugar
3 tablespoons plain yogurt
Grated zest of 2 oranges
Fresh mint or pineapple sage leaves, for
  serving (optional)

Mix together all the ingredients in a bowl using a spoon, or in a food processor, until fluffy and evenly combined. Store, covered, in the refrigerator for up to 1 week before serving. Serve on a bed of aromatic herb leaves, if desired.

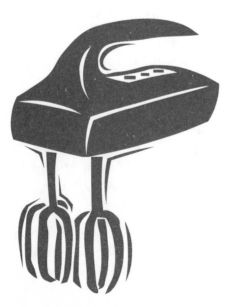

Whole Wheat–Bran Bread with Dates

Whole Wheat–Bran Bread is a coarse-textured, mildly sweet loaf made with no added butter or oil. Considering how economical the ingredients are, the resulting flavor of this loaf is distinctive. Serve year-round, plain or toasted, with coffee, fruit salads, and soft cheeses.

Makes two 8-by-4-inch loaves

2¼ cups whole wheat flour

1¾ cups wheat bran

¼ cup packed light brown sugar

1½ teaspoons baking soda

½ teaspoon baking powder

½ teaspoon salt

1¾ cups buttermilk

1 large egg

⅓ cup light molasses

⅔ cup chopped pitted dates

1 · Preheat the oven to 350°F. Grease and flour two 8-by-4-inch loaf pans. In a large bowl, combine the flour, bran, brown sugar, baking soda, baking powder, and salt.

2 · In a small bowl, combine the buttermilk, egg, and molasses. Beat with a whisk until frothy. Add the dates and stir to combine. Pour over the dry ingredients. Stir with a large spatula just until moistened.

3 · Pour the batter into the prepared loaf pans. Bake in the center of the oven for 60 to 70 minutes, or until a cake tester inserted into the center of the loaves comes out clean. The top surface will be crusty. Let the loaves rest in the pans for 15 minutes. Turn the loaves out of the pans onto a rack, then turn them right side up to cool completely. Wrap tightly in plastic wrap and let sit at room temperature overnight before serving.

Steamed Brown Bread with Dried Blueberries

Traditionally made by cooking the bread in a tightly covered mold in simmering water to form a cylindrical-shaped loaf, brown bread is pure Americana. Developed during the colonial period to utilize native corn, along with small amounts of locally grown rye and molasses imported from the West Indies, the loaf perfectly complemented a big pot of savory baked beans. Use two 1-pound coffee cans topped with foil for the high loaf, or a European-style metal pudding mold with a clamp lid for a more decorative shape. Serve this ultra-moist bread sliced into rounds spread with cream cheese or tangy kefir cheese, available at deli counters in some grocery stores or in natural foods stores. Slices of this bread are also great toasted.

Makes two 1-pound loaves

1 cup dried blueberries (see page 340 for mail-order source)

3 tablespoons golden rum

1 cup yellow cornmeal, preferably stone-ground

1 cup graham or whole wheat flour

1 cup unbleached all-purpose flour

2 teaspoons baking soda

½ teaspoon salt

2 cups buttermilk

¾ cup light molasses, warmed slightly for easier pouring

1 large egg

1 · In a small bowl, combine the blueberries and the rum. Let stand at room temperature 1 hour to macerate.

2 · Generously grease two 1-pound coffee cans and line the bottoms of each with a circle of parchment paper.

3 · In a large bowl, combine the cornmeal, graham or whole wheat flour, unbleached flour, baking soda, and salt. In a 4-cup measure or in a bowl, combine the buttermilk, molasses, and egg. Stir with a whisk. Pour the buttermilk mixture into the dry ingredients and add the plumped blueberries. Beat well until evenly moistened.

4 · Scrape the batter into the prepared molds, filling each no more than two-thirds full. Cover tightly with foil held in place by thick rubber bands. Place

on a rack in a deep kettle. Add boiling water to a depth of 1 to 2 inches up the sides of the molds. Cover pot and adjust heat to a low simmer. Steam for 2 hours, or until a cake tester inserted into the center of each loaf comes out clean. Add more boiling water, if necessary, during the steaming if too much evaporates.

5 · Preheat the oven to 400°F. When the breads are done, remove the foil tops from the molds and place the loaves in the oven for no more than 5 minutes, to dry slightly. Remove the bread from the cans, peel off the parchment paper, and place the loaves on their sides on a rack to cool. Serve warm, sliced into rounds. Store, wrapped in plastic wrap, at room temperature for up to 3 days.

NOTE: *These loaves also can be baked in a conventional 350°F oven for 40 to 50 minutes in two 8-by-4-by-3-inch loaf pans, but the consistency will be a bit drier, and the top of the loaves will be crusty.*

VARIATION:

Steamed Applesauce Brown Bread

Substitute 1 cup of unsweetened applesauce for 1 cup of the buttermilk in Step 2. If the dough seems a bit dry, depending on the consistency of your applesauce, add a few more tablespoons of buttermilk. Continue to mix and bake as directed.

Gingerbreads

Gingerbreads

Along with dried clove flower buds, giant nutmeg seeds, ground cassia bark (cinnamon), and peppercorns, sacks of dried ginger originally came to Europe from remote islands in the Indian Ocean. Highly precious imports utilized as a money standard, ginger and the other spices traveled via the Arab merchant land caravans and Venetian sea trade routes. The high demand for these Oriental spices inspired many sea voyages by Portuguese and English sailors, since these spices were literally worth their weight in gold.

Gingerroot, also known as *singabera* in Sanskrit, is originally native to Bengal, India, and southern China and transplanted easily to the warm climate of southern Europe. The Spanish were the first to carry the lilylike plant to the West Indies, where it is now widely cultivated. Jamaican ginger (*zingiber*) in particular is highly prized throughout the world.

Looking clearly like the palm of a human hand with fingers, ginger holds a distinguished position in Western as well as Eastern medicinal lore, attributed with healing powers whether used fresh or dried and finely ground. The root of the perennial plant is dug up when the plant is about a year old, then simply washed and sun-dried before being ready for use.

Gingerbread is often called the oldest baked sweet in the world since it was baked in ancient Greece many centuries before Christ. Recipes for the spiced bread were preserved during the Dark Ages in monasteries. Early American bakers knew the sweet as "gyngerbredde," and the Pilgrims adapted the recipes they brought with them to a variety of native ingredients, such as dried pumpkin flour, cornmeal, and honey. Leavening was pearlash, a vegetable ash often made from pea and bean stalks, which was commonly combined with molasses. Gingerbread could either be made with a thin boiling water–based batter that baked into soft and moist cakes, as we make it today, or with a stiff batter that baked into firm and dry-textured cookies or breads, like the sturdy French *pain d'épices*, English parkin, and Dutch honey and rye *koeks*.

One of the great pleasures of baking gingerbread is the warm, intoxicating fragrance that pervades your kitchen while it is baking. Use plenty of fresh ground ginger (buy a new bottle every 6 to 9 months) for the best flavor. One tablespoon of ground ginger may be substituted for one 2-inch piece peeled and finely grated fresh ginger (to make about ¼ cup), but the flavor will be quite different, because the powdered ginger has a more concentrated, hot, and fiery flavor.

Besides its blend of intensely aromatic spices, the true heart of good gingerbread is the molasses, which lends the bread its characteristic flavor, color, and soft texture. Use the unsulphured "Barbados" variety rather than "blackstrap," which is bitter. British cookbooks call for dark or light treacle, which is sometimes substituted for pure cane syrup or Lyle's Golden Syrup for a mellower flavor. In the making of white gingerbreads, sugar, maple syrup, or honey is substituted for the molasses.

Gingerbread is a cake you will rarely find in a bakery—it is a real homemade treat. It dresses up well with pureed fruit, sweet custard sauces, layers of good jam, chocolate glazes, fluffy lemon frosting, whipped cream, and cream cheese spreads.

Gingerbreads can be baked successfully into moist, spongy, spicy loaves in a wide variety of shallow metal, clay, porcelain, or glass baking pans. They can be eaten straight from an oven-to-table baking dish or turned out onto a plate and drizzled with glaze. Gingerbread's intense flavor mellows nicely after a day or two, but it is just as good eaten warm from the oven.

Classic Gingerbread

This is old-fashioned gyngerbredde, *just like the Colonial American housewives made it—dark with molasses and pungent with spices. It is what I whip up during the holidays or when a lot of children are coming for dinner. It is a simple recipe that does not need any embellishments, but it is also good with the addition of crystallized ginger or dates. I like the smooth, cakelike texture of this recipe, which is adapted from the recipe of my friend the home baker and entrepreneur Murray Jaffe, who knows the best recipe for every baked good in the American kitchen. In his words, "People go crazy for homemade gingerbread"—especially when it is accompanied by softly whipped cream.*

Makes one 8-inch cake

1⅔ cups unbleached all-purpose flour
2 teaspoons baking soda
2 teaspoon ground ginger
1 teaspoon ground cinnamon
¼ teaspoon ground cloves
⅛ teaspoon ground mace

¼ teaspoon salt
6 tablespoons (¾ stick) unsalted butter
½ cup packed dark brown sugar
½ cup light molasses
1 large egg
⅔ cup boiling water

1 · Preheat the oven to 350°F (325°F if you are using a Pyrex or dark-cast metal pan). Grease an 8-inch square, round, or springform pan or spray it with cooking spray. In a large mixing bowl, combine the flour, baking soda, spices, and salt. Set aside.

2 · In a large bowl with an electric mixer, cream the butter and brown sugar until flufffy, 3 minutes, scraping down the sides of the bowl as needed. Add the molasses and slowly blend. Add the egg and beat for 30 seconds.

3 · Add the flour mixture in three portions, alternating with the boiling water, and mix for 30 seconds on medium speed. Beat gently just until the ingredients are evenly incorporated, only about 1 minute. Do not overmix.

4 · Scrape the batter into the prepared pan, and tap the pan on the counter to smooth the top. Bake in the center of the oven until the top springs back

when touched and a cake tester inserted into the center comes out clean, 35 to 40 minutes. Let the cake cool in the pan on a rack for 20 minutes. Then run a knife around the edge to loosen the cake, turn it out onto the rack, and place it right side up to finish cooling. You can serve it right out of the pan, if you desire.

Pumpkin Gingerbread

Bake this stunning and moist cake in a square, rectangular, round, or even heart-shaped pan to showcase the crumb top. Adding cornmeal to the recipe (variation follows) makes a gently textured cake redolent of its New England roots. For an extra-special dimension, serve the warm cake topped with a cup of heavy cream that has been whipped to soft mounds with 3 tablespoons of maple syrup.

Makes one 9-inch cake

2½ cups unbleached all-purpose flour
½ cup whole wheat flour
1 cup sugar
1½ teaspoons ground ginger
1 teaspoon ground cinnamon
1 teaspoon fresh-ground nutmeg
¾ cup (1½ sticks) unsalted butter, cut into
   12 pieces

2 cups pureed fresh pumpkin (page 351) or
   one 16-ounce can pumpkin
2 large eggs
½ cup light molasses
⅓ cup buttermilk
1½ teaspoons baking soda

1 · Preheat the oven to 350°F. Grease a 9-inch square, round, or springform pan. In a large bowl, combine the flours, sugar, and spices. Cut in the butter pieces with your fingers, a pastry blender, or a heavy-duty electric mixer until the mixture makes coarse crumbs. Set aside ¾ cup of the crumbs for the topping, and make a well in the remaining crumbs.

2 · In another mixing bowl, combine the pumpkin, eggs, molasses, buttermilk, and baking soda with a whisk. Pour the pumpkin mixture into the well in the crumbs. Stir just until moistened.

3 · Pour the batter into the prepared pan. Sprinkle evenly with the reserved crumbs. Bake in the center of the oven until the top is firm to the touch and a cake tester inserted in the center comes out clean, about 40 to 45 minutes. Cool the cake in the pan on a rack. Serve warm.

VARIATION:

Pumpkin-Cornmeal Gingerbread

Substitute 1 cup fine-grind yellow cornmeal for an equal amount of flour in Step 1. Continue to mix, bake, and serve as directed.

Gingerbread with Stout

This tube cake gingerbread is the creation of my friend Rick Rodgers. Once while he was visiting food writer Bruce Aidells, who is a beer aficionado, they wondered how the intense flavor of stout, the cabernet sauvignon of beers, would work as the liquid in a gingerbread. The idea isn't new after all; I found old Irish recipes using porter ale (a weaker form of stout) in gingerbread, as well as in porter cake, a spicy fruitcake that is also soaked with stout after baking. The dark, dense, malty flavor of the stout ends up making a gourmet, yet old-fashioned, gingerbread that balances the inherent sweetness of the sugar and molasses. I like to use one of the special decorative fluted tube pans to make this cake look really special. Serve warm slices with a small dollop of Orange Hard Sauce (following) melting on the side.

Makes one 10-inch tube cake

1 bottle stout
2½ cups unbleached all-purpose flour
1 tablespoon ground ginger
2 teaspoons ground cinnamon
1½ teaspoons baking powder
½ teaspoon baking soda
½ teaspoon salt
1 cup (2 sticks) unsalted butter, at room temperature

1 cup packed light brown sugar
¼ cup packed dark brown sugar
2 large eggs
1 large egg yolk
1 cup light molasses
Powdered sugar, for dusting
Orange Hard Sauce (optional), following

1 · An hour before baking, open the bottle of stout and measure out ¾ cup. (You will not use the whole bottle: Cover the spout and refrigerate the leftover stout for up to one week, to use in other recipes, such as beef stew or a steamed pudding.) Let the ¾ cup stout stand for a full hour at room temperature, stirring occasionally, to allow the stout to go flat.

2 · Preheat the oven to 350°F (325°F if you are using a dark-cast metal pan). Grease and flour a 12-cup fluted tube pan. In a large mixing bowl, combine the flour, spices, baking powder, baking soda, and salt. Set aside.

3 · In a large bowl with an electric mixer, cream the butter and brown sugars until fluffy, 3 minutes, scraping down the sides of the bowl as needed. Add the eggs and beat for 30 seconds. Add the molasses and slowly blend.

4 · On low speed, add the flour mixture in three portions, alternating with the stout, and mixing for 30 seconds on medium speed after each addition. After the last addition, beat gently just until evenly incorporated, only about 1 minute. Do not overmix.

5 · Scrape the batter into the prepared pan. Bake in the center of the oven until the top springs back when touched and a cake tester inserted into the center comes out clean, 50 to 60 minutes. Let the cake cool in the pan on a rack for 10 minutes. Then invert onto the rack to finish cooling. Transfer to a serving platter, dust with sieved powdered sugar, and serve warm or at room temperature, with Orange Hard Sauce, if desired.

Orange Hard Sauce

Makes ½ cup sauce

4 tablespoons (½ stick) unsalted butter,
  at room temperature
Grated zest of ½ orange
¾ cup sifted powdered sugar
2 tablespoons brandy, bourbon, rum,
  orange liqueur, or cognac
½ teaspoon vanilla extract
Fresh-ground nutmeg, for sprinkling

1 · In a small bowl with an electric mixer, cream the butter, zest, and sugar until light and fluffy. Stir in the brandy and vanilla and beat until just smooth and incorporated.

2 · Scrape into a serving dish or plastic container, cover, and refrigerate until serving. Chill overnight to meld the flavors. The sauce will have a solid consistency. Before serving, grate fresh nutmeg over the top. To serve, scoop out a small spoonful and push the sauce out of the spoon using a butter knife.

Maple Gingerbread with Pumpkin Gelato

This is a spicy, complex flavored, cakey gingerbread. The spices blend with the bergamot in the Earl Grey tea, one of my favorite secret ingredients in quick breads, and the sweetener is a combination of molasses and maple syrup. The prunes work perfectly. A superb dessert, especially served with my cognac-laced "adult ice cream," accompanied by coffee.

Makes one 9-inch cake or twelve 4-inch cakes

2½ cups unbleached all-purpose flour

2 tablespoons instant espresso powder

1 tablespoon ground ginger

1 teaspoon ground cinnamon

½ teaspoon ground cloves

½ teaspoon fresh-ground nutmeg

¼ teaspoon ground black pepper

¼ teaspoon salt

½ cup (1 stick) unsalted butter

½ cup packed light brown sugar

½ cup light molasses

½ cup pure maple syrup

3 large eggs

2 teaspoons baking soda

¾ cup strongly brewed Earl Grey tea
 (can be decaf)

¾ cup chopped pitted prunes

Pumpkin Gelato, following

1 · Preheat the oven to 350°F (325°F if you are using a Pyrex or dark-cast metal pan). For one large cake, grease a 9-inch square, round cake, or springform pan. For the individual cake rounds, grease a 15-by-10-by-1-inch pan and line it with parchment paper. (When the cake is done, you'll cut out individual cakes using a biscuit cutter.) In a large mixing bowl, combine the flour, espresso, spices, pepper, and salt. Set aside. In a small saucepan, combine the butter, brown sugar, molasses, and maple syrup. Stir constantly over low heat until the butter is melted. Remove from heat.

2 · Make a well in the center of the dry ingredients and pour in the hot butter mixture. Add the eggs, one at a time, beating the mixture until smooth with a wooden spoon or electric mixer after the addition of each egg. Combine the baking soda and brewed tea. Pour over the batter and stir gently just until evenly incorporated. Fold in the prunes.

3 · Pour the batter into the greased 9-inch pan or spread the batter into the prepared 15-by-10-by-1-inch pan. Bake in the center of the oven until the top springs back when touched and a cake tester inserted into the center comes out clean, 35 to 40 minutes for the 9-inch cake or 25 to 30 minutes for the 15-by-10-inch cake. Let the cake cool in the pan on a rack. To make individual cake rounds, cut out 12 rounds from the 15-by-10-inch cake using a 4-inch plain or fluted biscuit or other decorative cutter (save the excess cake for snacks).

4 · To serve, place a wedge, square, or round of gingerbread on a dessert plate and top with two small scoops of Pumpkin Gelato.

Pumpkin Gelato

Makes 1 quart ice cream

1 quart vanilla ice cream
¾ cup canned pumpkin purée
1 teaspoon ground cinnamon
Pinch of ground cloves
Pinch of ground ginger
Pinch of ground allspice
1 tablespoon cognac

1 · Let the ice cream soften slightly at room temperature for 10 to 15 minutes. Transfer the ice cream to a bowl. With an electric mixer or by hand, beat the ice cream until just creamy.

2 · Add the pumpkin, spices, and cognac; blend on low speed until evenly distributed. Working quickly, scrape the ice cream back into the carton using a large rubber spatula. Refreeze for at least 6 hours before serving.

Gingerbread with Lemon and Raspberry Sauces

For sophisticated diners, serve this English-style moist spice cake accompanied by the bright-flavored Lemon and Raspberry Sauces (following), dollops of cold crème fraîche, and fresh tart berries. I make this recipe often for young diners and, in lieu of the sauces, serve it with hot, unsweetened applesauce. To serve the dessert to large groups, make the 15-by-10-inch sheet cake and cut it into individual rounds.

Makes one 9-inch cake or twelve 4-inch cakes

2½ cups unbleached all-purpose flour
2 tablespoons instant espresso powder
1 tablespoon ground ginger
1 teaspoon ground cinnamon
½ teaspoon ground cloves
½ teaspoon fresh-ground nutmeg
¼ teaspoon ground black pepper
¼ teaspoon salt
Grated zest of 1 lemon
½ cup (1 stick) unsalted butter
½ cup packed light brown sugar

½ cup light molasses
½ cup pure maple syrup
2 large eggs
2 teaspoons baking soda
1 cup boiling water
Raspberry Sauce, following
Lemon Sauce, following
1 cup crème fraîche, for serving
1 pint fresh raspberries, for serving
12 fresh mint sprigs, for garnish

1 · Preheat the oven to 350°F. Grease a 9-inch square, round, or springform pan or spray it with cooking spray. For the individual cake rounds, grease a 15-by-10-inch pan and line it with parchment paper. In a large mixing bowl, combine the flour, espresso, spices, salt, and lemon zest. Set aside. In a small saucepan, combine the butter, brown sugar, molasses, and maple syrup. Stir constantly over low heat until the butter is melted. Remove from heat.

2 · Make a well in the center of the dry ingredients and pour in the hot butter mixture. Add the eggs and immediately beat with a wooden spoon or electric mixer until smooth. Combine the baking soda and boiling water. Pour over the batter and stir gently just until evenly incorporated.

3 · For one large cake, pour the batter into the prepared 9-inch cake pan. Bake in the center of the oven until the top springs back when touched and a cake tester inserted into the center comes out clean, about 35 to 40 minutes. For the individual cake rounds, spread the batter into the prepared 15-by-10-by-1-inch pan and bake for 25 to 30 minutes. Let the cake cool in the pan on a rack.

4 · To serve: Cut the cake into squares or wedges. To make individual cake rounds, cut out 12 rounds from the 15-by-10-by-1-inch cake using a plain or fluted 4-inch round biscuit or other decorative cutter (save the excess cake for snacks). Place a spoonful of each fruit sauce on a dessert plate. Place a wedge, square, or round of gingerbread on top of the sauce. Top with cold crème fraîche, fresh raspberries, and a mint sprig.

Raspberry Sauce

Makes about 2 cups sauce

2 cups fresh raspberries or one 12-ounce
  package unsweetened frozen raspberries,
  thawed
3 tablespoons raspberry vinegar
¼ cup sugar or to taste

In a small bowl, sprinkle the berries
with the vinegar and sugar. Let stand
for 1 hour at room temperature. Pass
the mixture through a sieve to remove
the seeds. Refrigerate until serving.

Lemon Sauce

Makes about 1⅓ cups sauce

¼ cup fresh lemon juice
½ cup water, divided
½ cup sugar
Grated zest of 2 lemons
1 tablespoon cornstarch
3 tablespoons unsalted butter

Combine the lemon juice, ¼ cup of the
water, sugar, and zest in a medium
saucepan. Heat just until the sugar is
dissolved. Dissolve the cornstarch in
the remaining ¼ cup water. Add to the
hot lemon mixture. Over medium-high
heat, stir the mixture constantly with
a whisk until it comes to a full boil,
thickens, and becomes clear. Remove
the sauce from the heat and stir in the
butter until it melts. Serve the sauce
warm or at room temperature.

$\mathcal{F}$resh Apricot Gingerbread

This is an early summer, country-style gingerbread, with a batter embellished with ripe apricots. It is a marriage of spices and fruit that is quite unusual, but exceptionally complementary. Crystallized preserved ginger is classified as a confection rather than as a spice and is available in some grocery stores and in gourmet food stores. Serve the cake on a platter decorated with a bed of fresh apricot or fig leaves.

Makes one 10-inch tube cake

1 cup sour cream
½ cup (1 stick) unsalted butter, at room temperature
⅔ cup light molasses
½ cup granulated sugar
2 large eggs
3½ cups unbleached all-purpose flour
2 teaspoons baking soda
1 tablespoon ground ginger

1 teaspoon ground mace
1 teaspoon ground cinnamon
½ teaspoon cream of tartar
¼ teaspoon salt
12 ripe fresh apricots, halved, pitted, and each half snipped into 4 pieces
½ cup chopped pecans
2 pieces crystallized ginger, finely chopped
Powdered sugar (optional), for dusting

1 · Preheat the oven to 350°F. Grease a 10-inch fluted tube or tube springform pan or spray it with cooking spray. In a mixing bowl, combine the sour cream, butter, molasses, granulated sugar, and eggs. Beat hard with a wooden spoon or an electric mixer until smooth and well blended, about 1 minute.

2 · In another bowl, combine the flour, baking soda, spices, cream of tartar, and salt. Beat into the sour cream mixture until light and fluffy. Fold in the fresh apricots, pecans, and crystallized ginger with a large spatula.

3 · Pour the batter into the prepared tube pan. Bake in the center of the oven until the top springs back when touched and a cake tester inserted into the center comes out clean, about 45 to 50 minutes. Let stand in the pan for 10 minutes before turning the cake out onto a rack to cool completely before slicing. Dust with powdered sugar, if desired.

$\mathcal{P}$each Upside-Down Ginger Cake

Upside-down cakes have a reputation for being cloyingly sweet, which they need not be. Every summer I take advantage of the bounty of fresh fruit to make these delicate cakes embellished with a variety of seasonal fruits. Many sophisticated restaurants like Spago in Los Angeles and Chez Panisse in Berkeley offer these old-fashioned, seasonal cakes on their menus. The variations are endless. My favorite version was consumed at Eddy Jacks, a South-of-Market eatery in San Francisco. The cake was made with fresh figs and served in a pool of raspberry sauce. The baker said it was her grandmother's recipe, the kind of source that, I suspect, many of these old-fashioned cakes can be traced back to. This version, which uses fresh peaches, is also excellent made with fresh pineapple, papaya, apricots, or sweet cherries. A variation using oranges, cranberries, and raisins follows. Dress up this dessert with Amaretto Crème Anglaise (following), a delicate French custard sauce.

Makes one 9-inch cake

4 tablespoons (½ stick) unsalted butter
¾ cup packed light brown sugar
¼ teaspoon ground cinnamon
¼ teaspoon fresh-ground nutmeg
¼ teaspoon ground ginger
6 firm, ripe large peaches, peeled, pitted, and sliced thick (2 to 3 cups)
½ cup (1 stick) unsalted butter, at room temperature
½ cup granulated sugar
2 large eggs
3 tablespoons light molasses

1 teaspoon vanilla extract
1½ cups unbleached all-purpose flour
1½ teaspoons ground ginger
½ teaspoon ground cinnamon
¼ teaspoon ground cloves
¼ teaspoon fresh-ground nutmeg
½ teaspoon baking soda
¼ teaspoon salt
¼ cup boiling water
Amaretto Crème Anglaise (optional), following

1 · Preheat the oven to 350°F. Melt the 4 tablespoons butter in a small saucepan. When the butter is melted, stir in the brown sugar and spices. Continue to heat the mixture just until the brown sugar is melted. Pour it into a 9-inch ceramic or metal cake or springform pan and arrange the fresh peach slices in a single layer over the brown sugar–butter mixture. Set aside.

2 · To make the Ginger Cake batter: In a mixing bowl, cream the butter and sugar. Beat in the eggs, molasses, and vanilla extract until fluffy. In another bowl, combine the flour, spices, baking soda, and salt. Stir the dry ingredients into the creamed mixture, alternating with the boiling water, mixing just until creamy. Do not overbeat.

3 · Carefully spoon the batter over the peaches in the pan. Bake in the center of the oven for 30 to 40 minutes, or until a cake tester inserted into the center of the cake comes out clean. Cool the cake in the pan for 5 minutes before inverting onto a serving plate. Serve warm or at room temperature accompanied by Amaretto Crème Anglaise (following), if you wish.

Amaretto Crème Anglaise

Makes about 3 cups sauce

2 cups heavy cream
½ cup sugar
3 large eggs
¼ cup amaretto liqueur

In a saucepan or in a microwave oven, scald the heavy cream. In a mixing bowl or food processor combine the sugar and the eggs. Beat hard with a whisk or process until light colored and foamy. Whisking constantly, or with the food processor running, add the hot cream very slowly. Pour into a saucepan and place over medium heat. Cook the sauce gently, stirring constantly, until just slightly thickened. Pour into a bowl and stir in the amaretto. Cool slightly. Refrigerate, covered, until serving time.

VARIATION:

Cranberry-Orange Upside-Down Ginger Cake

Combine 2 cups of fresh cranberries and a whole seedless orange, peeled and cut into chunks, in the workbowl of a food processor. Pulse just to coarsely chop. Spoon the mixture in a single layer evenly over the brown sugar–butter mixture as directed in Step 1, then sprinkle with ½ cup golden raisins in place of the peaches. Continue to mix, bake, and serve as directed.

Blueberry Gingerbread with Cinnamon Ice Cream

Fresh blueberry gingerbread is really special for a summer dessert when served with Cinnamon Ice Cream and additional fresh berries. This is one of my favorite cakes: moist, spicy, and fruity. With the ice cream, it is ethereal.

Makes one 8-inch cake

1½ cups fresh blueberries, plus an additional 2 cups (1 pint) fresh blueberries, for serving
2 tablespoons sugar
3 tablespoons blueberry vinegar
1½ cups unbleached all-purpose flour
½ cup packed light brown sugar
1 teaspoon baking soda
2 teaspoons ground ginger
¼ teaspoon ground cinnamon
¼ teaspoon ground mace
¼ teaspoon salt
½ cup sour cream
½ cup (1 stick) unsalted butter, melted
2 large eggs
2 tablespoons pure maple syrup
Cinnamon Ice Cream, following

1 · In a bowl, gently toss the 1½ cups of blueberries with the sugar and vinegar. Let stand at room temperature for 1 hour.

2 · Preheat the oven to 350°F. Grease an 8-inch square or heart-shaped cake pan or springform pan, or spray it with cooking spray. In a mixing bowl, combine the flour, brown sugar, baking soda, spices, and salt. Drain the berries, reserving the juices, and set aside. In another bowl, stir the reserved juices into the sour cream. Add the melted butter, eggs, and maple syrup, combining with a whisk. Add ½ cup of the flour mixture and beat until smooth. Add the remaining flour mixture and beat just until smooth and fluffy.

3 · Spread two-thirds of the batter into the prepared pan. Arrange the macerated berries over the top. Spoon the remaining batter over them, without completely covering the fruit. Bake in the center of the oven for about 45 to 50 minutes, or until the top is dry and springy and a cake tester inserted into the center comes out clean. Let cake cool in the pan on a rack until serving time. Serve cut into wedges with one or two small scoops of Cinnamon Ice Cream and additional fresh berries spooned over each serving.

Cinnamon Ice Cream

Makes 1 quart ice cream

1 quart vanilla ice cream
2 tablespoons ground cinnamon

Let the vanilla ice cream soften slightly at room temperature for 10 to 15 minutes. Transfer the ice cream to a bowl. With an electric mixer or by hand, beat until *just* creamy. Add the cinnamon and blend until evenly distributed. Working quickly, scrape the ice cream back into the carton with a large spatula. Refreeze for at least 6 hours.

Chocolate Gingerbread with Bittersweet Glaze

This is the most decadent recipe in this collection, bringing the classic prim Puritan gingerbread into this century. This dense chocolate gingerbread is glazed with a thin layer of bittersweet chocolate. Serve it cut into wedges, with spoonfuls of Poached Ginger Prunes (following) alongside, if you like.

Makes one 9-inch cake

3 ounces unsweetened chocolate
½ cup light molasses
½ cup vegetable oil
4 tablespoons (½ stick) unsalted butter
2½ cups unbleached all-purpose flour
1 cup packed light brown sugar
1 teaspoon baking soda
1 teaspoon baking powder
1 teaspoon ground ginger

¼ teaspoon ground cinnamon
¼ teaspoon fresh-ground nutmeg
¼ teaspoon fresh-ground white pepper
¼ teaspoon salt
2 large eggs
1 cup buttermilk
1 teaspoon vanilla extract
Bittersweet Glaze, following
Poached Ginger Prunes (optional), following

1 · In a double boiler, place the chocolate, molasses, vegetable oil, and butter. Stir over low heat until the chocolate is melted and the mixture is smooth. Set aside.

2 · Preheat the oven to 350°F. Grease a 9-inch springform pan or spray it with cooking spray. In a mixing bowl, combine the flour, brown sugar, baking soda, baking powder, spices, and salt. In a small bowl, beat the eggs with a whisk until foamy. Add the buttermilk and vanilla extract.

3 · Make a well in the center of the dry ingredients and pour in the buttermilk-egg mixture. Stir to combine. Add the chocolate mixture. Beat with a wooden spoon or electric mixer until smooth.

4 · Pour the batter into the prepared pan. Bake in the center of the oven until the top springs back when touched and a cake tester inserted into the center comes out clean, about 35 to 40 minutes. Set the cake on a rack and remove

the springform sides. Prepare the Bittersweet Glaze and glaze as directed. Cool on a rack to set the glaze until time to serve. Serve with Poached Ginger Prunes, if desired.

Bittersweet Glaze

Makes about 1 cup glaze

6 tablespoons (¾ stick) unsalted butter
4½ ounces bittersweet or semisweet
  chocolate
1 tablespoon light corn syrup

In a double boiler, combine the butter, chocolate, and corn syrup over low heat, stirring with a whisk until the mixture is melted and smooth. Pour the glaze onto the center of the gingerbread and use a metal spatula or other tool to coat the cake in a few strokes, letting the glaze drip down the sides of the cake.

Poached Ginger Prunes

Makes about 2 cups fruit

12 ounces large pitted prunes
1 cup water
1 tablespoon minced crystallized ginger
2 strips fresh lemon rind
2 cinnamon sticks
½ teaspoon vanilla extract

1 · Combine all the ingredients in a small saucepan. Bring to a boil, cover, and simmer for 5 to 8 min-utes, or until the prunes are soft. The prunes can also be prepared in a microwave, if desired.

2 · Remove and discard the lemon rind and cinnamon sticks. Serve the prunes at room temperature or chilled, alongside the Chocolate Gingerbread.

Cornbreads

Cornbreads

Originally a finger-sized wild plant native to the Mexican highlands, corn traveled northward to the United States by three main corridors, growing immense seed heads over the centuries. The tropical route to Sonora and southern Arizona produced the heat- and drought-resistant crops still grown there today. The Sierra Madre corridor produced corn adapted to the highlands, with their subtropical rainy summers. An eastern corridor along the northeastern United States resulted in corn that in the 1920s became the base for hybridized dents, which today is our modern commercial corn crop known for the dimple that tops each kernel. Corn was already grown in a staggering number of varieties (food historians have isolated over a thousand pure strains) throughout the North and Central American continent when the Pilgrims landed on the New England coast.

In the Northeast, Native Americans used their own stockpiles of corn to teach Europeans settlers and traders how to grow and prepare flint field corn, the hard corn that is ground into meals. A milk was made from ground corn mixed with boiled chestnuts. Recipes adapted from the Indians became daily staples, including flat, dense *pones*, adapted from the Algonquin, which were shaped and baked on platters of wood; long-lasting hot-stone johnnycakes; flat cakes baked in the ashes of a hearth fire; corn porridge called *suppawn*, sweetened with crushed green corn stalks, which would later be called spoon bread; whole dried corn boiled with ashes to form smoky-flavored *hominy*; and *nookik*, hoecakes with salt roasted on greased rake blades.

The rich yellow and white cornmeals of colonial and Yankee kitchens are still popular in the Northeast. With a sweetening of honey, sugar, molasses, or maple syrup, they were originally baked in a "spider," a black iron frying pan with legs used on an open hearth. Yankee johnnycakes, originally unsweetened, dense griddle cakes baked on an iron hanging skillet, are still a favorite. Northeastern water-powered mills have been grinding local flint corn on their granite stones since the 1600s. Most early American mills, like Kenyon's and Gray's Grist Mill in Rhode Island, are still grinding and selling their quality products. Gray's has the distinction of grinding Narragansett Indian White Cap flint corn, the original delicious strain, often called "cow corn," grown when the Pilgrims landed.

The South stands by its pristine,

unsweetened white cornbreads made from water-ground Boone County White dent corn grown in the southern Corn Belt, from Ohio to southern Tennessee. Distinguished Southern cooks would never consider making their creamy coarse-ground grits, crusty corn sticks, corn dodgers, and fluffy spoon breads with Northern corn. Classic recipes abound: Generations have enjoyed fritter cornmeal batters pan-fried into hush puppies alongside fish; Arkansas corn flapjacks are legendary; and in neighboring New Orleans, Cajun-Creole cooking features hot yellow cornbreads and Caribbean-style cornbreads made with fresh coconut milk. To supply the area with fresh cornmeals, several local water-powered mills dating from the Civil War era have been refurbished, such as the War Eagle Mill in Arkansas.

Midwestern country kitchens have long used sweet, home-rendered lard to create blue-ribbon farm-style cornbreads and sugared muffins. During cattle drives or while traveling across the prairies, Western pioneer chuckwagons incorporated lots of yellow cornmeal into bacon-flecked breads made in covered cast-iron pots that baked over an open fire.

For centuries, the Southwest has used its indigenous calico blue, red, black, and speckled varieties of corn in making native breads and the tortillas learned from the Mexicans. Bakers and home cooks use yellow and white meals, often ground on native metate stone slabs or with wind-powered mills, for limey *masa* flour and baking powder cornbreads flavored with hot chiles and fresh corn kernels scraped off the cob. Since Native American religious beliefs include a reverence for local foods as the sustainers of life, corn is closely associated with tribal spiritual practices and their intense mythology.

Corn was also incorporated into the breads of Europe and beyond. Columbus brought the cultivated staple grain of the New World, *mahiz* (meaning the "stuff of life"), back to Europe on his first voyage. The Portuguese and Spanish took an immediate liking to Indian corn. The lusty Basque, Gascony, and Béarn wine-producing provinces of southern France are known as maize country, having grown the hard field corn since its introduction in the sixteenth century to make a cornmeal bread known as *méture*. *Pain de mais de sac* is a rustic Basque country bread steamed over a kettle of water. The northern regions of Italy bordering on Austria,

Lombardy, Veneto, and Piedmont grow and serve ground *gran turco* in the form of a dense yeasted *pain di mais* flavored with fruity olive oil. Corn traveled the sea trade routes to Africa, Turkey, and the Far East. It also followed the Ottoman Empire to Romania, where it is served today as *malai*, a yeasted cornbread with cottage or feta cheese. Not every cuisine favored breads made of corn. The Swiss, the Scandinavians, and the Dutch considered it exclusively an animal food, and the British preferred the cold weather grain crops such as barley and oats.

Although cornmeal was originally laboriously hand-ground between stones, American towns soon had their own municipal water-powered gristmills complete with heavy, imported French millstones. No one wanted to cook with grains from an unknown origin, so each farm grew its own grains, and then threshed and ground them at the local mill. Quality and purity was guaranteed. Today large commercial milling complexes grind kiln-dried hybrid corn grown on large corporate farms throughout the midwestern Corn Belt, although many bakers claim the meals lack the flavor, depth, and character of the now-rare varieties of stone-ground hominy, such as the northeastern Indian *tackhummin*, or southwestern adobe-oven roasted corns. These meals were made by grinding the entire kernel, rather than just the starchy endosperm, which is the method for processing modern degerminated meals.

All large-scale commercial corn-meals are now ground from the starchy-sweet hybrid dent corn. All types of cornmeal and corn flour can be used in quick breads. Baked goods made with cornmeal are crumbly in texture and a bit gritty. Because corn-meal is unique in flavor and texture, there is no substitute for it. The different grinds of cornmeal contribute to a variety of textures and crumb in the finished baked cornbread. The packaged steel-cut cornmeals available on grocery shelves are usually a medium grind, very good in flavor, and keep fresh a long time, as they are degerminated. For an exceptional flavor, use very fresh, water-ground meals, which are crushed between heavy granite stones and retain flecks of the the flavorful germ. These meals are available from small local mills or natural foods stores. Stone-ground cornmeals are usually available in a variety of grinds, and now, after centuries of unpopularity, a variety of colors are reappearing. All colors of cornmeal are interchangeable in recipes as long as the grind is similar, but the flavor will vary slightly. You can store your cornmeals in the refrigerator for up to about 6 months and in the freezer up to a year. Fresh meals will always smell sweet, never sour or rancid.

The most popular method of baking cornbread is in an 8- or 9-inch square or round pan, but there is a long history of using a seasoned 9-inch cast-iron skillet, which produces the crispest crust (especially on the bottom) and a moist interior. Most households used these skillets as a staple kitchen utensil in open hearth and wood stove cookery. Southerners especially like the round skillets that are divided into eight wedge-shaped sections, and the corn-stick-patterned pans, which hold enough cornbread to serve 4 to 6 diners. For baking in cast iron, heat the pan in the preheated oven for 5 minutes, remove with a thick oven mitt to prevent burns, then swirl with a tablespoon of solid shortening or butter to grease the pan. Then pour in the batter. Immediately return the

pan to the hot oven and bake until the top is dry to the touch and the bread pulls away from the sides of the pan. If you do not have a cast-iron skillet, you can substitute an 8-inch square or round pan, or a 9-inch pan for a thinner bread. Many of the recipes that follow are meant to be baked in these pans. Fourteen corn-shaped sticks or ten 3-inch muffins can also be made from these same batters.

Cornbreads are meant to be eaten fresh from the oven for the best flavor (once aptly described by food writer Richard Sax as tasting like "hot sunshine"), as they begin to stale quickly, but the leftovers are perfect for poultry stuffings. Cold, day-old cornbread is also good split, brushed with melted butter flavored with fresh garlic or crushed dried herbs, curry or chili powders, and broiled until lightly toasted. Wrapped tightly in plastic wrap and then foil, all cornbreads can be frozen for up to 2 months. Consider contributing a large pan of your own cornbread for your next potluck supper, outdoor picnic, or barbecue.

Yogurt Cornbread

One of my favorite breakfasts is a wedge of day-old Yogurt Cornbread, heated well, slathered with butter, and drizzled with some pure maple syrup. Alternatively, by adding a few teaspoons of poultry herbs to the batter, you can create the perfect base for a stuffing. To prepare the cornbread for making into stuffing, crumble it onto a flat pan or plate, cover loosely with a tea towel, and let air-dry overnight at room temperature before using.

Makes one 8-inch cornbread

1 cup fine-grind yellow or white cornmeal, preferably stone-ground
1 cup unbleached all-purpose flour
2 tablespoons sugar
½ teaspoon salt
½ teaspoon baking soda

Grated zest of 1 large orange
2 large eggs
¼ cup buttermilk
1¼ cups plain yogurt
4 tablespoons (½ stick) unsalted butter, melted, or ¼ cup corn oil

1 · Preheat the oven to 425°F. Grease an 8-inch springform or deep cake pan or spray it with cooking spray. Combine the cornmeal, flour, sugar, salt, baking soda, and orange zest in a large bowl.

2 · In a small bowl, mix the eggs, buttermilk, and yogurt with a whisk. Add to the dry ingredients and pour the melted butter over the top of the batter. Stir just until all the ingredients are moistened yet thoroughly blended. Take care not to overmix.

3 · Pour the batter into the prepared pan. Bake in the center of the oven for about 20 to 25 minutes, until golden around the edges and a cake tester inserted into the center comes out clean. Let stand for 15 minutes before cutting into thick wedges to serve.

Maple Pan Cornbread

Heat a seasoned 9-inch skillet in a pre-heated 425°F oven for 5 minutes, then swirl with a tablespoon of shortening or butter to grease. Immediately scrape in the Yogurt Cornbread batter. Sprinkle the surface with ½ cup (3 to 3½ ounces) coarsely chopped pure maple sugar candy. Return the skillet to the oven and bake as directed.

Bacon Cornbread

In a medium skillet, cook 1 cup diced smoked bacon or Italian pancetta (about 4 to 5 slices) until crisp. Drain on paper towels and add to the Yogurt Cornbread batter in Step 2. Bake as directed.

Berry Cornbread

Fold 1½ cups rinsed fresh raspberries, blueberries, or blackberries into the Yogurt Cornbread batter in Step 2. Bake as directed.

Black Olive Cornbread

Add 1 cup chopped California or imported black olives to the Yogurt Cornbread batter in Step 2. Scrape the batter into a greased 9-by-5-inch loaf pan. Bake about 35 to 40 minutes, until the bread tests done.

Apple Cornbread

Add 1½ cups peeled, cored, and coarsely chopped tart cooking apples such as Granny Smith or Fuji (about 2 whole) to the Yogurt Cornbread batter in Step 2. Bake as directed.

Rice Cornbread

Add 1 cup cold, cooked brown, wild, or white rice to the Yogurt Cornbread batter in Step 2. Bake as directed.

Fresh Corn Kernel and Cornmeal Bread

Use a fresh stone-ground cornmeal to make this exceptionally moist bread, which is studded with plump, golden kernels of corn fresh off the cob. If you decide to make twenty individual corn sticks from this batter, preheat the greased cast-iron molds while making the batter. Bake for 12 to 15 minutes. This bread is also nice baked into individual Cornmeal Savarins (variation follows). The effect is stunning.

Makes one 8-inch tube cornbread

1 cup fine-grind white or yellow cornmeal, preferably stone-ground

1 cup unbleached all-purpose flour

¼ cup sugar

2½ teaspoons baking powder

1¼ teaspoons hot red pepper flakes

¼ teaspoon salt

2 large eggs, separated

⅔ cup milk

⅔ cup heavy cream or evaporated milk

½ cup (1 stick) unsalted butter, melted

2 cups fresh or frozen baby white or yellow corn kernels

1 · Preheat the oven to 375°F. Grease an 8-inch heavy-gauge aluminum tube or Bundt pan or spray it with cooking spray. Combine the cornmeal, flour, sugar, baking powder, red pepper flakes, and salt in a large bowl.

2 · In a small bowl, mix the egg yolks, milk, heavy cream, butter, and corn kernels with a whisk. Add the egg yolk mixture to the dry ingredients. Stir with a wooden spoon just until all ingredients are moistened yet thoroughly blended, taking care not to overmix. The batter will be lumpy. With an electric mixer, beat the egg whites to form soft peaks in a small bowl. With a spatula, gently fold the whites into the batter, just until there are no more streaks.

3 · Scrape the batter into the prepared pan. Bake in the center of the oven for about 45 to 50 minutes, until golden around the edges and a cake tester inserted into the center comes out clean. Turn the bread out of the pan onto a rack to cool. Let stand 15 minutes before cutting into thick slices to serve.

Cornmeal Savarins

A savarin is characterized by the shallow ring mold it is baked in. While savarins are usually sweet cakes, this is a savory rendition. Fill the centers of these individual cornbreads with sautéed vegetables or creamed seafood or use them as unique little bowls for fresh fruit.

Makes 16 individual cornbreads

Preheat the oven to 375°F. Spray sixteen 3¼-inch metal *savarin* molds, Mary Ann molds, miniature scalloped Bundt pans, or miniature plain tube pans with cooking spray. Fill each with about 3 tablespoons to ¼ cup of the Fresh Corn Kernel and Cornmeal Bread batter and place the molds on two baking sheets. Bake in the center of the oven until a cake tester inserted into the centers of the individual cornbreads comes out clean, about 12 to 15 minutes. Loosen the edges with a small knife and turn out the *savarins* onto a rack to cool. Serve immediately. (The *savarins* can be frozen in plastic freezer bags for up to 1 month and reheated just before serving.)

Green and Red Pepper Cornbread

A variety of chiles are essential to the cuisine of the Southwest, and they are often used in baking for unusual savory fillings. This bread combines sweet bright red bell peppers with a thick-fleshed mild green chile and spikes it all with a dash of jalapeño in a rich sour cream batter. For a more authentic flavor, use masa harina, *the cornmeal ground from hominy and used for making tortillas, available in the flour section of supermarkets or in ethnic grocery stores. Serve this hearty bread for a casual lunch with fresh tomato soup and a simple tossed green salad.*

Makes one 8-inch cornbread or one 9-inch skillet cornbread

2 tablespoons corn oil

½ red bell pepper, cored, seeded, and cut into thin strips about 1 inch long

½ mild green chile pepper, such as Anaheim, New Mexico, or poblano, cored, seeded, and cut into thin strips about 1 inch long

½ small hot green chile pepper, such as jalapeño, cored, seeded, deveined, and minced

¾ cup unbleached all-purpose flour

¾ cup fine-grind yellow cornmeal, preferably stone-ground, or *masa harina*

3 tablespoons sugar

2 teaspoons baking powder

½ teaspoon baking soda

½ teaspoon ground cumin

½ teaspoon salt

1 large egg

1 cup sour cream

½ cup shredded Monterey Jack cheese

1 · Preheat the oven to 400°F. If you are using an 8-inch springform pan or pie plate, grease it or spray it with cooking spray. Heat the corn oil in a small skillet and add the bell pepper and chiles. Cover and cook over low heat until tender, about 5 minutes. Remove from heat.

2 · Combine the flour, cornmeal, sugar, baking powder, baking soda, cumin, and salt in a large bowl. In a small bowl, beat together the egg, sour cream, and cooked chiles with any excess oil. Mix the wet ingredients into the dry ingredients just until evenly combined. Take care not to overmix. The batter will be lumpy. If you are using a 9-inch cast-iron skillet, place it in the oven to preheat for 5 minutes.

3 · Pour the batter into the prepared pan or into the preheated skillet. Bake in the center of the oven for 15 minutes. Sprinkle with the shredded cheese and return to the oven for about 10 minutes longer. When done, the corn-bread will be golden around the edges, and a cake tester inserted into the center will come out clean. Let stand for 15 minutes before cutting into wedges to serve.

Skillet Cornbread with Walnuts

Skillet cornbreads are the grandparents of all quick bread cornbreads. Colonial American cook-books always contain recipes for skillet breads, baked on a trivet over an open fire, then, in later times, in the descending heat of the oven built into the side of the brick fireplace that graced every kitchen hearth. This cornbread is still as good today as in generations gone by. If you do not have a cast-iron skillet, you can use a 9-inch round heavy ceramic or metal baking dish. Just be sure to preheat the pan.

Makes one 9-inch cornbread

2 tablespoons unsalted butter
1 tablespoon vegetable oil
1 cup medium-grind yellow or white
  cornmeal
1 cup unbleached all-purpose flour
½ cup chopped walnuts
1 teaspoon baking powder

1 teaspoon baking soda
1 teaspoon salt
½ teaspoon cream of tartar
½ cup milk
One 8-ounce can cream-style corn
1 large egg

1 · Preheat the oven to 425°F. Place the butter and oil in a 9-inch cast-iron skillet.

2 · In a bowl, combine the cornmeal, flour, walnuts, baking powder, baking soda, salt, and cream of tartar. In a 4-cup measuring cup or in a bowl, combine the milk, cream-style corn, and egg. Pour the milk mixture into the dry ingredients and stir with a large wooden spoon until just combined. Place the skillet in the oven for 5 minutes to melt the butter and preheat the skillet.

3 · With heavy oven mitts, remove the skillet from the oven and scrape the batter into it. Smooth the top to make it even. Return the skillet to the center of the oven and bake for 20 to 25 minutes, until the cornbread is golden around the edges, and a cake tester inserted into the center comes out clean. Let stand for 10 minutes before cutting into thick wedges and serving warm.

Sweet-Potato Cornbread with Orange Butter

Sweet potatoes add a lush texture and delicate color to traditional cornbread, although Fresh Pumpkin Puree (page 351) may be substituted, if desired. A great way to use leftover baked "sweets," this bread is good with turkey or spicy black bean soup on a blustery day. Serve warm, dripping with Orange Butter (following).

Makes one 9-inch cornbread

1 cup unbleached all-purpose flour
½ cup fine-grind yellow or white cornmeal,
  preferably stone-ground
1 teaspoon baking powder
½ teaspoon baking soda
½ teaspoon salt
⅛ teaspoon ground allspice
⅛ teaspoon ground mace

2 large eggs
1 cup pureed baked sweet potatoes or ruby
  yams, cooled
¼ cup corn oil
3 tablespoons pure maple syrup
½ cup buttermilk
Orange Butter (optional), following

1 · Preheat the oven to 375°F. Grease a 9-inch round springform or square cake pan. Combine the flour, cornmeal, baking powder, baking soda, salt, and spices in a large bowl.

2 · In a small bowl, mix the eggs, sweet potatoes, corn oil, maple syrup, and buttermilk with a whisk. Add the mixture to the dry ingredients. Stir just until all ingredients are moistened yet thoroughly blended. Take care not to overmix.

3 · Pour the batter into the prepared pan. Bake in the center of the oven about 20 to 25 minutes, until the cornbread is golden around the edges and a cake tester inserted into the center comes out clean. Let stand for 15 minutes before cutting into thick wedges. Serve with Orange Butter (following), if desired.

Orange Butter

Makes ½ cup butter

½ cup (1 stick) unsalted butter, at room
  temperature
Grated zest of 1 large orange

In a small bowl using the back of a
spoon, or in a blender or food processor, cream the butter and zest until
fluffy and well combined. Store,
covered, in the refrigerator for up to
1 week. Bring to room temperature
before serving.

Maple–Whole Wheat Johnnycake with Blueberries

This is a Northern-style cornbread using ground yellow cornmeal, gently sweetened and full of juicy, ripe berries. In comparison, Southern-style cornbreads are characteristically white and contain no added sweetening in their batters. Whole wheat johnnycakes are popular in Nova Scotia and New England, where maple sugar trees grow profusely. Locals say maple sweetenings are unequalled by any others in the world; these sweeteners are a common addition to cornbreads from that area. Serve for brunch with Maple Butter (following), if desired, fresh juices, and scrambled eggs, or for Sunday night supper with pumpkin soup. Cornbreads do not keep well, so plan to mix, bake, and serve your bread the same day it is made.

Makes one 9-inch cornbread

1¼ cups fine-grind yellow cornmeal, preferably stone-ground

1 cup whole wheat pastry flour

1 tablespoon baking powder

½ teaspoon salt

2 large eggs

¾ cup buttermilk

¼ cup pure maple syrup

4 tablespoons (½ stick) unsalted butter, melted

1½ cups fresh or frozen, unthawed, blueberries

Maple Butter (optional), following

1 · Preheat the oven to 400°F. Grease a 9-inch springform or deep cake pan or square Pyrex pan, or spray with cooking spray. (Reduce oven temperature by 25° if using a Pyrex pan.) Combine the cornmeal, flour, baking powder, and salt in a large bowl.

2 · In a small bowl, mix the eggs, buttermilk, and maple syrup together with a whisk. Add to the dry ingredients, and pour the melted butter over it. Stir with a wooden spoon just until all ingredients are moistened yet thoroughly blended. Take care not to overmix. With a rubber spatula, gently fold in the blueberries.

3 · Pour the batter into the prepared pan. Bake in the center of the oven for about 20 to 25 minutes, until the cornbread is golden around the edges and

a cake tester inserted into the center comes out clean. Let stand for 15 minutes before cutting into thick wedges. Serve with Maple Butter, if desired.

Maple Butter

Makes ½ cup butter

½ cup (1 stick) unsalted butter, at room
   temperature
3 tablespoons pure maple syrup

In a small bowl using the back of
a spoon, or in a blender or food
processor, cream the butter and
maple syrup until fluffy and well
combined. Store, covered, in the
refrigerator for up to 3 days. Bring
to room temperature before serving.

Cranberry-Walnut Cornbread

Cranberries and walnuts are one of my favorite fruit-and-nut combinations. Fresh cranberries arrive in the supermarkets in late September, packaged in 12-ounce plastic bags. They can be frozen and used in baking year-round. Their tart, crunchy nature makes for a hearty cornbread with a delicate, fruity flavor.

Makes one 9-by-5-inch loaf

1 cup fine-grind yellow cornmeal, preferably
  stone-ground
1 cup unbleached all-purpose flour
¾ cup packed light brown sugar or
  granulated maple sugar
½ teaspoon salt
½ teaspoon baking soda

Grated zest of 1 large orange
1 cup fresh cranberries, coarsely chopped
1 cup (4 ounces) walnuts, chopped
2 large eggs
1 cup buttermilk
6 tablespoons (¾ stick) unsalted butter,
  melted

1 · Preheat the oven to 425°F. Grease a 9-by-5-inch loaf pan or spray it with cooking spray. Combine the cornmeal, flour, brown or maple sugar, salt, baking soda, and orange zest in a large bowl. Add the cranberries and the walnuts.

2 · In a small bowl, mix the eggs and buttermilk with a whisk. Add to the dry ingredients and pour the melted butter over the top. Stir just until all ingredients are moistened and thoroughly blended. Take care not to overmix.

3 · Pour the batter into the prepared pan. Bake in the center of the oven for about 35 to 40 minutes, until the cornbread is golden around the edges and a cake tester inserted into the center comes out clean. Let stand for 15 minutes before cutting into thick slices to serve.

Steamed Pecan Cornbread

Steaming cornbread over a hot-water bath results in a beautifully moist texture. For an added dimension of flavor, toast the cornmeal gently on a baking sheet or in a heavy, dry skillet in a 325°F oven for 15 to 20 minutes, stirring occasionally, until it turns a pale golden brown. Transfer immediately to a bowl to stop the cooking process, and let the cornmeal cool before making the batter. Slice Steamed Pecan Cornbread into fat rounds and serve fresh or toasted with honey and butter.

Makes two 1-pound loaves

1 cup fine-grind yellow cornmeal, preferably stone-ground

2 cups unbleached all-purpose flour

1 cup (4 ounces) pecans, finely chopped

2 teaspoons baking soda

½ teaspoon salt

2 cups buttermilk

½ cup pure maple syrup

2 large eggs

1 · Generously grease two 1-pound coffee cans and line the bottom of each with a circle of parchment paper.

2 · In a large bowl, combine the cornmeal, flour, pecans, baking soda, and salt. In a 4-cup measure or in a bowl, combine the buttermilk, maple syrup, and eggs. Stir with a whisk. Pour into the dry ingredients. Beat well until evenly moistened.

3 · Scrape the batter into the prepared molds, filling them no more than two-thirds full. Cover each tightly with foil held in place by thick rubber bands. Place the molds on a rack in a deep kettle. Add boiling water to a depth of 1 to 2 inches up the sides of the molds. Cover pot and adjust heat to a low simmer. Steam for about 2½ hours, or until a cake tester inserted into the center of each loaf comes out clean. Add more boiling water during the steaming, if necessary, if too much evaporates.

4 · Preheat the oven to 400°F. When the breads are done, remove the foil tops from the molds and place the molds in the center of the oven for no more

than 5 minutes to dry slightly. Remove the bread from the cans, peel off the parchment paper, and place the loaves on their sides on a rack to cool. Serve warm, sliced into rounds. Store, wrapped in plastic wrap, at room temperature for up to 3 days.

NOTE: *These breads can also be baked in a conventional 350°F oven for 40 to 50 minutes in two 8-by-4-by-3-inch loaf pans, but the consistency will be a bit drier and there will be a crusty top surface.*

Country Whole Wheat Cornbread

This is the recipe I use when making cornbread for a large crowd. Although it uses whole wheat pastry flour rather than unbleached white flour, it bakes into moist, light, and flavorful bread. Feel free to reduce or eliminate the brown sugar if you desire. I bake the cornbread in a 12-inch round pan, but you can also use a 13-by-9-inch rectangular pan, or, for a thin bread, in a 16-by-13-inch sheet pan (bake for 10 minutes less). It serves ten hearty eaters. Serve this cornbread hot for brunch with some Hazelnut Honey Butter (following) melting over the wedges, if desired. For dinner, split and fill the cornbread, as for a shortcake, with creamed lobster in season and garnish with a sprinkle of paprika and lemon wedges.

Makes one 12-inch cornbread

3½ cups fine-grind yellow cornmeal, preferably stone-ground

2 cups whole wheat pastry flour

½ cup packed light brown sugar or granulated maple sugar

2 teaspoons baking powder

1½ teaspoons baking soda

1 teaspoon salt

4 large eggs

3 cups buttermilk

¾ cup (1½ sticks) unsalted butter, melted

Hazelnut Honey Butter (optional), following

1 · Preheat the oven to 325°F. Grease a 12-inch springform or deep cake pan, or spray it with cooking spray. Combine the cornmeal, flour, brown or maple sugar, baking powder, baking soda, and salt in a large bowl.

2 · In a small bowl, mix the eggs and buttermilk with a whisk. Add to the dry ingredients and pour the melted butter over the top. Stir just until all ingredients are moistened yet thoroughly blended. Take care not to overmix.

3 · Pour the batter into the prepared pan. Bake in the center of the oven for about 45 to 50 minutes, until the cornbread is golden around the edges and a cake tester inserted into the center comes out clean. Let stand for 15 minutes before cutting it into thick wedges. Serve with Hazelnut Honey Butter, if desired.

Hazelnut Honey Butter

Makes about 1 cup butter

¼ cup whole hazelnuts
½ cup (1 stick) unsalted butter, at room
  temperature
⅓ cup honey

1 · Preheat the oven to 350°F. Spread
the hazelnuts in a baking pan and
bake until lightly toasted, about
8 minutes. Place the nuts in the
center of a clean kitchen towel,
fold the towel over, and rub the
hazelnuts to remove their skins.
Let cool.

2 · In a blender or in a food processor
fitted with the metal blade, blend
all the ingredients until smooth,
stopping as necessary to scrape
down the sides of the container.
Place the butter in a covered container and store in the refrigerator
for up to 1 week. For the best
flavor, let the butter stand for 1
hour at room temperature before
serving.

Italian Polenta Cornbread with Sun-Dried Tomatoes and Basil

Polenta is a coarse cornmeal that is a staple in northern Italy. Indian meal traveled to Italy during the 1500s and rapidly became a popular, unpretentious peasant food also known as gran turco, *the "Turkish grain." In Italy today, it is grown in yellow-, white-, and copper-colored varieties that are ground into polenta. This recipe makes a Tuscan-style, basil-scented, rustic* pane di polenta. *Sun-dried Roma tomatoes can be bought marinated in oil or as dehydrated slices; either type is fine for this recipe. Use a good-quality fresh, whole-milk mozzarella as the exquisite final touch.*

Makes one 10-inch or 13-by-9-inch cornbread or one 10-inch skillet cornbread

2 ounces dry-pack sun-dried tomatoes
  or ¼ cup oil-packed sun-dried tomatoes
1 large shallot, chopped
4 tablespoons (½ stick) unsalted butter or
  oil from oil-packed sun-dried tomatoes
1¼ cups unbleached all-purpose flour
¾ cup polenta or coarsely ground yellow
  cornmeal, preferably stone-ground
½ teaspoon salt
½ teaspoon baking powder

½ teaspoon baking soda
2 tablespoons minced fresh basil
¼ teaspoon ground cumin
3 large eggs
½ cup sour cream
One 17-ounce can baby corn kernels,
  undrained
1 cup (4 ounces) coarsely shredded or
  diced whole-milk or smoked mozzarella
  cheese

1 · Preheat the oven to 400°F. If you are using a 10-inch springform pan or a 13-by-9-inch baking dish, grease the pan or spray it with cooking spray. If you are using dry-pack sun-dried tomatoes, place them in a small bowl and cover them with boiling water. Let stand for 10 minutes to soften; drain and chop. If using oil-packed tomatoes, drain the tomatoes, reserving the oil, and chop. In a small skillet, sauté the shallot in the butter or reserved tomato oil until softened. Remove from the heat and set aside.

2 · Combine the flour, polenta or coarse cornmeal, salt, baking powder, baking soda, basil, and cumin in a large bowl.

3 · In a small bowl, mix the eggs, sour cream, corn with its liquid, sautéed shallots and butter or oil, chopped sun-dried tomatoes, and cheese with a wooden spoon. Add to the dry ingredients and stir just until all the ingredients are moistened and thoroughly blended. Take care not to overmix; the batter will be thin. If you are using a skillet to bake the cornbread, place the greased skillet in the oven for 5 minutes to preheat.

4 · Pour the batter into the prepared pan or baking dish or into the the hot 10-inch skillet. Bake in the center of the oven for about 30 to 35 minutes, until the cornbread is golden around the edges and a cake tester inserted into the center comes out clean. Let stand for 15 minutes before cutting into thick wedges to serve.

Blue Cornbread with Goat Cheese and Green Chiles

This sophisticated cornbread is ideal for serving to a discriminating group of diners. Laced with spicy chiles, it is not too sweet, with a buttery consistency and crumbly texture. The goat cheese creates delightful, creamy pockets of flavor. Serve it with baked beans, corn on the cob, and a large mixed raw-vegetable salad with a tomato vinaigrette.

Makes one 10-inch or 13-by-9-inch cornbread or one 10-inch skillet cornbread

¾ cup (1½ sticks) unsalted butter, at room temperature

¼ cup sugar

1 cup fine- to medium-grind blue cornmeal (*harina de mais azul para tortillas*)

4 large eggs

1½ cups unbleached all-purpose flour

1 tablespoon baking powder

1 teaspoon salt

One 15-ounce can cream-style corn

1 poblano or Anaheim green chile, roasted, peeled, seeded, and minced, or one 4-ounce can diced green chiles, drained

5½ ounces fresh goat cheese, such as Chabis or Montrachet, crumbled

1 · Preheat the oven to 375°F. If you are using a 10-inch springform pan or a 13-by-9-inch baking dish, grease the pan or spray it with cooking spray. In a large bowl using an electric mixer, beat the butter and sugar until creamy. Add the cornmeal and beat until blended. Add the eggs, one at a time, beating until fluffy after each addition.

2 · In another bowl, combine the flour, baking powder, and salt. Add the mixture to the cornmeal batter and beat well with the electric mixer. Fold in the corn, chile, and crumbled goat cheese until evenly distributed. If you are using the cast-iron skillet, place it in the oven for 5 minutes to preheat, then swirl a tablespoon of solid shortening or butter in it to grease it.

3 · Pour the batter into the prepared pan or hot skillet. Bake in the center of the oven for about 35 to 40 minutes, until the cornbread is golden around the edges and a cake tester inserted into the center comes out clean. Let stand for 15 minutes before cutting into thick wedges to serve.

$\mathcal{K}$asha Cornsticks

I consider kasha, toasted buckwheat groats, an acquired taste. But when it is added into a corn-meal batter with some toasted sesame seeds, its assertive taste becomes delightful. A basket of these cornsticks is sure to delight at any meal, with egg dishes for breakfast, with a soup or salad at lunch, or with a chicken dinner. This recipe is straight off the box of Wolff's kasha and has been a favorite for decades. If you don't have a corn-stick pan, you can make this as a corn-bread in a 9-inch pan.

Makes about 20 cornsticks

1 cup milk
½ cup whole kasha
4 tablespoons (½ stick) unsalted butter
2 tablespoons sesame seeds
1 cup unbleached all-purpose flour

⅔ cup yellow cornmeal, stone-ground, if
   possible
4 teaspoons baking powder
½ teaspoon salt
¼ cup honey
1 large egg

1 · Scald the milk in a 4-cup Pyrex measuring cup in the microwave oven, or in a small saucepan on the stovetop. Add the kasha and butter. Stir to melt the butter and let the mixture stand until lukewarm on the counter, about 40 minutes. Place the sesame seeds in a dry skillet over medium heat. Shaking the pan, toast the sesame seeds until they turn light golden, 3 to 4 minutes. Remove from the pan and let cool.

2 · Preheat the oven to 425°F. Grease two cornstick pans or plan on baking a second batch in the same pan (ten to a pan; you will be making about twenty cornsticks). In a mixing bowl, combine the flour, cornmeal, baking powder, toasted sesame seeds, and salt.

3 · In a 4-cup measuring cup or in a bowl, combine the milk-kasha mixture, the honey, and the egg, and stir into the dry ingredients with a large wooden spoon until just combined.

4 · Spoon the batter into the prepared cornstick pan molds, until level with the top of the pan. Bake in the center of the oven for 15 to 20 minutes, until the cornsticks are golden around the edges and firm to the touch. Let stand 10 minutes before unmolding.

Coffee Cakes

Coffee Cakes

Coffee cakes are an American passion, a homey concoction crossing a muffin and a cake, neither too sweet nor too rich. They are never frosted like regular cakes, but may be drizzled with frosting, glazed with jam, dusted with an ethereal layer of powdered sugar, or sport a spice- or nut-enhanced crumb top. They are excellent showcases for seasonal fresh fruit. Often referred to as "morning cakes," they offer a wide range of delightfully versatile interpretations on the simple butter cake, but need not be restricted to breakfasting. They satisfy the "I baked it from scratch" urge most cooks get at one time or another. In the world of cake baking, these cakes are by far the easiest to prepare, and they enable even a beginning baker to produce a cake that tastes as wonderful as it looks. These recipes, such as Blueberry Cheese Crumbcake and Fresh Apple Coffee Cake, reflect pure nostalgic American traditions, with simple batters made in the same manner as they were decades ago, when home baking was a country art, as well as a necessity.

The beginning of the eighteenth century brought coffee, tea, and chocolate drinks to the upper classes of Europe, and baked goods were the natural accompaniment. Coffee time and teatime became an established small meal for all classes of society, and toasted breads, tea cakes, and scones with jam were all very popular. High tea in Britain, the Viennese *Kaffeejause*, and the German home *Kaffeetisch* all featured favorite simple to elaborate baking-powder cakes, served unadorned or covered with precious spices, sugared crumbs, nuts, chestnuts, orchard fruits, or sweet cheese. German, Swiss, Austrian, and Hungarian home bakers were proud of their hospitality and the high quality and artistic presentation of their tables. From this era we have inherited many of the basic styles and recipes still prepared today.

Coffee cakes are simple batters leavened with baking powder, baking soda, or both, mixed in one bowl, baked in the center of a preheated oven, and often served from the pan as soon as they've cooled enough not to scorch the fingers. Batters are mixed briskly by hand or with an electric mixer until fluffy and scraped into a well-greased pan. Coffee cakes all contain the same basic ingredients: butter or vegetable oil; eggs; sugar or some other sweetening; flour; milk, sour cream, or buttermilk; leavening; and one or more flavorings creamed together to create a moist, rich cake after baking. The proportion of these ingredients varies slightly from recipe to recipe and dictates the finished flavor and texture of each individual cake, so take care to measure the ingredients as directed.

A coffee cake should be baked immediately after mixing. To avoid overbaking, always set the timer for 5 to 10 minutes before the end of the suggested baking time to start testing with a toothpick or metal cake tester for doneness. If the edges have pulled away from the sides of the pan, it is a good indication that the cake is baked. A coffee cake may be quite fragile or very moist when it comes directly out of the oven, but it then cools on a rack into a delicate or richly dense cake. A wire or wooden cooling rack is important here; it allows the air to circulate fully around the cake. A properly cooled cake sets and contracts enough to either turn out of the pan to finish cooling or to cut into serving pieces. To unmold a cake that doesn't have a crumb topping, loosen the sides with a knife or spatula, if necessary. Place a wire cake rack over the top rim of the cake pan. Place your outstretched palm against the rack to secure it and gently turn the pan upside down onto the rack. The cake will release onto the rack. Carefully remove the pan

and allow the cake to finish cooling. A cake left to cool for too long will form a crusty outer layer, so don't leave a cake out unwrapped for more than a few hours. Each recipe will specify the best handling techniques.

For baking a wide range of coffee cakes, collect a selection of lightweight aluminum, Pyrex, rustic stoneware, imported porcelain, or antique metal baking dishes in a variety of sizes and shapes in addition to the standard round, square, or rectangular pans. This is the place to use those beautifully crafted fluted tube molds, square angel food pans, fluted tin tart pans, scalloped Turk's-head molds, and heavy aluminum Bundt pans. Antique stores often turn up the simple, early models of central tunnel-cake pans made of beaten tin, or elaborately embossed ones made of fired clay or copper that were used for special-occasion baking. Cakes look extraordinarily stately made in these pans, turned out of the pan and served from a pedestal cake plate. The center tube may be filled with flowers or whole fresh berries to create a centerpiece.

Most coffee cakes keep well at room temperature for up to 3 days (please refrigerate cakes with cheese toppings), but they also freeze well for 2 to 3 weeks if they are allowed to cool completely first, and are tightly wrapped in plastic wrap and then in foil, which retains the moist, crumbly texture and full flavor. To defrost, let the coffee cake stand at room temperature fully wrapped but slightly open, to allow the excess moisture to evaporate. Serve at room temperature or warm first, unwrapped, in a 350°F oven for 10 to 15 minutes, depending on the size of the cake.

Good not only for brunch, coffee cakes may also be served as a casual dessert or afternoon repast. They're great picnic fare and make wonderful gifts because they are easy to wrap and pack. And coffee cakes needn't be served just with coffee. Brewed and iced English teas, savory coffee substitutes derived from malt and chicory, an array of herbal teas, or even a glass of cold milk or fresh juice are all worthy partners to these delicious cakes.

Fresh Apple Coffee Cake

Fresh Apple Coffee Cake is luscious and extravagant in flavor. Since it is a large cake, it is important that it be baked in a pan with a center tube, such as an angel food cake pan, scalloped Bundt pan, or highly decorative fluted kugelhopf *mold. In early fall I make it with homegrown Rome Beauty apples, but any firm tart cooking apple, such as a Granny Smith or Winesap, will do nicely. The cake needs no embellishment, since the fruit adds a fragrant touch to the orange-scented batter.*

Makes one 10-inch tube cake

4 cups peeled, cored, and coarsely chopped
   tart cooking apples (4 to 5 apples)
⅓ cup packed light brown sugar
1½ tablespoons ground cinnamon
3 cups unbleached all-purpose flour
1¾ cups granulated sugar

1 tablespoon baking powder
½ teaspoon salt
Grated zest of 1 orange
4 large eggs
1 cup vegetable oil
½ cup orange juice

1 · Preheat the oven to 375°F. Grease and flour a 10-inch plain tube pan, fluted *kugelhopf* mold, or Bundt pan and set aside. In a small bowl, combine the apples with the brown sugar and the cinnamon. Set aside.

2 · In a medium bowl, combine the flour, sugar, baking powder, salt, and orange zest.

3 · With an electric mixer, balloon whisk, or blender, beat the eggs and oil until thick and creamy, about 2 minutes at high speed. Add the egg and oil mixture to the dry ingredients along with the orange juice and beat just until moistened, but thoroughly blended. Do not overmix, but there should be no lumps or dry spots.

4 · Pour one-third of the batter over the bottom of the prepared tube pan. Cover evenly with half the apple mixture and then pour another one-third of the batter over the apples. Use a spatula to smooth the batter over the apples to cover completely. Repeat with the remaining apples and batter, ending with a smooth layer of batter.

5 · Bake in the center of the oven for 60 minutes. Cover loosely with a piece of aluminum foil and bake an additional 15 minutes, or until a cake tester inserted into the center comes out clean. Remove from the oven and cool in the pan on a rack for about 1 hour. Turn out onto a rack to cool completely before serving. Securely wrapped, this cake freezes well.

Banana Coffee Cake

Although we are used to banana quick breads, a banana coffee cake is rare. Bananas ripen off the tree as they travel from the Latin American tropics to our grocery stores. Somehow every household seems to end up with some overripe ones. Instead of tossing them, make this coffee cake. I especially like to use Cook's Cookie Vanilla here; it has a fruity flavor from the combination of Tahitian vanilla and Bourbon vanilla. This is a coffee cake that even the kids will love. If you would like to add a chocolate glaze, which complements the banana to perfection, drizzle the cake with the Bittersweet Glaze on page 59.

Makes one 10-inch tube cake

¾ cup (1½ sticks) unsalted butter, at room temperature
1½ cups sugar
2 large eggs
1 cup (8 ounces) sour cream
2 teaspoons vanilla extract
3 medium ripe bananas, mashed
3 cups unbleached all-purpose flour

2 teaspoons baking powder
½ teaspoon baking soda
½ teaspoon salt
½ cup pecans, finely chopped
½ cup packed light brown sugar
1¼ teaspoons ground cinnamon
Powdered sugar, for dusting

1 · Preheat the oven to 350°F. Grease and flour a 12-cup Bundt or fluted tube pan.

2 · Cream the butter and sugar until light and fluffy in the bowl of a heavy-duty electric mixer. Add the eggs, one at a time, beating thoroughly after each addition. Add the sour cream, vanilla extract, and bananas, and beat until just smooth.

3 · In another bowl, combine the flour, baking powder, baking soda, and salt. Gradually add the dry ingredients to the creamed mixture and beat well until fluffy, thick, and light colored. There should be no lumps or dry spots.

4 · Combine the pecans, brown sugar, and cinnamon in a small bowl. Pour about half of the batter into the prepared pan. Sprinkle with half of the nut

mixture. Spoon the remaining batter over the nut mixture and then sprinkle the top with the remaining nut mixture.

5 · Bake in the center of the oven for 55 to 60 minutes, or until a cake tester inserted into the center comes out clean, and the top of the cake is no longer shiny. Let the cake stand in the pan for 10 minutes before turning it out of the pan onto a rack to cool. Let cool completely before slicing. Dust with powdered sugar before serving.

Spiced Brown Sugar–Pecan Coffee Cake

This is a soft-textured buttermilk cake with a crunchy nut topping that is a must for the quick-bread baker's repertoire. I often substitute macadamias or blanched slivered almonds for the pecans, but the buttery flavor of pecans infuses the whole cake with a taste all its own. Spiced Brown Sugar–Pecan Coffee Cake is what is known as an old-fashioned "keeping cake," as it is naturally preserved by the buttermilk and can be stored tightly wrapped in plastic wrap and foil at room temperature for up to 5 days before serving.

Makes one 8-inch cake

Spiced Pecan Crumb Topping
¼ cup packed light brown sugar
¼ cup granulated sugar
½ cup unbleached all-purpose flour
½ teaspoon ground cinnamon
½ teaspoon ground mace
½ teaspoon ground ginger
6 tablespoons (¾ stick) cold unsalted butter, cut into pieces
2 cups (8 ounces) pecans, coarsely chopped

Coffee Cake
4 tablespoons (½ stick) unsalted butter
½ cup packed light brown sugar
½ cup granulated sugar
2 large eggs
2 teaspoons vanilla extract
2 cups unbleached all-purpose flour
1 teaspoon baking powder
1 teaspoon baking soda
¼ teaspoon salt
1 cup buttermilk

1 · Preheat the oven to 350°F. Line the bottom of an 8-inch springform pan, an 8-inch fluted ceramic *clafouti* baking dish, or a 2-inch-deep removable-bottom tart pan with parchment paper and grease the sides.

2 · To make the crumb topping: Combine the sugars, flour, and spices in a small bowl or the workbowl of a food processor. Cut in the butter with your fingers or process just until the mixture forms coarse crumbs. Add the pecans and set aside.

3 · To make the coffee cake: In a bowl using a wooden spoon, or in the bowl of a heavy-duty electric mixer, cream the butter and sugars until fluffy. Add the eggs and vanilla extract. Beat until smooth. In another bowl, combine

the flour, baking powder, baking soda, and salt. Add to the creamed mixture, alternating with the buttermilk. Beat hard until the batter has a creamy consistency, about 1 minute.

4 · Scrape half of the batter into the prepared pan. Sprinkle evenly with half of the Spiced Pecan Crumb Topping. Spoon the remaining batter over and sprinkle with the remaining crumb topping. Bake in the center of the oven until a cake tester inserted into the center comes out clean, about 40 to 45 minutes. Remove the cake from the oven and let it cool in the pan on a rack. To serve, remove the sides of the springform pan or serve from the baking dish, as desired.

▲ Cranberry-Hazelnut Coffeecake

STREUSEL:

¼ cup sifted cake flour
¼ cup packed brown sugar
¼ cup chopped hazelnuts
½ teaspoon ground cinnamon
1 tablespoon butter or stick margarine, melted

CAKE:

1⅔ cups sifted cake flour
1 cup granulated sugar
1½ teaspoons baking powder
¼ teaspoon baking soda
¼ teaspoon salt
1 teaspoon vanilla extract
1 (8-ounce) carton fat-free sour cream, divided
1 large egg
1 large egg white
5 tablespoons butter or stick margarine, softened

REMAINING INGREDIENTS:

Cooking spray
2 cups fresh cranberries, chopped

1. Preheat oven to 350°.

2. To prepare streusel, lightly spoon ¼ cup flour into a dry measuring cup; level with a knife. Combine ¼ cup flour and next 4 ingredients (¼ cup flour through 1 tablespoon butter) in a bowl; toss well. Set aside.

3. To prepare cake, lightly spoon 1⅔ cups flour into dry measuring cups; level with a knife. Combine 1⅔ cups flour and next 4 ingredients (1⅔ cups flour through salt), stirring well with a whisk. Combine vanilla, ¼ cup sour cream, egg, and egg white in a small bowl; stir with a whisk. Place remaining sour cream and 5 tablespoons butter in a large bowl; beat with a mixer at medium speed until well-blended (about 2 minutes). Add flour mixture to butter mixture alternately with egg mixture, beginning and ending with flour mixture.

4. Spread half of batter into a 9-inch springform pan coated with cooking spray. Sprinkle cranberries over batter. Spread remaining batter over cranberries. Sprinkle streusel mixture over batter. Bake at 350° for 45 minutes or until a wooden pick inserted in center comes out clean. Cool on a wire rack. Yield: 10

Cranberry–Almond Coffee Cake

My girlfriend once bought a slice of cranberry coffee cake at the Oakville Grocery in Palo Alto, California. She raved about it, and that was enough for me to want to make a cranberry–sour cream coffee cake of my very own. This recipe uses canned whole cranberry sauce, rather than fresh cranberries, so you can make it all year round.

Makes one 10-inch tube cake

3 cups unbleached all-purpose flour
1½ teaspoons baking powder
1½ teaspoons baking soda
½ teaspoon salt
¾ cup (1½ sticks) unsalted butter, at room
 temperature
1½ cups granulated sugar
3 large eggs
2 teaspoons almond extract
1½ cups sour cream

One 16-ounce can whole-berry cranberry
 sauce
½ cup slivered almonds

Almond Glaze
¾ cup sifted powdered sugar
1 to 2 tablespoons warm sweetened
 condensed skim milk
½ teaspoon almond extract

1 · Preheat the oven to 350°F. Grease and flour a 10-inch plain or fluted tube pan, and set aside. In a medium bowl, combine the flour, baking powder, baking soda, and salt.

2 · In the bowl of a heavy-duty electric mixer, cream the butter and granulated sugar until light and fluffy. Add the eggs, one at a time, beating thoroughly after each addition. Add the almond extract and sour cream, and blend just until smooth. Gradually add flour mixture and beat well until fluffy and smooth, yet thick.

3 · With a large spatula, scrape a third of the batter into the prepared pan. Break up the cranberry sauce with a spoon, and spoon a third of it over the batter. Repeat the layering two more times, ending with the cranberry sauce, and sprinkle the top with the slivered almonds.

4 · Bake in the center of the oven for 60 to 65 minutes, or until a cake tester inserted into the center comes out clean. Let the cake stand in the pan for 5 minutes.

5 · While the cake cools, make the glaze. Place the powdered sugar in a small bowl and whisk in the sweetened condensed milk and the almond extract until the mixture is smooth and of a pourable consistency. Adjust the consistency of the glaze by adding more warm milk, a few drops at a time, if needed.

6 · Turn the cake out onto a rack placed over a piece of wax paper, to catch the drips. Drizzle immediately with the glaze while the cake is warm. Let stand until cool before slicing.

Blueberry Cheese Crumbcake

Blueberry Cheese Crumbcake is one of those little gems of the baking world. It is a sublime combination of elements: fruit, cake, cheese, and ample crumbly topping—a harmony of tastes that is really pleasing to the palate. It is temptingly rich and decadent, with each element lending distinctive flavor and texture. I also like the cake made with fresh tart raspberries, big boysenberries, pitted Bing cherries, or homegrown red currants, when they're available.

Makes one 10-inch cake

Cheese Filling
8 ounces cream cheese, at room
  temperature
⅓ cup sugar
2 tablespoons fresh lemon juice
1 large egg
1 tablespoon unbleached all-purpose flour

Crumb Topping
1¼ cups unbleached all-purpose flour
  (can be half whole wheat pastry flour,
  if desired)
½ cup sugar
½ teaspoon ground cinnamon
6 tablespoons (¾ stick) cold unsalted butter,
  cut into small pieces

½ cup (1 stick) unsalted butter, at room
  temperature
⅔ cup sugar
2 large eggs
1½ teaspoons vanilla extract
1½ cups unbleached all-purpose flour
1½ teaspoons baking powder
¼ teaspoon salt
½ cup milk
1 pint fresh blueberries, rinsed and well
  drained

1 · Preheat the oven to 350°F. Grease and flour a 10-inch springform pan and set aside.

2 · To make the cheese filling: In a bowl, beat the cream cheese with a wooden spoon or electric mixer until creamy. Beat in the sugar, lemon juice, egg, and flour. Beat until smooth, about 1 minute. Set aside.

3 · To make the crumb topping: In a small bowl, combine the flour, sugar, and cinnamon. Cut in the butter with a fork or your fingers until coarse crumbs are formed. Set aside.

4 · To make the cake batter: In a bowl with a wooden spoon, or in the bowl of a heavy-duty electric mixer, cream the butter and sugar until fluffy. Add the eggs and vanilla extract and beat well. In a small bowl, combine the flour, baking powder, and salt. Beat the dry ingredients into the creamed mixture in two additions, alternating with the milk. Beat until smooth and fluffy.

5 · Spread the batter into the prepared pan, building the sides up slightly. Sprinkle the surface of the batter with 1 cup of the blueberries and spoon over the cheese filling. Scatter the remaining 1 cup blueberries over the surface. Sprinkle the top evenly with the crumb topping and press it gently into the blueberries and cheese mixture.

6 · Bake in the center of the oven for 60 to 70 minutes, or until the top is golden, the cheese filling is set, and the cake pulls away from the sides of the pan slightly. Cool the cake in the pan on a rack for 30 minutes before removing the sides and serving.

Fresh Pineapple Crumbcake

This is my basic fresh-fruit crumbcake, as sumptuous as it is simple. Fresh pineapple, a juicy fruit I find is not used often enough in baking, makes this cake very special. Pineapples are tropical fruit, even though they are named for the fir tree's pinecone. They are grown in areas nicknamed "pineapple paradises"—Hawaii, the West Indies, Mexico, and Florida. You could also use sliced apples, peach halves, plum halves, fresh blueberries (a favorite with everyone), or fresh or canned cherries in place of the pineapple.

Makes one 9-inch-square cake

Crumb Topping
1¼ cups unbleached all-purpose flour
⅓ cup sugar
3 tablespoons packed dark brown sugar
1 teaspoon ground cinnamon or apple pie spice
½ cup (1 stick) cold unsalted butter, cut into pieces

½ cup (1 stick) unsalted butter, at room temperature
⅔ cup sugar

1 large egg
2 large egg yolks
1½ teaspoons vanilla extract
3 tablespoons plain yogurt
1¼ cups unbleached all-purpose flour
1 teaspoon baking powder
½ teaspoon baking soda
¼ teaspoon salt
1 medium fresh pineapple (about 2 pounds) or 20 ounces precut fresh pineapple

1 · Preheat the oven to 350°F (325°F for a Pyrex glass or dark-finish pan). Line a 9-inch-square baking pan with parchment paper, and grease the paper and the sides of the pan. Set aside.

2 · Prepare the crumb topping: In the bowl of an electric mixer, combine the flour, sugars, and cinnamon or apple pie spice. Cut in the cold butter on low speed until coarse crumbs are formed. Pour the crumb topping into a small bowl and set aside. If not using immediately, refrigerate until needed.

3 · To make the cake batter: Without cleaning the mixing bowl, cream the butter and sugar until fluffy. Add the egg and yolks, one at a time, beating after

each addition. Then add the vanilla extract, and beat well on medium speed for 30 seconds; the mixture will be loose. Add the yogurt and mix until blended; the mixture will look curdled. Add the flour, baking powder, baking soda, and salt. Beat on low speed for 30 seconds, then increase the speed to medium and beat for at least 1 minute, until thick, creamy, and fluffy.

4 · If you are using a whole pineapple, peel it and cut it in half lengthwise. Remove the core and cut the fruit into ½ inch slices. If you are using the precut fruit, cut it in half lengthwise, discard the core, then slice it into half-rings.

5 · Pour the batter into the prepared pan and use a metal spatula or knife to spread the batter evenly (it will be a bit stiff). Arrange the half-rings slightly overlapping one another in two rows on top of the batter. Place any extra slices sideways between the two rows. Sprinkle the top evenly with the crumb topping.

6 · Bake in the center of the oven for 50 to 55 minutes, or until the cake pulls away from the sides of the pan slightly, and a cake tester inserted into the center comes out clean. Let the cake cool in the pan on a rack for at least 30 minutes before serving warm in squares out of the pan, or wrapping it tightly with plastic to serve later at room temperature.

Apricot and Prune Coffee Cake

This coffee cake has shown up in many versions in the decades since it won the blue ribbon for the best cake in a Midwest baking contest. The dried apricots and prunes are a surprisingly delightful taste combination. Serve this cake sprinkled with powdered sugar, if desired, and accompanied by mugs of extravagant Mexican hot chocolate for brunch.

Makes one 10-inch tube cake

1 cup (6 ounces) dried apricots
1 cup (8 ounces) pitted dried prunes
Boiling water
1 tablespoon all-purpose flour, for dusting the fruit
¾ cup (1½ sticks) unsalted butter, at room temperature
1¼ cups granulated sugar
4 large eggs
3 cups unbleached all-purpose flour
2½ teaspoons baking powder

1 teaspoon baking soda
½ teaspoon salt
1 cup sour cream
2 teaspoons vanilla extract

Nut Crumb Topping
⅔ cup packed light brown sugar
½ cup finely chopped walnuts
1 tablespoon ground cinnamon
1 tablespoon unbleached all-purpose flour

1 · Preheat the oven to 350°F. In a small bowl, cover the apricots and prunes with boiling water to plump. Let stand for 10 minutes. While the fruit macerates, grease and flour a 10-inch tube pan. Drain the dried fruit and, using oiled kitchen shears or a knife, coarsely chop the prunes and dice the apricots. Toss them with the tablespoon of flour and set aside.

2 · In the bowl of a heavy-duty electric mixer, cream the butter and granulated sugar until light and fluffy. Add the eggs, one at a time, beating thoroughly after each additon.

3 · In another bowl, combine the flour, baking powder, baking soda, and salt. Gradually add the dry ingredients to the creamed mixture, alternating with the sour cream, and adding the vanilla with one of the sour cream additions. Beat well until just smooth. There should be no lumps or dry

spots, although the mixture may look curdled. Fold in the chopped fruit with a spatula.

4 · To make the Nut Crumb Topping: Combine the brown sugar, walnuts, cinnamon, and flour in a small bowl. With a large spatula, scrape a third of the batter into the prepared pan. Sprinkle with half of the topping. Repeat with another third of the batter and the remaining topping, finishing with the remaining batter.

5 · Bake in the center of the oven for 65 to 75 minutes, or until a cake tester inserted into the center comes out clean, and the top of the cake is no longer shiny. Let the cake stand in the pan for 10 minutes before turning it out of the pan onto a rack to cool completely.

*I*talian Lemon and Anise Sweet Bread

My favorite Italian flavors—lemons, walnuts, anise, and raisins—are the spirited Mediterranean additions to this barely sweet cake, which you will be proud to serve for a festive occasion. It also toasts nicely after a day or two.

Makes one 10-inch tube cake

6 large eggs
2 cups granulated sugar
¾ cup vegetable oil
4½ cups unbleached all-purpose flour
2 tablespoons baking powder
Grated zest of 2 lemons

¾ teaspoon salt
1 cup milk
2 teaspoons anise extract
1 cup golden raisins
1 cup (4 ounces) walnuts, coarsely chopped
Powdered sugar, for dusting

1 · Preheat the oven to 350°F. Grease and flour a 10-inch plain or fluted tube pan and set it aside. With an electric mixer, blender, or balloon whisk, beat the eggs, granulated sugar, and oil on high speed or briskly by hand until thick and creamy, about 2 minutes.

2 · In another bowl, combine the flour, baking powder, lemon zest, and salt. Combine the milk and anise extract in a measuring cup. Add the egg mixture to the dry ingredients, alternating with the milk mixture. Beat just until moistened but thoroughly blended. Do not overmix, but there should be no lumps or dry spots. Fold in the raisins and the walnuts until evenly combined.

3 · Pour the batter into the prepared tube pan. Bake in the center of the oven until a cake tester inserted into the center comes out clean, 55 to 65 minutes. Remove the cake from the oven and let it stand in the pan for 15 minutes. Turn the cake out of the pan and onto a rack to cool slightly. Place the powdered sugar in a small sieve, place the rack over a piece of waxed paper, and dust the sugar over the cake while it is slightly warm. Transfer the cake to a serving plate. Serve slightly warm or at room temperature, cut into wedges. This cake freezes well for up to 2 months, but if you plan to freeze it, wait and dust it with the powdered sugar just before serving.

Jam Tea Cake

I have been baking this coffee cake in one form or another for last-minute breakfast guests for twenty years. It is a good way of using all those jars of exceptional store-bought jams that I tend to accumulate in the back of my refrigerator, but it is also an ideal showcase for the wonderful sweetness and flavor of homemade preserves. The small 6-inch cakes are particularly charming.

Makes one 8-inch cake or two 6-inch cakes

1½ cups unbleached all-purpose flour
⅓ cup sugar
1 teaspoon baking powder
½ teaspoon baking soda
Pinch of salt
4 tablespoons (½ stick) unsalted butter, melted

2 large eggs
½ cup sour cream
1½ teaspoons almond extract
½ to ⅔ cup thick fruit jam, preserves, or all-fruit spread
½ cup sliced almonds

1 · Preheat the oven to 350°F. Grease and flour an 8-inch springform pan, an 8-inch square cake pan, or two 6-inch springform pans, and set aside.

2 · In a mixing bowl, combine the flour, sugar, baking powder, baking soda, and salt. In another bowl, combine the butter, eggs, sour cream, and almond extract with a whisk. Add to the dry ingredients and beat until smooth and fluffy.

3 · Spread the batter evenly into the prepared pan then cover with spoonfuls of the jam, dotting it over the surface of the batter. Insert a butter knife straight into the batter and gently swirl a few times to distribute the jam slightly through the batter. Sprinkle with the almonds.

4 · Bake in the center of the oven until a cake tester inserted into the center comes out clean, about 40 to 45 minutes for the 8-inch pan or 25 to 30 minutes for the 6-inch pans. If you're using a springform pan or pans, let the cake stand for 10 minutes before removing the springform sides. Serve warm or at room temperature.

Marbled Chestnut–Sour Cream Coffee Cake

Vanilla- and chestnut-flavored batters are baked together to form a quintessential coffee cake that is excitingly different, yet exceptionally simple to mix and bake. Be certain to obtain sweetened crème de marron *puree, often available in the jam or specialty food section of supermarkets, rather than unsweetened chestnut puree. I have served this cake with fresh jumbo strawberries for dessert, as well as for brunch. A fluted pan, known as a* kugelhopf *mold, will bake the batter into a handsome cake that is suitable for presenting on a pedestal cake stand, but the plain tube pan, also known as an angel food cake pan, will make a cake that is just as beautiful.*

Makes one 10-inch Bundt or tube cake, or two 9-by-5-inch loaves

3 cups unbleached all-purpose flour
1½ teaspoons baking powder
1½ teaspoons baking soda
¼ teaspoon salt
½ cup (1 stick) unsalted butter, at room temperature
1¼ cups granulated sugar
3 large eggs
1 tablespoon vanilla extract
2 cups sour cream

One 8.75-ounce can imported French sweetened chestnut spread (*crème de marron*) or 1 cup plus 1 tablespoon homemade chestnut puree (page 331)
2 ounces (⅓ cup) semisweet or bittersweet chocolate chips
3 tablespoons powdered sugar, for dusting
1½ teaspoons unsweetened cocoa, for dusting

1 · Preheat the oven to 325°F. Grease and flour a 10-inch plain or fluted tube pan or Bundt pan or two 9-by-5-inch loaf pans and set aside.

2 · In a medium bowl, combine the flour, baking powder, baking soda, and salt. Set aside. In a large bowl, cream the butter and granulated sugar with a wooden spoon or electric mixer until light and fluffy. Add the eggs, one at a time, beating thoroughly after each addition. Add the vanilla extract and sour cream, blending just until smooth.

3 · Gradually add the dry ingredients to the sour cream and egg mixture and beat well until fluffy and smooth yet thick, about 2 minutes. There should

be no lumps or dry spots. Remove 1 cup of the batter and place it in a small bowl. Add the chestnut spread and chocolate chips. Stir briskly to combine evenly.

4 · If you are using the tube pan, with a large spatula, scrape half the batter into the prepared pan. Gently top with half of the chestnut and chocolate batter. Layer the remaining batter over the top and finish with the remaining chestnut and chocolate batter. Or scrape one quarter of the batter into each of the prepared loaf pans. Gently top with one quarter of the chestnut and chocolate batter. Divide the remaining batter between the two pans, and finish each with the remaining chestnut and chocolate batter. Place a butter knife straight down into the batter and gently swirl around the pan once or twice, distributing the chestnut and chocolate batter.

5 · Bake in the center of the oven for 60 to 65 minutes for the tube pans and 45 to 50 minutes for the loaves, or until a cake tester inserted into the center comes out clean, and the top of the cake is no longer shiny. Let the cake stand in the pan for 15 minutes before turning the cake out of the pan and onto a rack, right side up, to cool completely. Combine the powdered sugar and the cocoa in a small sieve, place the rack over a piece of waxed paper, and dust the mixture over the cake. Transfer the cooled cake to a serving plate. Serve at room temperature, cut into wedges. This cake freezes well for up to 2 months, but if you plan to freeze it, wait and dust it with the cocoa and powdered sugar just before serving.

Peach and Almond Torte

An adaptation of a recipe for Pfirsichtorte mit Mandeln *that appeared years ago in the women's section of a newspaper in the Black Forest region of West Germany, this is a baking specialty of my friend Jutta. It has a flavor I find utterly irresistible, with peach halves sunk into a ground almond–laced batter. I was always dropping hints to Jutta to bake it for me, so she finally gave me the original recipe written in grams and centimeters. After adapting the ingredient amounts for my American kitchen, I can now make it for myself. Use blanched fresh peaches or nectarines during the summer, but canned peaches are also fine during the winter. Serve this cake warm for brunch or as a dessert with a scoop of vanilla ice cream.*

Makes one 9-inch cake

4 large peaches (about 1¼ pounds) or one 29-ounce can peach halves in light syrup, drained and patted dry

1½ cups unbleached all-purpose flour

1½ cups whole unblanched almonds

1½ teaspoons baking powder

1 teaspoon ground cinnamon

1 cup (2 sticks) unsalted butter, at room temperature

1 cup sugar

4 large eggs

½ teaspoon almond extract

1 · If using fresh peaches, fill a deep, medium-size saucepan with water and bring to a boil. Add the peaches and blanch them for 10 to 15 seconds. Remove with a slotted spoon and cool under running water. Place on a cutting board, slip off the skins, cut the peaches in half, and pit them. Drain on paper towels. If the peaches are very tart, sprinkle them with some sugar. Set aside at room temperature.

2 · Preheat the oven to 350°F. Grease and flour a 9-inch springform pan and set it aside. Place the flour and the almonds in the workbowl of a food processor fitted with a metal blade and process until a flour is formed. The almonds will be finely ground. Alternatively, grind the almonds separately using a nut grinder or blender, then combine them with the flour. In a mixing bowl, combine the almond flour, baking powder, and cinnamon.

3 · In another bowl, cream the butter and sugar until light and fluffy. Add the eggs, one at a time, beating thoroughly after each addition. Add the almond extract. Gradually add the flour-nut mixture and beat well until a fluffy, smooth, and quite thick batter is formed. There should be no lumps or dry spots. Spread the batter evenly into the prepared pan. Cover the surface evenly with the peach halves, with the flat sides down.

4 · Bake in the center of the oven until the cake begins to pull away from the sides of the pan, the center springs back when gently touched, and a cake tester inserted into the center comes out clean, about 55 to 60 minutes. Let the cake stand for 10 minutes before removing the springform sides. Serve warm or at room temperature, cut into wedges. This cake is best eaten the same day it is made.

Fresh Fruit Cobbler

This fruit cobbler is certainly one of the simplest coffee cakes to make. The cobbler is low in sugar, baking up into an appealing fruit-laden cake that is as flavorful as it is tender. It is based on traditional German everyday coffee-time cake recipes known as kuchens, the simple cakes leavened with backpulver, *the baking powder used in German, Swiss, and Austrian baking.*

One of my favorite fruits for this recipe is pitted fleshy, sweet Tartarian cherries from my local farmer's market. Peeled and pitted ripe summer peaches in combination with Santa Rosa plums, apricots, or nectarines; field-grown red rhubarb; delicate winter pears; even sliced bananas or big Watsonville raspberries are also nice. For the adult palate, try substituting a complementary fruit brandy for 2 tablespoons of the milk.

This recipe makes an 8-inch cake or two 6-inch cakes, or it doubles perfectly to be baked in a 12-inch round or a 13-by-9-inch rectangle. The cobbler can be frozen for up to 2 weeks and reheated, although it is best served the day it is made, either warm or at room temperature, accompanied by a pitcher of cold heavy cream.

Makes one 8-inch cake or two 6-inch cakes

4 tablespoons (½ stick) unsalted butter, at room temperature
½ cup sugar
1 large egg
1 cup unbleached all-purpose flour
1 teaspoon baking powder
¼ teaspoon salt
½ cup milk
1½ teaspoons vanilla extract

About 3 cups pitted and halved or sliced fresh fruit, such as plums, peaches, cherries, pears, or nectarines
Juice of ½ lemon

Cinnamon Sugar:
¼ cup sugar
1 teaspoon ground cinnamon

1 · Preheat the oven to 350°F. Grease and flour an 8-inch springform pan, two 6-inch springforms, or an 8-inch square pan, and set aside. In a bowl with a wooden spoon, or in the bowl of a heavy-duty electric mixer, cream the butter and sugar until fluffy. Add the egg and beat well.

2 · In another bowl, combine the flour, baking powder, and salt. In a measuring cup, combine the milk and vanilla extract. Beat the dry ingredients into the creamed mixture in two additions, alternating with the milk. Beat until smooth and fluffy.

3 · Spread the batter evenly into the prepared pan. Cover with all of the fruit to create a thick layer, and drizzle with the lemon juice. In a small bowl, combine the sugar and the cinnamon, and sprinkle evenly over the fruit.

4 · Bake in the center of the oven until the fruit is bubbly and a cake tester inserted into the center comes out clean, about 40 to 45 minutes for the 8-inch pans or 25 to 30 minutes for the 6-inch pans. Serve warm or at room temperature, straight from the pan.

Muffins

Muffins

A muffin is easily defined: It is a quick bread baked in a pan designed for single servings. Known as a "Little Muff" in centuries past, muffins warmed the hands that held them nestled inside a lady's fur muff on cold days. Corn, blueberry, bran, banana, and apple muffins seem to be among the most favored recipes. But the gently sweet muffin medley just begins with these, and the limitless assortment grows with combinations of your favorite ingredients: apple and oats, bananas and chocolate, maple and cranberry, orange with dates, and cinnamon with nuts. Whatever the ingredients, I've never known a diner to refuse a homemade crumb-top gem.

The basic techniques for making muffins are very simple. The wet ingredients are beaten as long as you like, and the dry ingredients are mixed in a separate bowl to evenly distribute the leavenings. Some oil or melted butter is necessary to create the tender, coarse crumb typical of most muffins. Some muffin recipes call for creaming the butter and sugar as for a cake, which results in a finer texture. Acidic liquids, such as buttermilk, yogurt, molasses, and citrus, also create a tender crumb and balance the flavor of the leaveners.

Nutritious grains and brans are often soaked in liquid to soften before being added to the batter.

The liquid and dry mixtures are combined just until the batter holds together, no more than about 15 seconds. Do not worry about lumps and clumps. They are natural. The less a muffin is beaten, the better. An overbeaten muffin is tough and flat, with undesirable tunnels on the inside.

Although muffins are usually round, they can be made in a wide variety of sizes and shapes. I enjoy them made in individual heart shapes or in the cast-iron gem pans that are shaped like a variety of fruits. Look for unusual rectangular-shaped muffin pans, popular from the last century, in antique stores, or substitute miniature bread pans. My specialty heart mold has 5 connected cups that hold the same amount of batter ($\frac{1}{8}$ cup) as a standard 2¾-inch muffin cup. Standard round cups come in pans of 6, 12, and 24 connected cups. The larger pans, easily available from restaurant supply houses, are nice if you have a big family and a big oven. Muffins can also be made in mega 3¼-inch oversized-cup pans or 1⅝-inch to 2-inch miniature-cup pans, with the batter making half or double the yield, respectively. (Commercial muffin shops make a muffin size that seems to fall in between the oversized and the standard by custom ordering their pans from restaurant suppliers.) The large muffins will need to bake for 5 to 7 minutes longer than standard size muffins; the mini-muffins 5 to 7 minutes less.

For thick batters, fill greased, sprayed, or paper-lined muffin cups until the batter is level with the tops of the cups, using a ¼-cup-capacity ladle, an ice-cream scoop, or a large spoon. For very thin batters, filling the cups three-quarters full works nicely to prevent overflowing. If not all the cups are used, pour some water into the empty cups to keep the muffin tin from buckling and to enlarge the baked muffins with a bit of added oven moisture. Muffin batters made with only baking powder can be mixed and kept in the refrigerator for up to 3 days successfully. After more than three days the leavening loses its punch and the flour breaks down, resulting in an unappetizing grayish tinge.

Bake muffins in the center of a preheated, never cold, oven. The lower rack seems to consistently brown the bottoms too much, and the top rack cooks the tops faster than the rest of the muffin, so use a middle rack to bake each muffin evenly. An oven that

is too hot will create asymmetrically shaped muffins, with the sides of the muffins extending above the cups. Although most muffins bake at about 400°F, temperatures can vary. If a batch of muffins is becoming asymmetrical or browning too quickly, decrease the heat by 25°F. Conversely, muffins will be leaden and will not rise if the oven temperature is too low.

Muffins are done when the tops are domed and dry to the touch, the sides have pulled away from the pan slightly, and a cake tester inserted into the center of one muffin comes out clean. The muffins on the outside of the tin may bake a few minutes faster than those in the center. After removing from the oven, let the muffins sit a minute or two to allow them to shrink a bit from the sides of the pan. Then remove the muffins from the cups, loosening them with a knife if they do not come out easily, and turn them upside down onto a rack to cool. If they stay in the pan any longer, moisture will become trapped and the bottoms will be soggy.

Muffins are best eaten fresh the day they are made, but they freeze perfectly. After they have cooled completely, store them in plastic freezer bags in your freezer for up to 3 months. Keep a supply on hand, ready for reheating on the spur of the moment. Reheat frozen muffins in a microwave oven for a minute or less, or in a conventional oven, at 350°F, wrapped in foil, for 10 to 15 minutes.

Cherry-Almond Muffins

Cherries and almonds are natural flavor mates, as this muffin beautifully illustrates. Cherries need to be pitted carefully, as the juice splatters relentlessly. Use fresh cherries during the early summer, and, for later use, freeze pitted whole cherries for up to 12 months in freezer bags. One pound of stemmed, unpitted cherries equals about 3 cups. If you use a fresh sour cherry, such as an English Morello or Montmorency, increase the sugar in this recipe to ½ cup.

Makes 10 muffins

6 tablespoons (¾ stick) unsalted butter, at
  room temperature
¼ cup sugar
3 large eggs
2 teaspoons almond extract
2 cups unbleached all-purpose flour
2 teaspoons baking powder

1 teaspoon baking soda
¼ teaspoon salt
½ cup milk
1½ cups (about ½ pound) pitted fresh
  sweet cherries, such as red Bings,
  Black Tartarians, or yellow Royal Anns

1 · Preheat the oven to 375°F. Grease ten standard 2¾-inch-diameter muffin cups. In a large bowl, combine the butter and sugar, and cream with a spoon or an electric mixer for 1 minute, or until light colored. Add the eggs one at a time and beat for another minute, until the batter is thick and light colored. Add the almond extract.

2 · In another bowl, combine the flour, baking powder, baking soda, and salt. With a large spatula or an electric mixer, add the dry ingredients to the creamed mixture, alternating with the milk, mixing just until evenly moistened, using no more than 15 to 20 strokes. Fold in the cherries.

3 · Spoon the batter into each muffin cup until just level with the top of the pan. Bake in the center of the oven until the tops are browned and feel dry and springy, and a cake tester inserted into the center of a muffin comes out clean, 20 to 25 minutes. Do not overbake. Let the muffins rest in the pans for 5 minutes before turning them out onto a rack to cool. Serve them the day they are made or freeze them in plastic freezer bags for up to 3 months.

Orange–Chocolate Chip Muffins

The beautiful word orange *comes from a word that is just about as old as time,* naranga, *which means "fragrant" in ancient Sanskrit. I love that the orange is a fruit of fertility in the tropics, and, certainly, when it is paired here with chocolate, which attracts a lover as surely as a bee's nose is drawn to the center of a pollen-rich flower, we have the perfect muffin to serve at a wedding brunch or to that special someone. This sour cream muffin is cakelike, sweet, and rich, almost like a cupcake—just the way I like it. I adapted this recipe from one I got from my girl-friend Rosemarie, who is a prodigious baker and a confirmed chocoholic.*

Makes 10 muffins

2 cups unbleached all-purpose flour
2 tablespoons orange zest
1¼ teaspoons baking powder
½ teaspoon baking soda
½ teaspoon salt
½ cup (1 stick) unsalted butter, at room temperature

1 cup sugar
2 large eggs
½ cup sour cream
½ cup orange juice
1 teaspoon vanilla extract
4 ounces semisweet chocolate chips

1 · Preheat the oven to 375°F. Grease ten standard 2¾-inch-diameter muffin cups. In a large bowl, combine the flour, zest, baking powder, baking soda, and salt.

2 · In another bowl with an electric mixer, beat the butter and sugar for 1 minute, until fluffy. Add the eggs and beat. Combine the sour cream, orange juice, and vanilla extract. Pour the egg mixture and the sour cream–orange juice mixture into the dry ingredients and stir with a large spatula just until moistened, using no more than 15 to 20 strokes. The batter will be lumpy. Fold in the chocolate chips.

3 · Immediately spoon the batter into each muffin cup until level with the top of the pan. Bake in the center of the oven for 20 to 25 minutes, until the tops are browned and feel dry and springy, and a cake tester inserted into the center of a muffin comes out clean. Do not overbake. Let the muffins rest in the pan for 5 minutes before turning out onto a rack to cool. Serve them the day they are made or freeze them in plastic freezer bags for up to 3 months.

Sour Cream–Apple Muffins

Exciting and sublime, cakelike apple muffins with a crisp sugar crust, tart chunks of fruit, and the soulful dimension of spicy cinnamon are an ever-popular choice. The all-American home-spun apple is certainly the commonest of fruits, perfect for baking. From crisp lime green Granny Smiths and Pippins to the blushing red, honey-sweet McIntosh, the fruit is comforting and satisfying. Apples are harvested throughout the summer months in the world's temperate zones, but cold-storage methods enable us to have firm, fresh fruit year-round. Make certain to fill the batter to the tops of the cups, so that the baked muffins sport a queen-sized dome.

Makes 12 muffins

Streusel Topping
½ cup packed light brown sugar
⅓ cup unbleached all-purpose flour
4 tablespoons (½ stick) cold unsalted butter

2 cups unbleached all-purpose flour
¾ cup granulated sugar
1 tablespoon baking powder
¾ teaspoon baking soda
1 teaspoon ground cinnamon
¼ teaspoon fresh-ground nutmeg

¼ teaspoon ground allspice
¼ teaspoon ground cloves
¼ teaspoon salt
½ cup walnuts, chopped
2 tablespoons dried currants
2 large eggs
4 tablespoons (½ stick) unsalted butter, melted
1½ cups sour cream
2 cups (2 large) cored and chopped tart green apples

1 · Prepare the Streusel Topping: In a small bowl with a pastry blender or fork, or in a food processor, combine the brown sugar and flour. Cut the butter into chunks. Add to the sugar and flour mixture and cut in until coarse crumbs are formed. Set aside. Preheat the oven to 375°F. Grease twelve standard 2¾-inch-diameter muffin cups.

2 · In a large bowl, combine the flour, granulated sugar, baking powder, baking soda, spices, salt, walnuts, and currants. In another bowl, combine the eggs, melted butter, and sour cream with a whisk until well blended. Add the chopped apples and sour cream and egg mixture to the dry ingredients

and stir just until the ingredients are evenly moistened, no more than 15 to 20 strokes.

3 · Spoon the batter into each muffin cup, until level with the top of the pan. Bake in the center of the oven until the tops are browned and feel dry and springy, and a cake tester inserted into the center of a muffin comes out clean, 20 to 25 minutes. Do not overbake. Let the muffins rest in the pan for 5 minutes before turning out onto a rack to cool. Serve them the day they are made or freeze them in plastic freezer bags for up to 3 months.

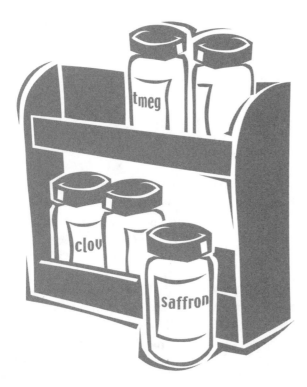

Banana, Coconut, and Macadamia Nut Muffins

I love using the ubiquitous banana in many different types of quick breads. Since the banana is a tropical fruit, it pairs naturally with all sorts of other tropically grown fruits and nuts. And, of course, the coconut, the most widely used fruit in the world, seems to go well with almost anything. I think you will find the trio of banana, coconut, and macadamia nuts outright addictive. Luckily for us, macadamia nuts are now available in many well-stocked grocery stores in the bulk aisle, and are sold unsalted. If you buy a jar of salted ones instead, just rinse them under cold water and drain them on paper towels. After I rinse the nuts I put them in the oven for a few minutes to dry them out, but this is optional.

Makes 10 muffins

2 cups unbleached all-purpose flour
½ cup unsweetened shredded coconut
1 tablespoon baking powder
½ teaspoon baking soda
½ teaspoon ground cinnamon
½ teaspoon fresh-ground nutmeg
½ teaspoon salt
½ cup chopped raw unsalted macadamia nuts

½ cup (1 stick) unsalted butter, at room temperature
½ cup sugar
2 large eggs
2 large ripe bananas, mashed (to make about 1 cup)
1 teaspoon vanilla extract

1 · Preheat the oven to 375°F. Grease ten standard 2¾-inch-diameter muffin cups. In a large bowl, combine the flour, coconut, baking powder, baking soda, spices, salt, and nuts.

2 · In another bowl beat the butter and sugar with an electric mixer for 1 minute, until fluffy. Add the eggs and then the mashed banana and vanilla extract and beat. Pour the wet ingredients into the flour mixture and stir with a large spatula just until moistened, using no more than 15 to 20 strokes. The batter will be lumpy.

3 · Immediately spoon the batter into each muffin cup until level with the top of the pan. Bake in the center of the oven for 20 to 25 minutes, until the tops are brown and feel dry and springy to the touch, and a cake tester inserted

into the center of a muffin comes out clean. Do not overbake. Let the muffins rest in the pan for 5 minutes before turning them out onto a rack to cool. Serve them the day the are made or freeze them in plastic freezer bags for up to 3 months.

Sour Cream–Peach Muffins

Exciting and sublime, cakelike muffins with a crisp sugar crust, sweet chunks of fruit, and the soulful dimension of spicy cinnamon are an ever-popular combination. The peaches, or nectarines, should be ripe, but still firm. Make certain to fill the batter to the tops of the cups so that the baked muffins sport a queen-sized dome.

Makes 12 muffins

Oat Streusel Topping
⅓ cup packed light brown sugar or date sugar
¼ cup rolled oats
3 tablespoons unbleached all-purpose flour or whole wheat pastry flour
½ teaspoon ground cinnamon
5 tablespoons cold unsalted butter or soy margarine, cut into pieces

2 cups unbleached all-purpose flour
⅓ cup packed light brown sugar
1 tablespoon baking powder
½ teaspoon baking soda
1 teaspoon ground cinnamon
¼ teaspoon fresh-ground nutmeg
¼ teaspoon ground allspice
¼ teaspoon ground cloves
¼ teaspoon salt
2 large eggs
⅓ cup canola oil
1¼ cups sour cream
1½ cups (1 to 2 large) peeled, pitted, and coarsely chopped fresh ripe peaches or nectarines

1 · Prepare the Oat Streusel Topping: In a small bowl with a pastry blender or fork, or in a food processor, combine the sugar, oats, flour, and cinnamon. Add the butter or soy margarine pieces and cut in until coarse crumbs form. Set aside. Preheat the oven to 375°F. Grease twelve standard 2¾-inch-diameter muffin cups.

2 · In a large bowl, combine the flour, sugar, baking powder, baking soda, spices, and salt. In another bowl, combine the eggs, oil, and sour cream with a whisk until well blended. Add the chopped peaches or nectarines and egg–sour cream mixture to the dry ingredients and stir just until evenly moistened, no more than 15 to 20 strokes.

3 · Spoon the batter into each muffin cup until just level with the top of the pan. Sprinkle the top of each with some Oat Streusel Topping. Bake in the center of the oven until the tops are browned and feel dry and springy, and a cake tester inserted into the center of a muffin comes out clean, 20 to 25 minutes. Do not overbake. Let the muffins rest in the pan for 5 minutes before turning them out onto a rack to cool. Serve them the day they are made or freeze them in plastic freezer bags for up to 3 months.

Raspberry Cornmeal Muffins

I consider this a muffin that merges earthiness with a touch of glitter. Cornmeal and raspberries: simple and flawless. If your raspberries are very tart, sprinkle them with some of the sugar and macerate for 15 minutes to sweeten them up before folding them into the batter.

Makes 9 muffins

1¼ cups unbleached all-purpose flour
¾ cup fine-grind yellow cornmeal, preferably
  stone-ground
⅔ cup sugar
2 teaspoons baking powder
½ teaspoon baking soda

¼ teaspoon salt
Grated zest of 1 lemon
1 cup milk
2 large eggs
⅓ cup corn oil
1½ cups fresh red or golden raspberries

1 · Preheat the oven to 400°F. Grease nine standard 2¾-inch-diameter muffin cups. In a large bowl, combine the flour, cornmeal, sugar, baking powder, baking soda, salt, and zest.

2 · In another bowl, beat the milk, eggs, and corn oil with a whisk or an electric mixer for 1 minute. Pour the wet ingredients into the dry ingredients and stir with a large spatula just until moistened, using no more than 15 to 20 strokes. Gently fold in the raspberries, taking care not to break them up. The batter will be lumpy.

3 · Spoon the batter into each muffin cup until just level with the top of the pan. Bake in the center of the oven until the tops are browned and feel dry and springy, and a cake tester inserted into the center of a muffin comes out clean, 20 to 25 minutes. Do not overbake. Let the muffins rest in the pan for 5 minutes before turning them out onto a rack to cool. Serve them the day they are made or freeze them in plastic freezer bags for up to 3 months.

VARIATION:

Cornmeal Muffins with Cranberries and Golden Raisins

Substitute 1 cup chopped fresh cranberries and ½ cup golden raisins for the fresh raspberries in Step 2. Continue to mix and bake as directed.

Blueberry–Blue Corn Muffins

Popular in the Southwest for centuries as part of religious ceremonies and as a beloved culinary ingredient, blue cornmeal is now available nationwide. Blue corn, like yellow, red, and white corn, has its own unique flavor. Blue corn is naturally very hardy, and it does not need to be sprayed with pesticides of any kind while growing. When you buy blue corn flour, also known as harinilla, you are supporting small New Mexican farms, the primary growers of blue corn. Although blue is an unusual color in food, take a chance here if this ingredient is new to you. Its flavor and aroma are very sweet.

Makes 10 muffins

1 cup fresh blueberries, picked over

2 to 4 tablespoons granulated sugar

1 cup blue corn flour

1 cup unbleached all-purpose flour

¼ cup fine-grind yellow cornmeal, preferably stone-ground

¼ cup packed light brown sugar

1 tablespoon baking powder

¼ teaspoon salt

1 cup milk

½ cup sour cream

2 large eggs

4 tablespoons (½ stick) unsalted butter, melted

¼ cup granulated sugar mixed with 1 teaspoon ground cinnamon, for sprinkling

1 · In a small bowl, sprinkle the blueberries with granulated sugar to taste and let macerate for 15 minutes.

2 · Preheat the oven to 375°F. Grease ten standard 2¾-inch-diameter muffin cups. In a large bowl, combine the flours, cornmeal, brown sugar, baking powder, and salt.

3 · In another bowl, beat the milk, sour cream, eggs, and melted butter with a whisk or an electric mixer for 1 minute. Pour the wet ingredients into the dry ingredients and stir with a large spatula just until moistened, using no more than 15 to 20 strokes. The batter will be lumpy.

4 · Spoon the batter into each muffin cup until half full. Sprinkle each with a thick layer of berries. Cover the berries with batter until it is just level with

the top of the pan. Sprinkle with the cinnamon sugar. Bake in the center of the oven until the tops are browned and feel dry and springy, and a cake tester inserted into the center of a muffin comes out clean, 20 to 25 minutes. Do not overbake. Let the muffins rest in the pan for 5 minutes before turning them out onto a rack to cool. Serve them the day they are made or freeze them in plastic freezer bags for up to 3 months.

Everyday Maple Bran Muffins

This bran muffin is made with the unsweetened, high-fiber, whole-bran commercial cereals easily found in supermarkets. The cereal works perfectly, giving the muffin a unique double-bran flavor that is not too sweet for everyday breakfasts. I usually make double batches to bring to friends or to share with the children who show up at my screen door when the aromas waft out during baking.

Makes 10 muffins

1½ cups buttermilk
2 large eggs
4 tablespoons (½ stick) unsalted butter, melted
¼ cup sunflower seed or other vegetable oil
¼ cup pure maple syrup
1½ cups All-Bran whole-grain cereal
1 cup chopped dried apricots

¼ cup dried cranberries
1 cup unbleached all-purpose flour
½ cup wheat bran or oat bran
¼ cup packed light brown sugar
1 teaspoon baking powder
1 teaspoon baking soda
¼ teaspoon salt
½ cup raw sunflower seeds

1 · Preheat the oven to 400°F. Grease ten standard 2¾-inch-diameter muffin cups. In a large bowl, combine the buttermilk, eggs, melted butter, oil, maple syrup, and All-Bran cereal. Stir with a whisk until evenly moistened. Add the dried apricots and cranberries. Let stand at room temperature 5 to 10 minutes.

2 · In another bowl, combine the flour, wheat or oat bran, sugar, baking powder, baking soda, salt, and sunflower seeds. Add the dry ingredients to the buttermilk and egg mixture and stir with a large spatula or spoon just until evenly moistened, using no more than 15 to 20 strokes.

3 · Spoon the batter into each muffin cup until just level with the top of the pan. Bake in the center of the oven until the tops are browned and feel dry and springy, and a cake tester inserted into the center of a muffin comes out clean, 20 to 25 minutes. Do not overbake. Let the muffins rest in the pan for

5 minutes before turning them out onto a rack to cool. Serve them the day they are made or freeze them in plastic freezer bags for up to 3 months.

VARIATION:

Blueberry Bran Muffins

Add 3 tablespoons orange juice concentrate to the wet ingredients in Step 1. Substitute 1½ cups fresh or unthawed frozen blueberries for the dried apricots, sunflower seeds, and cranberries. Continue to mix and bake as directed.

Buckwheat and Hazelnut Muffins

Buckwheat is really an acquired taste, but I find these muffins an easy and delicious way to prepare this hardy ethnic grain. Because buckwheat is so sturdy, it is a commercial crop that is grown without chemical pesticides, making a flour that is very pure. It is incredibly nutritious, with twice the amount of B vitamins as whole wheat flour, and it is low in calories. If you can find it, use dark buckwheat honey in place of the maple syrup. Serve these muffins with fresh fruit and hot tea.

Makes 9 muffins

1½ cups unbleached all-purpose flour
⅓ cup buckwheat flour
¼ cup rolled oats
¼ cup chopped toasted hazelnuts
2 teaspoons baking powder
½ teaspoon baking soda

¼ teaspoon salt
1 cup buttermilk
4 tablespoons (½ stick) unsalted butter, melted
¼ cup pure maple syrup
2 large eggs

1 · Preheat the oven to 400°F. Grease nine standard 2¾-inch-diameter muffin cups. In a large bowl, combine the unbleached flour, buckwheat flour, rolled oats, hazelnuts, baking powder, baking soda, and salt.

2 · In another bowl, beat the buttermilk, melted butter, maple syrup, and eggs with a whisk or an electric mixer for 1 minute. Pour the buttermilk and egg mixture into the dry ingredients and stir with a large spatula just until moistened, using no more than 15 to 20 strokes. The batter will be lumpy.

3 · Spoon the batter into each muffin cup until just level with the top of the pan. Bake in the center of the oven until the tops are browned and feel dry and springy, and a cake tester inserted into the center of a muffin comes out clean, 20 to 25 minutes. Do not overbake. Let the muffins rest in the pan for 5 minutes before turning them out onto a rack to cool. Serve them the day they are made or freeze them in plastic freezer bags for up to 3 months.

Rye Muffins with Orange and Fennel

I like to include some savory muffins in my repertoire of recipes. Uniquely flavored rye breads and crackers shaped rather like tortillas are featured extensively in Scandinavian folk recipes. The following muffin, adapted from a recipe by East Coast food writer Leslie Land, reflects the flavoring of Vørtlimpor, a Swedish holiday bread that often uses beer or ale as the liquid ingredient. Serve these muffins with Honey-Almond Cheese (following) for breakfast, or with butter and a hearty soup for dinner.

Makes 9 muffins

1¼ cups unbleached all-purpose flour
¾ cup medium or light rye flour
¼ cup packed light brown sugar
1 tablespoon baking powder
½ teaspoon fennel seeds, crushed
½ teaspoon whole aniseed
¼ teaspoon salt

Grated zest of 1 orange
1 cup milk
2 large eggs
4 tablespoons (½ stick) unsalted butter, melted
3 tablespoons light molasses
Honey-Almond Cheese (optional), following

1 · Preheat the oven to 375°F. Grease nine standard 2¾-inch-diameter muffin cups. In a large bowl, combine the flours, brown sugar, baking powder, fennel seeds, aniseed, salt, and zest.

2 · In another bowl, beat the milk, eggs, melted butter, and molasses with a whisk or an electric mixer for 1 minute. Pour the milk and egg mixture into the dry ingredients and stir with a large spatula just until moistened, using no more than 15 to 20 strokes. The batter will be lumpy.

3 · Spoon the batter into each muffin cup until just level with the top of the pan. Bake in the center of the oven until the tops are browned and feel dry and springy, and a cake tester inserted into the center of a muffin comes out clean, 20 to 25 minutes. Do not overbake. Let the muffins rest in the pan for 5 minutes before turning them out onto a rack to cool. Serve them the day they are made, with Honey-Almond Cheese, if you like, or freeze them in plastic freezer bags for up to 3 months.

Honey–Almond Cheese

Makes about 1¼ cups cheese

¼ cup whole toasted almonds
4 ounces cream cheese, at room
   temperature
1 cup plain kefir cheese or cottage cheese
3 tablespoons honey

Grind the almonds in a food processor. Add the cheeses and honey, processing just until evenly combined. Store, covered, in the refrigerator for up to 1 week.

Black Olive and Goat Cheese Muffins

This muffin is a rustic dinner gem with Italian flavors, my contribution to cucina povera. Use an imported or domestic pitted olive as your taste dictates. This recipe also makes eighteen 1⅛-inch miniature muffins, which are good for serving with cocktails. Pair these muffins with smoked turkey and fresh fruit for picnics.

Makes 9 muffins

2¼ cups unbleached all-purpose flour
2 tablespoons fine-grind yellow cornmeal, preferably stone-ground
2 teaspoons baking powder
Pinch of salt
1 cup milk
¼ cup olive oil

2 large eggs
½ cup coarsely chopped, pitted black olives
¼ cup drained oil-packed, sun-dried tomatoes, chopped
6 ounces plain, herb, or chive goat cheese, cut into 9 pieces and rolled into balls
9 walnut halves

1 · Preheat the oven to 375°F. Grease nine standard 2¾-inch-diameter muffin cups. In a large bowl, combine the flour, cornmeal, baking powder, and salt.

2 · In another bowl, beat the milk, olive oil, and eggs with a whisk or an electric mixer for 1 minute. Pour the milk and egg mixture into the dry ingredients and stir with a large spatula just until moistened, using no more than 15 to 20 strokes. Gently fold in the olives and tomatoes. The batter will be lumpy.

3 · Spoon the batter into each muffin cup until half full. Press a ball of goat cheese on top of the batter in each cup. Spoon the remaining batter over the cheese until mounded just level with the top of the pan. Place a walnut half on top of each muffin. Bake in the center of the oven until the tops are browned and feel dry and springy, and a cake tester inserted into the center of a muffin comes out clean, 20 to 25 minutes. Do not overbake. Let the muffins rest in the pan for 5 minutes before turning them out onto a rack to cool. Serve them the day they are made or freeze them in plastic freezer bags for up to 3 months.

$\mathcal{T}$omato Corn Muffins with Melting Cheese Hearts

These savory tomato muffins are filled with a cube of a favorite white melting cheese as a finishing touch. Serve them with main dish chicken salads, or with a corn and black bean salad with a chili vinaigrette.

Makes 9 muffins

1¾ cups unbleached all-purpose flour
½ cup medium-grind yellow cornmeal
2 tablespoons sugar
1 tablespoon baking powder
¼ teaspoon salt
2 ripe plum tomatoes, seeded and diced

1 cup milk
2 large eggs
¼ cup fruity olive oil
3 ounces mozzarella cheese, cut into 9 cubes

1 · Preheat the oven to 375°F. Grease nine standard 2¾-inch-diameter muffin cups. In a large bowl, combine the flour, cornmeal, sugar, baking powder, and salt. Add the diced tomatoes and toss to distribute evenly.

2 · In another bowl, combine the milk, eggs, and olive oil with a whisk. Pour into the flour mixture and stir with a large spatula just until moistened, using no more than 15 to 20 strokes. The batter will be lumpy.

3 · Fill the muffin cups half full and place a cube of cheese in the center. Cover with the remaining batter until mounded just level with the top of the pan. Bake in the center of the oven for 20 to 25 minutes, or until the tops are golden and feel dry and springy to the touch. Cool in the pan for 5 minutes before turning them out to cool on a rack. Serve them warm or freeze them in plastic freezer bags for up to 3 months.

Zucchini-Basil Baby Cakes

Basil, an herb from the mint family, is considered an omen of happiness in Mediterranean cuisines and is also a popular flavoring. All of my gardening friends have surplus squash and basil to share at the end of the summer, to my delight. Homegrown zucchini is very sweet and an excellent ingredient for adding moisture to quick breads. These savory muffins are best served to happy diners the day they are made. Serve alongside egg dishes, hot and cold soups, or salads.

Makes six 3¼-inch baby cakes

2½ cups unbleached all-purpose flour
1 tablespoon sugar
1 teaspoon baking powder
1 teaspoon baking soda
¼ teaspoon salt
Grated zest of 1 lemon
¾ cup buttermilk

2 large eggs
3 tablespoons olive oil
2 tablespoon Pernod liqueur
1¼ cups (2 medium) coarsely grated unpeeled zucchini, drained on paper towels
¼ cup chopped fresh basil
⅓ cup grated Parmesan cheese

1 · Preheat the oven to 375°F. Grease six oversized 3¼-inch-diameter muffin cups. In a large bowl, combine the flour, sugar, baking powder, baking soda, salt, and zest.

2 · In another bowl, beat the buttermilk, eggs, olive oil, and liqueur with a whisk or an electric mixer for 1 minute. Pour the buttermilk and egg mixture into the dry ingredients and stir with a large spatula just until moistened, using no more than 15 to 20 strokes. Gently fold in the grated zucchini and basil until evenly distributed. The batter will be lumpy.

3 · Spoon the batter into each muffin cup until just level with the top of the pan. Sprinkle each with a tablespoon of the Parmesan cheese. Bake in the center of the oven until the tops are browned and feel dry and springy, and a cake tester inserted into the center of a muffin comes out clean, 20 to 25 minutes. Do not overbake. Let the muffins rest in the pan for 5 minutes before turning out onto a rack to cool. Serve them the day they are made or freeze them in plastic freezer bags for up to 3 months.

Pancakes and Crêpes

Pancakes and Crêpes

Pancakes

Americans call them flapjacks, hotcakes, flannel cakes, johnnycakes, but the Europeans have the strong tradition of pancakes that patented them all. The popular fluffy American breakfast pancakes are direct descendants of the Dutch *pannekoen* brought to New Amsterdam hundreds of years ago. The pancake's European origins go back even further; they were originally a symbol of the Christian Eucharist wafer.

Almost every culture has its own unique pancake variation. The French have immortalized the oversized wheat crêpe; in Gaelic Brittany savory griddlecakes, *krampouz*, are often made with a splash of brandy and lemon juice or with thick farm-style dairy cottage cheese. Scots still make a "girdle" oatcake, and the Welsh, a large barley-meal pancake. Rich Shrovetide pancakes have been eaten before Lent from England to Russia since the Middle Ages. Russians make wheat as well as buckwheat *blini*, a miniature crêpe perfect for entertaining; the Germans created *pfankuchen* and puffy oven "Dutch Babies"; the Austrians love the soufflelike *nockerln*; and Swedes serve a traditional Thursday night supper of pea soup and thin *pannkakor* rolled with tart lingonberry jam inside. Upper-class Viennese created the women-run *mehlspeiskőchins* kitchens, specializing in a pancake dessert course made of flour, eggs, butter, and milk. Hanukkah is celebrated with grated potato *latkes* topped with applesauce and sour cream. The Italians have chestnut flour pancakes, *castagnaccio*, often served in place of potatoes, or as a Tuscan-style dessert with olive oil, pine nuts, walnuts, orange peel, rosemary, and raisins in the batter, served hot from the griddle with scoops of fresh ricotta cheese. Hungarians make the popular *palacsintas*, and even the Chinese make a crêpelike scallion pancake. American lumber camps made hearty flannel cakes, also known as a "string of flats," household words. All describe the familiar pancake, a thin, thinner, or thinnest batter that is baked on a lightly greased hot griddle until bubbles break the surface, turned once, and served immediately.

The first colonial settlers were taught by local Native Americans to make griddlecakes from Rhode Island Narragansett maize. These griddlecakes soon became a staple, known among the settlers as johnnycakes. The origin of the word "johnnycake" is still disputed today. Some say it is from "Shawnee cake," after the native northeastern tribes who taught traveling

French and English trappers how to make the daily hoecakelike bread. Pancakes prevailed as the household bread in homes with no ovens, only an open hearth. They utilized gluten-free flours and meals, such as oats, barley, buckwheat, and corn, that did not stretch and rise high like ones made with wheat. Each household owned a slate bakestone, or English "bak-stun," under which a fire could be built and onto which batters would be ladled. Even today, New Englanders enjoy their corn johnnycakes and "lace cakes," a thin johnnycake batter that crinkles around the edges as it cooks, made from finely ground Rhode Island stone-ground cornmeal in much the same manner as their ancestors did.

From such a rich history, pancakes somehow evolved to be exclusively Sunday morning or overnight-guest breakfast fare. Since they are easy to make and there are so many different ways to prepare them, pancakes are a favorite hearty food to cook for a crowd. But today, frugal epicureans use the versatile griddlecake for any meal, as a vehicle for mashed and grated vegetables, nutty-flavored whole grains, tangy cheeses, or fresh fruits and nuts. Pancakes may be thick, thin, small, large, rolled, cut into pie-shaped wedges, embellished with vegetables, or sweetened for dessert. Although the long-favored topping for a griddlecake is maple syrup and sweet pats of butter, it is easy to be creative with other favorite flavors, such as warm honey, fruit-flavored butters, hot applesauce, buttered syrups, stewed fruit, liqueur-flavored sauces, thick cream, melted cheese, shaved maple sugar, and a variety of luscious savory sauces. Homemade Fruit Syrups (page 354) are quickly made and easily stored in the refrigerator, a great way to use up less-than-perfect and overripe fruits during the summer months and a less sweet, more full-flavored alternative to commercial toppings.

Pancake batters do well when made a few hours in advance and refrigerated until baking. Gently and quickly assemble the batter, paying no attention if there are a few lumps. All-purpose flour is a standard ingredient, but many bakers also use cake flour for a lighter-than-air texture. If the batter is leavened only with baking powder, not baking soda, it can be made the night before, refrigerated, and ladled cold onto the greased, hot griddle. If a batter looks and feels too thick, thin it with a tablespoon or two of liquid; if it is too thin, whisk in an extra tablespoon or so of flour until the consistency looks right to you. For the busy baker, there is a recipe for a Buttermilk Griddle Mix (page 141). This recipe allows you to premix the dry ingredients, making a mix similar to commercial pancake mixes, such as Aunt Jemima's, but gives you control over the amounts of fiber, fat, sodium, and sugar in the mix. Once you have this mixture on hand, you can quickly prepare Sunday Pancakes (page 149) or waffles (page 208) with a minimum amount of fuss.

Unless otherwise specified in the recipes, for even cooking use a large, heavy aluminum sauté pan with a nonstick surface, a cast-iron skillet, or an electric, cast-iron, or soapstone griddle to make your pancakes. A soapstone griddle has a copper-rimmed blue-green surface that retains heat and needs no additional greasing. It is a very special lifetime investment for the pancake buff.

Before cooking the pancakes, preheat the baking surface over medium-high to high heat. The age-old system for testing whether a griddle surface is hot enough is to drizzle it with a few drops of cold water. When the surface is sufficiently hot, the water will dance over it. If the water evaporates immediately, the surface is too hot, and if the water sits and boils, the surface is definitely too cool. When the surface is hot, lightly grease it once for the first batch. One of the best ways to grease the griddle is to lightly rub the end of a firm stick of butter or margarine once across the hot surface, but you can also brush it with vegetable oil. A cold pan can be lightly coated with a cooking spray.

Next, pour the required amount of batter onto the hot griddle and let it cook for about 2 minutes, unless otherwise specified in the recipe. Using the amount of batter specified in each recipe to form each cake is important for even, thorough cooking. When bubbles appear across the pancake surface and the edges are slightly dry, check the underside for an even browning, and turn once. The second side takes only half the amount of time to cook as the first does. Serve the pancakes immediately or keep them warm in a 200°F oven, covered loosely with foil to prevent drying, until all cakes are cooked and ready to serve. It is important that pancakes be kept warm in a single layer or, if stacked, separated by a tea towel or paper towels to prevent sogginess. Pancakes can also be cooled, wrapped in plastic freezer bags, and frozen for impromptu reheating in a toaster or microwave oven.

Old-Fashioned Buttermilk Pancakes

Here lies the perfect American hotcake, flapjack, or pancake in all its glory. When you walk into your kitchen to prepare pancakes, first put on some hot water for a pot of tea and some music to match your mood while assembling the ingredients. Set a skillet on the stove and sauté some corncob-smoked bacon or fresh turkey sausage patties. Cut some cool fruit of any sort, such as melon or berries, or perhaps pour a small glass of juice. Set the table with a pitcher of syrup and a mound of sweet butter. As the sun rises higher in the sky, heat up the old soapstone griddle and ladle on the batter. Then summon your breakfasters, who will assemble gladly at the table, forks in hand, to await the arrival of fresh, hot pancakes. The variations that follow this recipe are sensational, so try them too.

Makes twelve 4-inch pancakes

2 cups unbleached all-purpose flour
1 teaspoon baking soda
Large pinch of salt
2¼ cups buttermilk

3 large eggs
4 tablespoons (½ stick) unsalted butter,
  melted, or vegetable oil

1 · Combine the flour, baking soda, and salt in a mixing bowl. In another bowl, whisk together the buttermilk, eggs, and melted butter or oil. Add the buttermilk and egg mixture to the dry ingredients, stirring just until combined. Do not overmix; the batter will have small lumps. If you are making one of the variations, gently fold in any additional ingredients at this time.

2 · Heat a griddle or heavy skillet over medium heat until a drop of water skates over the surface, and lightly grease the pan. Using a ¼-cup measure as a scoop for each pancake, pour the batter onto the griddle. Cook until bubbles form on the surface, the edges are dry, and the bottom is golden brown, about 2 minutes. Turn once, cooking the opposite side until golden, about 1 minute. The second side will take half the amount of time to cook as the first side does. Serve the pancakes immediately or keep them warm in a 200°F oven until ready to serve.

VARIATIONS:

Multi-Grain Buttermilk Pancakes

Substitute 1 heaping tablespoon *each* stone-ground cornmeal, toasted wheat germ, rolled oats, rolled barley flakes, and oat bran for ¼ cup of the unbleached all-purpose flour in Step 1. Mix and cook as directed.

Rice Buttermilk Pancakes

Stir ⅔ cup cooled, cooked white or brown rice into the batter at the end of Step 1. Mix and cook as directed.

Strawberry Buttermilk Pancakes

Fold 1½ cups sliced fresh strawberries into the batter at the end of Step 1. Mix and cook as directed.

Banana Buttermilk Pancakes

Distribute 1 cup sliced fresh banana over the batter after the pancakes have been ladled onto the griddle. Mix and cook as directed.

Vanilla-Millet Buttermilk Pancakes

Add ⅓ cup raw whole millet and 1½ teaspoons vanilla extract to the batter in Step 1. Mix and cook as directed.

Homemade Buttermilk Griddle Mix Pancakes

Makes twelve 4-inch pancakes

2 large eggs
3 tablespoons unsalted butter or margarine, melted, or vegetable oil
¾ cup water

1½ cups Buttermilk Griddle Mix, following
½ cup berries, grated zucchini, or chopped nuts (optional)

1 · In a bowl, whisk together the eggs, butter, margarine, or oil, and water. Add the griddle mix and stir until just blended. Do not overmix; the batter will have small lumps. Gently fold in any additions at this time, if you are using them.

2 · Heat a griddle or heavy skillet over medium heat until a drop of water skates over the surface, and lightly grease the pan. Using a ¼-cup measure as a scoop for each pancake, pour the batter onto the griddle. Cook until bubbles form on the surface, the edges are dry, and the bottom is golden brown, about 2 minutes. Turn once, cooking the opposite side until golden brown, about 1 minute. The second side will take half the amount of time to cook as the first side does. Serve immediately or keep warm in a 200°F oven until ready to serve.

Buttermilk Griddle Mix

Makes about 6 cups mix

3 cups unbleached all-purpose flour
1 cup whole wheat pastry flour
1 cup dried buttermilk or goat's milk powder
½ cup wheat bran flakes, oat bran, or wheat germ
½ cup fine-grind yellow or blue cornmeal, preferably stone-ground
¼ cup sugar (optional)
1 tablespoon baking powder

1 tablespoon baking soda
1 teaspoon salt

In a plastic container with an airtight lid, combine all the ingredients and stir with a whisk or spoon until evenly mixed. Store in a cool, dry place for up to 3 months.

Vineyard Pancakes

These pancakes could be aptly named Jim's Make-Them-from-Scratch-Quick Pancakes. They are the specialty of Jim Spaulding, the husband of my literary agent, Martha. She often requests them for breakfast in their Calistoga home before heading out to work in their grape vineyards. Martha heats the pure maple syrup, ordered by mail from New York State, in the microwave oven for a minute while Jim mixes the mild-flavored batter and heats the griddle. Please note that the batter stands for 3 minutes to give the baking powder time to start bubbling, and that the batter should not be stirred down before ladling it onto the hot griddle.

Makes twelve 4-inch pancakes

1 cup unbleached all-purpose flour, divided
⅓ cup whole wheat flour
½ teaspoon salt
2 tablespoons buckwheat flour or fine-grind yellow cornmeal

1 cup nonfat milk
1 large egg
2 tablespoons vegetable oil, such as canola, safflower, peanut, or corn
1½ teaspoons baking powder

1 · Combine half of the unbleached flour, the whole wheat flour, buckwheat or cornmeal, and milk in a mixing bowl. Stir in the egg and oil. Add the remaining ½ cup unbleached flour and baking powder, stirring gently just until combined. Do not overmix; the batter will have small lumps. Let the batter stand for 3 minutes at room temperature.

2 · Heat a griddle or heavy skillet over medium heat until a drop of water skates over the surface, and lightly grease the pan. Using a ¼-cup measure or a large spoon as a scoop for each pancake, pour the batter onto the griddle. Cook until bubbles form on the surface, the edges are dry, and the bottom is golden brown, about 2 minutes. Turn once, cooking the opposite side until golden, about 1 minute. The second side will take half the amount of time to cook as the first side does. Serve the pancakes immediately or keep them warm in a 200°F oven until ready to serve.

Autumn Persimmon Pancakes

There are two types of persimmons available in the fall in American markets and at produce stands. One is firm and shaped like a tomato; the other is large and round with a pretty pointed tip and gets translucent and mushy when ripe. The latter is the Hachiya persimmon, the one that is perfect for these pancakes. Although persimmon pudding is a favorite way to use this neglected fruit, once you use it in these pancakes, you will have another delightful alternative to using pumpkin or applesauce in spicy-sweet baked goods.

Makes twelve 4-inch pancakes

1 cup unbleached all-purpose flour
1 tablespoon packed light brown sugar
2 teaspoons ground cinnamon or apple pie
  spice
1 teaspoon baking powder
½ teaspoon baking soda

½ teaspoon salt
1 cup buttermilk
1 large egg
2 tablespoons vegetable oil
1 soft, ripe Hachiya persimmon, peeled
  (to yield 1 cup pulp)

1 · Combine the flour, brown sugar, cinnamon, baking powder, baking soda, and salt in a mixing bowl. In another bowl, whisk together the buttermilk, egg, oil, and persimmon pulp. Add the buttermilk-persimmon mixture to the dry ingredients, stirring just until combined. Do not overmix; the batter will have small lumps.

2 · Heat a griddle or heavy skillet over medium heat until a drop of water skates over the surface, and lightly grease the pan. Using a ¼-cup measure as a scoop for each pancake, pour the batter onto the griddle. Cook until bubbles form on the surface, the edges are dry, and the bottom is golden brown, about 2 minutes. Turn once, cooking the opposite side until golden, about 1 minute. The second side will take half the amount of time to cook as the first side does. Serve the pancakes immediately or keep them warm in a 200°F oven until ready to serve.

Cornmeal-Yogurt Pancakes

A stack of gently crunchy cornmeal pancakes is simple and delicious. Serve them alongside chicken-apple sausages, with a wedge of chilled melon, fresh sweet butter, and maple syrup for a memorable breakfast. A very special touch is smooth and tangy homemade Fruit Syrup (page 354), which can be made with overripe as well as fresh-picked fruit.

Makes twelve 4-inch pancakes

2 cups plain yogurt
2 large eggs
¼ cup milk
¼ cup corn oil
1¼ cups medium-grind yellow cornmeal,
  preferably stone-ground

¾ cup unbleached all-purpose flour
2 tablespoons sugar
2 teaspoons baking soda
¼ teaspoon salt

1 · Combine the yogurt, eggs, milk, and corn oil in a mixing bowl with a whisk. In another bowl, combine the cornmeal, flour, sugar, baking soda, and salt. Add the yogurt and egg mixture to the dry ingredients, stirring just until combined. Do not overmix; the batter will have small lumps.

2 · Heat a griddle or heavy skillet over medium heat until a drop of water skates over the surface, and lightly grease the pan. Using a ¼-cup measure as a scoop for each pancake, pour the batter onto the griddle. Cook until bubbles form on the surface, the edges are dry, and the bottom is golden brown, about 2 minutes. Turn once, cooking the opposite side until golden, about 1 minute. The second side will take half the amount of time to cook as the first side does. Serve the pancakes immediately or keep them warm in a 200°F oven until ready to serve.

*A*pple Oatcakes

Apples are a year-round fruit in California because cold storage is so efficient, but for a treat, use apples that have been fresh picked. Use an all-purpose, firm-fleshed cooking apple, such as Granny Smith, Rome Beauty, Golden Delicious, or Pippin, for these lowfat breakfast cakes. The batter is essentially prepared the night before serving, leaving only the leavenings to be added just before baking. This is a recipe I got at the Sonoma Mission Inn in the 1980s.

Makes twelve 4-inch pancakes

1½ cups water
½ cup (1 stick) unsalted butter
1 teaspoon ground cinnamon
½ teaspoon fresh-ground nutmeg
½ teaspoon salt
1 teaspoon vanilla extract
¾ cup packed brown sugar
1 cup rolled oats

⅓ cup toasted wheat germ
2 large eggs
1 medium apple, peeled, cored, and
  coarsely grated
1 cup unbleached all-purpose flour
1 teaspoon baking powder
1 teaspoon baking soda

1 · In a small saucepan, bring the water to a boil. Add the butter, spices, salt, vanilla, and brown sugar. Whisk in the oats and wheat germ. Cover, remove from heat, and let cool for 20 to 30 minutes.

2 · With a spatula, scrape the oat mixture into a bowl and beat with an electric mixer or by hand with a whisk. Add the eggs, grated apple, and flour. Beat until well mixed. Cover and refrigerate overnight.

3 · Just before cooking, stir the baking powder and baking soda into the bowl. Thin the batter with extra water if it has become too thick overnight. Heat a griddle or heavy skillet over medium heat until a drop of water skates over

the surface, and lightly grease the pan. Using a ¼-cup measure as a scoop for each pancake, pour the batter onto the griddle. Cook until bubbles form on the surface, the edges are dry, and the bottom is golden brown, about 2 minutes. Turn once, cooking the opposite side 1 minute. The second side will take half the amount of time to cook as the first side does. When done, the pancakes will look more moist than regular hotcakes and will have a lacy edge. Serve them immediately or keep them warm in a 200°F oven until ready to serve.

Whole Wheat–Blueberry Buttermilk Pancakes

People tend to gather together more often for dinner than for breakfast, but when they do sit down together for a morning meal, whole wheat pancakes are perfect for satisfying early morning appetites, especially if you plan a day at the beach or a hike in the woods before lunch. Whole wheat pancakes have a nutty, heartier nature than pancakes made with just unbleached flour. The blueberries are an important ingredient in this recipe, providing a counterpoint of taste and texture. Freeze your own blueberries during the summer season, unrinsed, in airtight plastic bags. Serve these pancakes with maple syrup and butter or, for special occasions, Yogurt Chantilly (following) and more fresh berries.

Makes sixteen 4-inch pancakes

1 cup unbleached all-purpose flour
¾ cup whole wheat flour
1 tablespoon packed light brown sugar
1 teaspoon baking powder
1 teaspoon baking soda
½ teaspoon ground cinnamon
¼ teaspoon salt
2 cups buttermilk

2 large eggs
¼ cup vegetable oil
¼ teaspoon vanilla extract
1½ cups fresh or canned, drained blueberries, or one 12-ounce package unsweetened, frozen blueberries, unthawed
Yogurt Chantilly (optional), following

1 · Combine the flours, brown sugar, baking powder, baking soda, cinnamon, and salt in a mixing bowl. In another bowl, whisk together the buttermilk, eggs, oil, and vanilla extract. Add the buttermilk and egg mixture to the dry ingredients, stirring just until combined. Do not overmix; the batter will have small lumps. Let the batter stand at room temperature for 15 minutes. Gently fold in the blueberries, taking care not to break them.

2 · Heat a griddle or heavy skillet over medium heat until a drop of water skates over the surface, and lightly grease the pan. Using a ¼-cup measure as a scoop for each pancake, pour the batter onto the griddle. Cook until bubbles form on the surface, the edges are dry, and the bottom is golden brown, about 2 minutes. Turn once, cooking the opposite side until golden,

about 1 minute. The second side will take half the amount of time to cook as the first side does. Serve the pancakes immediately or keep them warm in a 200°F oven until ready to serve. Accompany with Yogurt Chantilly, if desired.

Yogurt Chantilly

Makes about 3 cups topping

1 cup heavy cream, whipped to form soft
  peaks
1 cup vanilla yogurt

Using a balloon whisk or large spatula, gently combine the whipped cream and yogurt in a bowl. Chill for up to 8 hours, covered, until serving.

Sunday White Whole Wheat Pancakes

Since King Arthur Flour began distributing white whole wheat flour, it has become a standard pantry item. White whole wheat is just a different strain of wheat, grown in Kansas. The outer husk is pale compared to the red husk on our regular spring and winter wheat, so even the flour ground from the whole grain is white. Sometimes it is hard to know how to use a new flour; this pancake recipe is a perfect introduction to the mild flavor of white whole wheat. I like that these pancakes can just be stirred together quickly without any fuss. Pass the syrup and butter, please.

Makes sixteen 4-inch pancakes

1¾ cups white whole wheat flour
¼ cup brown rice flour, barley flour, cornmeal, buckwheat flour, or oat flour
2 tablespoons packed light brown sugar
1 tablespoon toasted wheat germ
2 teaspoons baking powder
1 teaspoon baking soda

1 teaspoon salt
2 cups buttermilk
½ teaspoon vanilla extract
2 large eggs
2 tablespoons vegetable oil
2 tablespoons unsalted butter, melted

1 · Combine the flours, brown sugar, wheat germ, baking powder, baking soda, and salt in a mixing bowl. In another bowl, whisk together the buttermilk, vanilla extract, eggs, oil, and butter. Add the buttermilk and egg mixture to the dry ingredients, stirring just until combined. Do not overmix; the batter will have small lumps.

2 · Heat a griddle or heavy skillet over medium heat until a drop of water skates over the surface, and lightly grease the pan. Using a ¼-cup measure as a scoop for each pancake, pour the batter onto the griddle. Cook until bubbles form on the surface, the edges are dry, and the bottom is golden brown, about 2 minutes. Turn once, cooking the opposite side until golden, about 1 minute. The second side will take half the amount of time to cook as the first side does. Serve the pancakes immediately or keep warm in a 200°F oven until ready to serve.

Four-Grain Sour Cream Pancakes

Sour cream adds a luxurious texture to this healthy morning pancake made with a combination of wheat, corn, oats, and barley flakes. Barley flakes are toasted and rolled pearl barley, a cereal grain that can be used exactly like rolled oats. Corn flour and barley flakes are available at natural foods stores and some whole foods supermarkets. Serve Four-Grain Sour Cream Pancakes with warm Whole-Blueberry Syrup (following), a very special topping made with Asti Spumante, the fruity Italian dessert wine.

Makes eighteen 4-inch pancakes

2 cups buttermilk

½ cup sour cream

2 teaspoons baking soda

2 tablespoons corn oil

2 large eggs

1 cup unbleached all-purpose flour

½ cup rolled oats

¼ cup corn flour

¼ cup barley flakes

1 teaspoon ground cardamom

½ teaspoon baking powder

¼ teaspoon salt

1 cup blueberries or 1 banana (optional), chopped

Whole-Blueberry Syrup (optional), following

1 · Combine the buttermilk, sour cream, and baking soda in a mixing bowl with a whisk. Stir until foaming stops. Add the oil and eggs, and whisk in. In another bowl, combine the unbleached flour, oats, corn flour, barley flakes, cardamom, baking powder, and salt. Add the buttermilk mixture to the dry ingredients, stirring just until combined. Do not overmix; the batter will have small lumps. Gently fold in the blueberries or banana at this time, if you are using them.

2 · Heat a griddle or heavy skillet over medium heat until a drop of water skates over the surface, and lightly grease the pan. Using a ¼-cup measure as a scoop for each pancake, pour the batter onto the griddle. Cook until bubbles form on the surface, the edges are dry, and the bottom is golden brown, about 2 minutes. Turn once, cooking the opposite side until golden, about 1 minute. The second side will take half the amount of time to cook

as the first side does. Serve the pancakes immediately or keep them warm in a 200°F oven until ready to serve. Accompany with Whole-Blueberry Syrup, if desired.

Whole-Blueberry Syrup

Makes 2 cups syrup

½ cup Asti Spumante sparkling wine or water
5 tablespoons sugar
Zest and juice of 1 orange
1 tablespoon cornstarch
2 teaspoons water
2 cups fresh blueberries, picked over, or one 12-ounce package frozen unsweetened blueberries

Place the wine or water, sugar, and orange zest and juice in a medium saucepan. Bring to a boil, then reduce heat to medium. In a small bowl, beat together the cornstarch and the water until smooth. Add to the hot wine mixture and stir constantly with a whisk until the mixture has thickened slightly and become clear. Immediately add the blueberries and cook until the blueberries are heated through. Serve immediately. The sauce can be stored in a covered container in the refrigerator for up to 3 weeks.

Buckwheat Pancakes with Maple-Nut Syrup

This is a light-textured buckwheat flour pancake that will have a wide appeal at breakfast. Serve these pancakes with warm Maple-Nut Syrup and cold cranberry juice, or for a lavish brunch during the holidays serve them with imported chestnuts in syrup. Transform them into a sophisticated dinner: Top stacks of pancakes with sour cream or crème fraîche along with cold caviar, smoked salmon, or smoked trout, and wash it all down with cold champagne. The secret to the excellent flavor of these pancakes is a small amount of musky buckwheat flour. For even lighter pancakes, separate the eggs and fold in the stiffly beaten egg whites last.

Makes sixteen 4-inch pancakes

1¾ cups unbleached all-purpose flour
¼ cup dark buckwheat flour
2 tablespoons rolled oats
1 teaspoon baking powder
1 teaspoon baking soda
Grated zest of 1 orange

¼ teaspoon salt
1½ cups buttermilk
4 large eggs
3 tablespoons unsalted butter, melted
Maple-Nut Syrup (optional), following

1 · Combine the flours, rolled oats, **baking powder**, baking soda, zest, and salt in a mixing bowl. In another bowl, whisk together the buttermilk, eggs, and melted butter. Add the buttermilk and egg mixture to the dry ingredients, stirring just until combined. Do not overmix; the batter will have small lumps. Let the batter rest at room temperature for 15 minutes.

2 · Heat a griddle or heavy skillet over medium heat until a drop of water skates over the surface, and lightly grease. Using a ¼-cup measure or a large spoon as a scoop for each pancake, pour the batter onto the griddle. Cook until bubbles form on the surface, the edges are dry, and the bottom is golden brown, about 2 minutes. Turn once, cooking the opposite side until golden, about 1 minute. The second side will take half the amount of time to cook as the first side does. Serve the pancakes immediately or keep them warm in a 200°F oven until ready to serve. Accompany with warm Maple-Nut Syrup, if desired.

Maple–Nut Syrup

Makes about 1 cup syrup

¾ cup pure maple syrup
½ cup pecans, toasted lightly and chopped
2 tablespoons unsalted butter
Splash of vanilla extract

In a small saucepan or microwave-proof bowl, combine all the ingredients. Heat over low heat or warm on full power in a microwave oven until the butter is melted and the nuts are warmed. Stir to incorporate the butter, if needed. Serve immediately.

VARIATIONS:

Blueberry Buckwheat Pancakes

Add 2 cups fresh or unsweetened, frozen blueberries, unthawed, to the batter in Step 1. Mix and cook as directed.

Banana Buckwheat Pancakes

Add 1 cup chopped or mashed fresh banana to the batter in Step 1. Mix and cook as directed.

Hopi Blue Corn Hotcakes with Fruit Salsa

*This is a traditional recipe for blue cornmeal pancakes that a friend brought to me from Second Mesa on the Hopi Indian Reservation in northeast Arizona. The Hopi are part of the tribes of Western Pueblo that also include the Zuni and Acoma, all of whom grow their sacred corn in an arid landscape. Please note that blue corn flour, also known commercially as **harinella**, is called for in this recipe rather than a coarser-grind cornmeal. There is a big difference in texture between the two, as well as in the finished product each makes. Substitute ⅔ cup fine-grind blue cornmeal and ⅓ cup unbleached all-purpose flour for the 1 cup blue corn flour if you are unable to find it in your local natural foods store. Serve these hotcakes with tangy, fresh Fruit Salsa (following) to wake up your taste buds.*

Makes twelve 3-inch hotcakes

1 cup blue corn flour
1 tablespoon sugar
1 tablespoon baking powder
¼ teaspoon salt
1 cup milk

2 large eggs
3 tablespoons corn oil
½ cup berries or pine nuts (optional)
Fruit Salsa (optional), following

1 · Combine the blue corn flour, sugar, baking powder, and salt in a mixing bowl. In another bowl, whisk together the milk, eggs, and corn oil. Add the milk and egg mixture to the dry ingredients, stirring just until combined. Do not overmix; the batter will have small lumps. Let the batter stand for 10 minutes at room temperature. Gently fold in the berries or pine nuts, if you are using them.

2 · Heat a griddle or heavy skillet over medium heat until a drop of water skates over the surface, and lightly grease the pan. For each hotcake, ladle 2 tablespoons of batter onto the griddle. Cook until bubbles form on the surface, the edges are dry, and the bottom is golden brown, about 2 minutes. Turn once, cooking the opposite side until golden, about 1 minute. The second side will take half the amount of time to cook as the first side does.

Serve the hotcakes immediately or keep them warm in a 200°F oven until ready to serve. Accompany with Fruit Salsa, if desired.

Fruit Salsa

Makes about 2½ cups salsa

2 medium fresh or canned peaches, peeled, pitted, and chopped, or 1 pint fresh or thawed frozen raspberries or strawberries, coarsely mashed

2 medium ripe pears, such as Bartlett or Comice, cored and chopped

½ cup dark or light raisins, currants, dried cherries, dried cranberries, or dried blueberries

2 tablespoons orange juice

2 tablespoons honey, or to taste

2 tablespoons raspberry vinegar

Combine all the ingredients and their juices in a small bowl and pour into a springtop jar or plastic storage container. Cover and store for up to 1 day in the refrigerator. Serve chilled.

Chili Corn Cakes

Chili Corn Cakes are a good accompaniment to grilled and roasted meats. They have a pro-nounced corn flavor that comes from the large proportion of cornmeal and fresh corn kernels in the batter. Homemade Chili Powder (page 331) gives a unique hint of spiciness, but you may use a good commercial brand, if you wish. Serve the corn cakes topped with a tablespoon of sour cream or plain yogurt and a drizzle of a sweet pepper jelly. For hors d'oeuvres, I often make the pancakes the size of a silver dollar and serve them with a thin slice of Red Pepper Butter (following). To transform this recipe into breakfast fare, substitute vanilla extract for the chili powder and serve with maple syrup.

Makes sixteen 4-inch cakes

¾ cup fine-grind yellow cornmeal, preferably stone-ground

1¼ cups unbleached all-purpose flour

1 teaspoon homemade Chili Powder (page 331)

2 teaspoons baking powder

2 teaspoons sugar

¼ teaspoon salt

2 cups milk

3 large eggs

¼ cup corn oil

4 tablespoons (½ stick) unsalted butter, melted

2 cups fresh or frozen, yellow or white corn kernels

Red Pepper Butter (optional), following

1 · Combine the cornmeal, flour, chili powder, baking powder, sugar, and salt in a mixing bowl. Make a well in the center of the mixture and add the milk and eggs to the dry ingredients, stirring just until combined. Drizzle with the oil and melted butter and gently mix. Fold in the corn with a spatula. Do not overmix; the batter will have small lumps.

2 · Heat a griddle or heavy skillet over medium heat until a drop of water skates over the surface, and lightly grease the pan. Using a ¼-cup measure or a large spoon as a scoop for each pancake, pour the batter onto the griddle. Cook until bubbles form on the surface, the edges are dry, and the bottom is golden brown, about 2 minutes. Turn once, cooking the opposite side until golden, about 1 minute. The second side will take half

the amount of time to cook as the first side does. Serve the corn cakes immediately or keep them warm in a 200°F oven until ready to serve.

Red Pepper Butter

Makes about 2 cups butter

1 cup (2 sticks) unsalted butter, at room
   temperature
One 7.5-ounce jar roasted red peppers,
   drained and patted dry
1 tablespoon fresh lemon juice
2 tablespoons chopped fresh Italian parsley

Puree all the ingredients in a blender or food processor until fluffy and smooth. Form into 2 narrow log shapes using plastic wrap to protect your hands. Wrap in clean plastic and twist the ends. Store, covered, in the refrigerator for up to 5 days or freeze for up to 6 months. Cut off slices as needed.

Savory Wild Rice Pancakes

Delicate and elegant is the best description of these silver dollar–sized gems. They nestle nicely next to sautéed vegetables and a roasted meat for a very special accompaniment to a main course. If you have friends who claim they don't like wild rice, this is the recipe to serve, since these pancakes have an appealing flavor and texture that are hard to resist. Serve plain or topped with Crème Fraîche (page 339). Frugal epicureans will rave.

Makes twenty 3-inch pancakes

4 tablespoons (½ stick) unsalted butter
1 medium shallot, minced
1 cup unbleached all-purpose flour
1 tablespoon baking powder
½ teaspoon salt

3 large eggs
1 cup milk
1½ cups cooked and cooled wild rice
  (page 355)

1 · Melt the butter in a medium skillet, add the shallot, and sauté until tender. Set aside.

2 · Combine the flour, baking powder, and salt in a bowl using a whisk, or in a food processor. Add the shallots and butter, eggs, and milk. Beat or process just until smooth. The batter will be thin, yet thicker than crêpe batter. Stir in the cooked wild rice.

3 · Heat a griddle or heavy skillet over medium heat until a drop of water skates over the surface, and lightly grease. For each pancake, ladle 2 tablespoons of batter onto the griddle. Cook until bubbles form on the surface, the edges are dry, and the bottom is golden brown, about 2 minutes. Turn once, cooking the opposite side until golden, about 1 minute. The second side will take half the amount of time to cook as the first side does. Serve the pancakes immediately or keep them warm in a 200°F oven until ready to serve.

Spinach Dinner Cakes

Luckily, the pancake is not relegated only to breakfast fare. These spinach pancakes are just as appealing as a first course, garnished with some sour cream and smoked fish or sautéed mushrooms, or for lunch alongside grilled sausages.

Makes twenty 3-inch pancakes

1¼ cups milk
1 cup unbleached all-purpose flour
1 teaspoon baking powder
½ teaspoon salt
½ teaspoon fresh-ground nutmeg
4 tablespoons (½ stick) unsalted butter, melted

2 large eggs
½ pound fresh spinach, washed, stemmed, and steamed, or one 9-ounce package frozen chopped spinach, thawed and drained
3 tablespoons chopped fresh Italian parsley

1 · Combine all the ingredients except the spinach and parsley in a blender or food processor and blend just until smooth. Transfer the batter to a bowl and scrape clean the canister of the blender or the workbowl of the food processor. Squeeze out the excess liquid from the spinach. In the blender canister or workbowl of the food processor, process the spinach and parsley until finely chopped. Add to the batter and stir until evenly blended. Let the batter rest for 1 hour at room temperature.

2 · Heat a griddle or heavy skillet over medium heat until a drop of water skates over the surface, and lightly grease. For each pancake, ladle 2 tablespoons of batter onto the griddle, spreading it into even circles with the back of the spoon. Cook until bubbles form on the surface, the edges are dry, and the bottom is golden brown, about 2 minutes. Turn once, cooking the opposite side until golden, about 1 minute. The second side will take half the amount of time to cook as the first side does. Serve the pancakes immediately or keep them warm in a 200°F oven until ready to serve.

Zucchini Pancakes

There is always room for one more recipe using abundant homegrown summer squashes. I some-times vary this recipe by combining delicious oblong yellow, pale green, and dark green Italian zuchettas *along with scalloped pattypan and yellow crookneck squashes, which gives the pan-cakes a slightly variegated color. This simple dinner pancake is a delicious complement to grilled meats, hot whole mushrooms with garlic, roasts, and even omelettes.*

Makes sixteen 2-inch pancakes

2 cups shredded unpeeled zucchini or other summer squash, drained for 10 minutes on paper towels

2 tablespoons chopped fresh Italian parsley

Salt

Fresh-ground pepper

1 large egg

½ cup unbleached all-purpose flour

1 teaspoon baking powder

Olive or other vegetable oil for frying

½ cup finely shredded imported or domestic Parmesan cheese, for sprinkling

1 · In a medium bowl, combine the zucchini, parsley, salt, pepper, and egg. Combine the flour and baking powder and add to the zucchini mixture; stir until combined. Let the batter stand at room temperature for 30 minutes.

2 · In a small, heavy skillet, heat ½ inch of oil until hot but not smoking. Drop the batter by tablespoonfuls into the oil. Cook until bubbles form on the surface, the edges are dry, and the bottom is golden brown, about 2 minutes. Turn once, cooking the opposite side until golden, about 1 minute. The second side will take half the amount of time to cook as the first side does. Drain the pancakes briefly on paper towels. Serve them immediately or keep them warm in a 200°F oven until ready to serve, sprinkled liberally with the Parmesan cheese.

Chinatown Green Onion Cakes

Staple Chinese breads are made with wheat, since the Chinese grow crops in Central Asia similar to the ones grown in our Great Plains. In Chinese cooking, savory bread rounds are often baked on griddles over an open fire and are assertively seasoned with scallions, garlic, lots of sesame seeds, or peppercorns. This one is a favorite from San Francisco's Chinatown, excellent with stir-frys.

Makes 3 onion cakes; 18 wedges

1 cup unbleached all-purpose flour
1 cup whole wheat pastry flour
1 teaspoon baking powder
1 teaspoon salt, plus extra for sprinkling
¾ cup ice water
⅓ cup brown rice flour, for dusting

2 tablespoons toasted sesame oil, for brushing
⅔ cup minced green onion (about 1 bunch), both white and green parts
⅓ cup peanut oil, or as needed, for frying

1 · In a medium bowl or the workbowl of a food processor, combine the flours, baking powder, and salt. Add the water, stirring vigorously or processing until the dough comes together in a ball.

2 · Place the dough on a lightly floured work surface and knead until a silky ball is formed, 1 to 2 minutes. Leave the dough ball on the work surface, cover with an overturned bowl, and let it rest for 1 hour to relax the dough. After the dough has rested, knead it a few times to smooth it out.

3 · On a work surface dusted with rice flour and using a rolling pin, roll out the dough ball into a flat 17-inch square about ⅛ inch thick. Brush with the sesame oil and sprinkle with the green onions and a bit of salt. Roll up tightly, jelly-roll-fashion, pinching the seams and ends. Cut into 3 equal portions. Using the palms of your hands, roll each portion of the filled dough back and forth to make an 18-inch-long rope. Coil the rope around itself to make a flat circular shape about 1 inch thick. Tuck under the outer end. Set aside, covered with plastic wrap, while you shape the other 2 portions. Using

a rolling pin on a floured surface, roll out each coiled round of dough into a 9-inch round circle with bits of green onion popping through.

4 · In a 9- or 12-inch cast-iron or nonstick large heavy skillet over medium-high heat, warm 2 tablespoons of the peanut oil. Place one green onion cake in the skillet and pan-fry for 2 minutes on each side, until lightly browned. Press with a metal spatula to keep deflating the bubbles while frying to help the cake bake evenly; it will puff slightly, and brown spots will fleck both sides. Transfer the cake to a paper towel–lined plate and cover to keep warm, or place, covered, in a 300°F oven until serving. Add 2 tablespoons more oil to the skillet and fry the next cake. Repeat for the third round of dough. Cut each bread into 6 wedges with a sharp knife and serve warm.

$\mathscr{P}$otato Latkes

Although everyone makes potato latkes for Hanukkah, the festival of lights, they are excellent year-round, and make a simple breakfast special anytime. Latke is Yiddish for "pancake." Use russets or other high-starch potatoes; they make a pancake that cooks up crisp and does not fall apart. Serve these pancakes very hot topped with cold unsweetened applesauce and sour cream.

Makes twelve 4-inch pancakes

1 medium onion
2 large russet potatoes (about 1½ pounds total)
1 large egg, lightly beaten
¼ to ½ cup unbleached all-purpose flour

1 teaspoon baking powder
Salt
Fresh-ground black pepper
½ cup canola oil

1 · Peel and shred the onion and potatoes using the large holes on a hand grater or the medium-holed grater disc on a food processor. The mixture will be mushy. Place in a mixing bowl and immediately add the egg, ¼ cup of the flour, baking powder, and salt and pepper to taste. Stir to combine evenly. Add the remaining flour in 1-tablespoon increments, as needed, to made a medium-thick batter.

2 · Pour ¼ inch of the canola oil into a large, heavy skillet; place over medium-high heat. Using a ¼-cup measure as a scoop for each latke, pour the batter into the skillet and flatten it slightly with the back of a spoon. Sauté until crisp and golden brown, about 5 minutes total, turning once about halfway through and adding more oil as needed. Drain the pancakes on paper towels. Serve immediately.

Potato-Spinach Pancakes with Goat Cheese

I have always had a fondness for crispy homemade potato pancakes, but these are the ultimate in elegant country food. The humble russet potato was the invention of Luther Burbank earlier in the twentieth century, and it has become the most widely grown variety of potato in the country. The russet's high starch content makes a pancake that cooks up crisp and does not fall apart. Serve these pancakes topped with cold unsweetened applesauce and leafy greens for a light meal or as a complement to simple roast chicken for a satisfying dinner.

Makes eight 4-inch pancakes

4 tablespoons (½ stick) unsalted butter, divided

1 large shallot, minced

6 large spinach or Swiss chard leaves, ribs removed, and leaves chopped

Salt

Fresh-ground black pepper

3 large russet potatoes (2½ to 3 pounds total)

2 large eggs, lightly beaten

3 tablespoons unbleached all-purpose flour

¼ cup vegetable oil

4 ounces goat cheese, such as Chabis or Montrachet, sliced into 8 pieces

Unsweetened applesauce (optional), chilled for serving

1 · In a large skillet, melt 2 tablespoons of the butter. Add the shallot and cook for 1 minute over medium heat to soften. Add the spinach or Swiss chard leaves, stirring until wilted, and carefully drain off any excess liquid, if there is any. Season with salt and pepper to taste.

2 · Peel and coarsely grate the potatoes; you should have about 2½ cups total. Transfer to a tea towel and wring out excess moisture. Place in a mixing bowl and add the eggs, flour, and spinach mixture. Stir to combine evenly.

3 · Wipe out the skillet with a paper towel and place over medium-high heat. Add the remaining butter and the oil and melt. For each pancake, drop the batter into the skillet by ¼-cup measure and flatten the patties slightly with the back of a spoon. Sauté the pancakes for about 5 minutes total, turning halfway through, until crisp and golden brown on both sides. While the second side is cooking, place a slice of the goat cheese over each pancake to melt slightly. Remove the pancakes from the pan, drain on paper towels, if necessary, and serve very hot accompanied by cold unsweetened applesauce, if desired.

Roasted Red Pepper Pancakes with Hot Goat-Cheese Sauce

Roasted Red Pepper Pancakes taste extravagant napped with silky Hot Goat-Cheese Sauce. For a celebration lunch, the pancakes may also be topped with cold California golden caviar and sour cream, or, for a less rich alternative, they may be topped with chopped garden-fresh chives with their colorful blosoms. Serve as a first course or alongside fresh corn on the cob and roasted meats or fish.

Makes ten 3-inch pancakes

1½ cups unbleached all-purpose flour
2½ teaspoons baking powder
½ teaspoon salt
3 large eggs, separated
1 cup milk

1 large red bell pepper, roasted, peeled, seeded, and minced (see page 352)
3 to 4 tablespoons unsalted butter, for sautéing
Hot Goat-Cheese Sauce, following

1 · In a bowl, combine the flour, baking powder, and salt. In a small bowl, whisk together the egg yolks and milk. Add the milk and egg mixture to the dry ingredients and beat well until evenly blended.

2 · In a clean bowl, beat the egg whites with an electric mixer or a balloon whisk until stiff peaks form. Fold the whites gently into the batter until no white streaks are visible. Fold in the minced roasted red pepper until evenly distributed.

3 · Heat a griddle or heavy skillet over medium heat until a drop of water skates over the surface. Using a tablespoon at a time for each batch, melt the butter in an even layer over the surface to grease. For each pancake, ladle 2 tablespoons of batter onto the griddle, making pancakes no more than 3 inches in diameter. Cook until bubbles form on the surface, the edges are dry, and the bottom is golden brown, about 2 minutes. Turn once, cooking the opposite side until golden, about 1 minute. The second side will take half the amount of time to cook as the first side does, and the pancakes will be quite light in texture. Serve immediately with Hot Goat-Cheese Sauce.

Hot Goat–Cheese Sauce

Makes 1¾ cups sauce

½ cup dry white wine
1 clove garlic, pressed
1 cup heavy cream
5 ounces fresh goat cheese
Pinch of fresh-ground white pepper

Combine the wine and garlic in a small saucepan. Bring to a boil, lower the heat to a simmer, and reduce the liquid to ¼ cup. Add the cream, goat cheese, and white pepper. Stir with a whisk until smooth. Use immediately or keep warm by setting in a hot-water bath for up to 2 hours.

Black Bean Pancakes

I think black beans, also called turtle beans when you buy them dry, are one of the best tasting beans. Of course, they are synonymous with Cuban cooking and Southwestern cuisine. Bean pancakes, made from leftover beans, are part of old-fashioned home cooking, from the days when every kitchen had its daily pot of beans bubbling on the back of the stove. Given how common they once were, I was surprised at how hard it was to find a recipe for bean pancakes. I think these are the perfect black bean pancakes—crisp on the outside and creamy on the in-side—a specialty of my friend Jacquie McMahan, author of numerous cookbooks on California Rancho and Mexican cooking, all of which include recipes handed down in her family. This one is from her grandmother and is cooked in olive oil, a staple oil in early California cooking. I wanted a bean pancake that could be made from canned beans for convenience, yet was still incredibly delicious. Serve these pancakes with brunch, alongside egg dishes, or as an accompaniment to roasted and barbecued meats for dinner.

Makes twelve 4-inch pancakes

1 clove garlic, minced

1 bunch green onions, white part and
  1 inch of the green part, minced

1 tablespoon olive oil

2⅓ cups drained canned black beans,
  divided

1 pickled jalapeño chile, minced

1 teaspoon red chili powder

½ teaspoon cumin seeds, toasted in a dry
  skillet and crushed in a mortar

¾ cup cooked brown rice or steamed barley,
  at room temperature

2 to 3 tablespoons fresh snipped cilantro

1 cup yellow cornmeal, for coating

About ¼ cup olive oil, for frying

½ cup regular, reduced-fat, or imitation sour
  cream, for garnish

Salsa, for topping

1 · Sauté the garlic and green onion in the olive oil for 4 to 5 minutes, until just softened. Do not brown. Purée 1 cup of the beans in a food processor. Place in a mixing bowl with the rest of the whole beans and mash together with a fork. Add the sautéed onion and garlic, jalapeño, chili powder, and cumin. Mash to combine. Stir in the rice or barley and the cilantro to taste. The mixture will be stiff enough to shape into patties.

2 · Place the cornmeal on a plate or sheet of waxed paper. Scoop out some of the bean mixture using with a ¼-cup measure as a scoop, and drop the batter onto the cornmeal. Use a spoon to turn it over, then flatten it slightly with the back of the spoon; both sides of the pancake should be coated with cornmeal.

3 · Lightly coat the bottom of a large, nonstick skillet with some of the olive oil; place over medium-high heat. Place 3 or 4 pancakes in the skillet. Sauté until crisp and golden brown around the edges, turning once with a wide metal spatula, about 2 minutes on each side, adding a teaspoon or two more oil as needed (I think the olive oil makes them taste especially good). The pancakes will still be creamy in the center. Serve immediately, topped with sour cream and some salsa.

Crêpes

Traveling in France decades ago was the first time I was introduced to crêpes (pronounced *crep* as in *yep*, rather than *crayp*). We often went to crêpe houses for dinner. There were pâte, cornichons, and French baguette pieces as appetizers; a main dish crêpe that was as big around as the over-sized dinner plate it was served on and was filled with a savory filling, such as ratatouille, or ham and Emmenthaler cheese; and then a sugar-crusted sweet dessert crêpe, available liberally doused with brandy and flamed at the table, with coffee to finish. On my jaunts to the local *l'épicerie*, a convenience store often not larger than a big closet packed with nice food, sort of a gourmet 7-11, as I handed my money over the counter for my daily yogurt, there would be flat piles of ready-made crêpes off to the side of the cash register wrapped in plastic wrap, ready to be taken home and filled.

Back in the states, I indulged my love of this delicate pancake at crêperies like the Magic Pan, or at the house of a friend who had gone to school in France. I was ecstatic to be invited to a brunch where my hostess had made homemade blintzes, a Jewish crêpe-type specialty, which she served with sour cream and blueberry preserves. Except for an occasional crêpe suzette, the showstopping orange-liqueur dessert crêpe that is flambéed tableside, on the menu of upscale old-style Continental restaurants, I found little trace of the food that is used much like homemade noodles and is very much loved in France. I craved the thin pancake filled with vegetables and topped with a creamy sauce. So I had to experiment on my own.

Crêpes comes from the word *crispus*, or curly or wavy, probably a reference to how the edges of a cooked crêpe look. In Hungary, crêpes are called *palacsintas* and are served in homes as well as restaurants; they are known as *crespelle* in Italy. Along with other types of pancakes, they are economical as well as elegant, a testament to the ability of European cooks to make a simple food a masterpiece of ingenuity as well as taste. It is said that crêpes are "the French cook's way to trans-form Sunday's roast chicken or ham into Monday's supper." No matter what filling you make, it must be moistened slightly with some sauce, melted butter, or soft cheese, and all the ingredients must harmonize with each other.

Crêpes can be sweet or savory, with sweet crêpes, *crêpes sucress*, including a bit of sugar, extra egg yolks, and a dash of brandy to make the batter a bit richer. The most famous crêpe desserts are crêpes bathed in suzette sauce, prepared in a chafing dish, and walnut crêpes, served in a pool of warm chocolate sauce, a dish that originated at Gundel's restaurant in Budapest, Hungary. There are many versions of each.

Crêpes are rich in milk and eggs, making them more protein-rich than starchy, but stock or beer can be substituted for the milk. Since they are so flexible, crêpes can be folded into halves or fourths, or rolled like a fat cigar into many different shapes around their filling, giving this humble pancake many different guises, from an appetizer bite to an Italian cannelloni casserole or *gâteau*, which is also called a crêpe cake, when individual pancakes are stacked one on top of another with moist fillings in between and served in wedges like a cake. A *gâteau* is a vegetarian's delight. At a wedding buffet I sampled a *gâteau* made with Gruyère and a béchamel sauce that was a solid 8 inches high, and delightfully filling as an entrée.

The most famous appetizer is the "beggar's purse," a 5-inch crêpe with a spoonful of créme frâiche and dab of caviar in the center, the edges gathered up to form a miniature bundle. A length of blanched chive or green onion is used to "tie" the pleated top. German crêpes, called *pfannkuchen*, are rolled up and cut into strips, placed into soup bowls, and served with clear hot consommé, a beautiful first course. A cross between American pancakes and the crêpe are tiny Russian and Scandinavian *blini*, often made with a bit of yeast and washed down with glasses of aquavit or vodka, and Swedish pancakes, *plättar*, both of which can be made in a special pan with shallow, small indentations for creating perfectly formed rounds (see page 199).

Crêpe batters showcase different flours beautifully, providing a perfect venue for their unique flavors. Although flours like whole wheat, chestnut, and garbanzo may be variations on the basic crêpe, the most famous is the hearty, oversized buckwheat crêpe called *krampouz*, which are native to the coast of Brittany, where they are street food and eaten dripping with butter or wrapped around a sausage.

Some batter recipes will have more liquid than flour, making a most delicate crêpe, but the standard is a 1-to-1 ratio of liquid to flour; the sturdiness of this crêpe is essential if you want to use it for a thick filling, such as for cannelloni or manicotti. All crêpe batters and the related pancakes can be prepared in advance, then filled and reheated. This is not true of regular pancakes; they must be eaten right off the griddle.

Specialty kitchen shops like Williams-Sonoma offer French steel crêpe pans at reasonable prices, often in pairs so you can have an assembly line of sorts, just like in restaurants (experienced crêpe makers bake on up to six pans at once), to make 6- to 7-inch crêpes efficiently. A crêpe pan is a flat pan with shallow, angled sides and a long, tilted handle, designed in the 1600s especially for the essential action of swirling the batter and turning the crêpe over. Dedicated crêpe makers use these pans only for making crêpes, nothing else. An ordinary black cast-iron skillet or nonstick sauté pan works just as well, but the pan must be heavy-weight, since the heat will be high and the pan must distribute it evenly. I generally use an 8- to 10-inch omelette pan with sloping sides, which I bought at a restaurant supply store; with a silverstone coating it requires minimal buttering. Any size pan from 6 to 8 inches to 12 to 20 inches in diameter, depending on the size of the crêpe you want to make, will do,

but remember that you have to be able to lift the pan to turn the crêpe. Many small crêpes will obviously take longer to make than larger crêpes, and will yield more crêpes per batch of batter. The larger the crêpe, the easier it is to tear it during the turning.

There are so many recipes for making and filling crêpes. I have included my favorites here, and fillings for them. All of the crêpe batters are cooked in exactly the same manner. If you make smaller crêpes, use 2 to 3 tablespoons of batter in a 6- to 7-inch pan, which yields about 20 crêpes per recipe; if you want big 9- to 10-inch crêpes, use ½ to ¾ cup batter and a 10- to 12-inch pan, which yields about 10 crêpes per recipe. Dinner crêpes are usually made in the larger size, and dessert, appetizer, and cannelloni crêpes are made in the smaller size. The recipe for Classic Crêpes, the first recipe in this section, gives the most detailed instructions for cooking crêpes.

If you are not going to use the crêpes you have made within a few hours, they should be refrigerated or frozen. Wrap the cooled crêpes in plastic or slip them into a self-sealing plastic bag and refrigerate them for up to 3 days, or freeze in plastic freezer bags for up to 1 month. Wrap the crêpes in stacks of as many as you will use at one time. Let refrigerated crêpes stand at room temperature for 1 hour before filling them so they won't tear as you separate them. If they have been frozen, the crêpes must be thawed in the refrigerator or on the kitchen counter and should be brought back to room temperature before they are separated, to avoid tearing. A package of 6 crêpes takes only 20 to 30 minutes to defrost. Delicate crêpes can be stacked with some waxed paper in between to keep them perfect. To reheat them, remove the waxed paper, wrap your stack in foil, and place it in a 325°F oven for 15 minutes. Warmed crêpes separate the easiest. You will need to warm the premade crêpes in this manner if you are going to fill them just before serving. You can also fill room-temperature crêpes if you are going to warm them in the oven after filling them.

Classic Crêpes

This is my basic crêpe recipe for filling, folding, and stacking crêpes that can then be served with savory or sweet fillings. I also like these crêpes made with flat beer for meat fillings. Unlike regular pancake batters, crêpe batters need to be beaten well to develop some of the gluten in the flour, so that the thin pancake will be strong enough to hold the filling. The batter, usually about the consistency of thick buttermilk, relaxes for an hour or so after the beating to relax the gluten again, making the crêpes tender to the bite after cooking. The secrets to perfect crêpes are having the pan at the correct heat, having the batter of the right consistency, and perfecting your quick wrist movements to distribute the batter over the bottom of the pan. Practice is the key here to gaining culinary confidence. As a caterer, I often had requests for crêpes and used the opportunity of making 50 crêpes per batch to get good at making them.
You can double or triple this recipe.

Makes about fifteen 7- to 8-inch crêpes

3 large eggs
1 cup milk
⅓ cup water

3 tablespoons unsalted butter, melted
1 cup unbleached all-purpose flour
¼ teaspoon salt

1 · Place all the ingredients, in the order given, in a deep bowl, the canister of a blender, or the workbowl of a food processor. Using a large wire whisk, an immersion blender, canister blender, or food processor, beat the batter vigorously by hand or on high until the mixture is smooth, 30 seconds. Scrape down the sides and bottom of the bowl or container once. Beat or blend 15 seconds longer. The batter should be the consistency of smooth, heavy cream. Adjust the consistency of the batter, if necessary, adding more milk or more flour. Cover and refrigerate the batter for 1 to 3 hours, allowing the starch to absorb the liquid and swell. (The batter can be prepared up to 1 day in advance. Bring the batter to room temperature and stir before using. If your batter is lumpy, strain it.)

2 · Assemble your work space with everything you will need for cooking the crêpes. Spread out a large clean kitchen towel on which to lay the crêpes after cooking (in Brittany there are ribbed wooden boards designed espe-

cially for this purpose). Set out a ¼-cup measuring cup for measuring out the batter, and a long metal spatula or wooden crêpe tongs for flipping. Have on hand a piece of paper towel, a natural bristle brush (one with plastic bristles will melt), or a piece of cloth for brushing the hot pan with a thin layer of oil.

3 · Brush an 8-inch crêpe pan, skillet, or nonstick frying pan with some oil or spray it with cooking spray (if you use cooking spray for oiling the pan between crêpes, be sure to remove the pan from the heat source as you spray), just enough to keep the batter from sticking. Heat the pan over medium-high heat until hot, but not smoking. Stir the batter a few times.

4 · Remove the pan from the heat and immediately ladle in 3 tablespoons of batter, tilting and rotating the pan quickly in all directions to coat the entire surface evenly with the batter. (If the batter does not spread quickly, it is too thick; thin it with some water. If the batter stiffens when poured into the pan, the pan is too hot.) If the crêpes have holes, fill them in with a few drops of batter; this is a common problem that disappears when you master the art of tilting the pan. If you have too much batter, just lift the pan and pour the excess back into the bowl of batter. Plan on a few uneven crêpes at first while you work on regulating the heat and thickness of the batter. (No matter how many years I have been making crêpes, it still takes a few to get the rhythm unless I make them every day. Sometimes it takes a few to get the right look.) Return the pan to the heat. In about 1 to 1½ minutes, the edges of the crêpe will be lightly browned and will lift up slightly from the pan. The top will be set and almost dry. Slide the long spatula under the crêpe and turn it carefully, to prevent tearing. Cook briefly, just until the underside is brown in spots but not crispy, 30 seconds. The second side is never as attractive in appearance as the first (when you fill crêpes, keep the side that was cooked first on the outside). The crêpes should remain soft; do not overcook them. Invert the pan and release the crêpe onto the clean dish towel. The process goes very quickly once you get going, and you can use two pans at once.

5 · Continue to make the crêpes in this manner, stirring the batter and greasing the pan lightly as needed before cooking each crêpe. If you will be using the crêpes within a few hours, cover them with another towel to keep them from drying out. Crêpes can also be refrigerated or frozen for longer storage.

Chicken and Mushroom–Filled Crêpes

This is a casserole that uses leftover chicken. You could also make it with turkey. It is topped with a French béchamel sauce, the delicious workhorse of a good cook's kitchen. It is a rave dinner party dish, rich and satisfying, served bubbling hot from the oven with steamed vegetables and a salad.

Serves 6

Filling
3 tablespoons unsalted butter
3 tablespoons olive oil
3 shallots, chopped
¾ pound fresh mushrooms, sliced
One 10-ounce package frozen spinach, thawed and squeezed dry
3 cups coarsely shredded cooked chicken
⅔ cup sour cream
2 tablespoons dry sherry

Sauce
6 tablespoons (¾ stick) unsalted butter
⅓ cup unbleached all-purpose flour
½ cup dry sherry

2 cups chicken broth
1 cup milk
¼ teaspoon fresh-ground white pepper
¾ cup grated Parmesan cheese
1 cup grated Swiss or Gruyère cheese, divided

1 recipe Classic Crêpes made with beer instead of milk and water

1 · Make the filling: Melt the butter and oil together in a large skillet. Add the shallots and sauté until soft. Add the mushrooms and sauté for 5 minutes, until cooked through. Remove from the heat and add the spinach. Stir to combine. Add the chicken. Combine the sour cream and the sherry and add to the chicken mixture. Stir to moisten evenly. (The filling can be prepared up to 6 hours before assembling the casserole, and refrigerated.)

2 · Make the sauce: Melt the butter in a heavy saucepan over medium heat. Add the flour and stir with a whisk until smooth. Cook for 30 seconds, stirring constantly. Add the sherry, chicken broth, milk, and white pepper. Cook over medium heat, stirring constantly, until the mixture comes to a boil and thickens. Reduce the heat to low and simmer for 1 minute. Add the Parmesan and half of the Swiss or Gruyère cheese. Stir to melt. Remove from the heat and cover with waxed paper or parchment to prevent a skin from forming.

3 · Preheat the oven to 350°F. Grease a large 15-by-10-inch ceramic casserole. To assemble the dish, lay a crêpe on a work surface and spoon some filling down one side. Roll up and place in the prepared casserole. Repeat with the other crêpes, laying the filled crêpes side by side. Cover with the sauce and sprinkle with the remaining Swiss or Gruyère cheese.

4 · Bake for 20 to 25 minutes, uncovered, until the sauce is bubbling and the cheese is slightly browned. The crêpes may need to bake an extra 15 minutes if the filling was very cold when the casserole was assembled. Serve immediately.

Crêpe Torta de la Mer

This is a stacked crêpe cake made with smoked salmon and an herbed cream cheese. If you can't find arugula, you can use fresh baby spinach instead. This recipe is wonderful for a summer first course with cold white wine, as a passed hors d'oeuvre, or a brunch side dish.

Serves 4; 8 wedges

10 Classic Crêpes or Buttermilk Crêpes (page 180)

5 ounces herbed cream cheese, such as Boursin or Rondelé, at room temperature

1 bunch fresh arugula leaves, washed, dried, and stemmed

2 plum tomatoes (6 to 8 ounces), thinly sliced

1 medium cucumber, peeled and thinly sliced

4 ounces smoked salmon, thinly sliced

1 · Set one crêpe on a serving plate. Spread it with a thin layer of the herbed cream cheese. Top with a single layer of arugula leaves, then a layer of tomato slices, a layer of cucumber slices, and some smoked salmon. Cover with a crêpe and press down to keep the stack even.

2 · Repeat the layering, ending with the last crêpe on top. Cover with plastic wrap and refrigerate until serving. Serve the torta the same day it is made, cut into 8 wedges.

Manicotti Crêpes

A savory crêpe is a perfect alternative to large tube pasta in Italian-style casseroles. The crêpe is incredibly delicate and less chewy than pasta. A traditional favorite, Manicotti Crêpes are good for Christmas eve dinner or a wedding buffet. This meatless casserole is a specialty of many very accomplished cooks. You can make the sauce a few days ahead and the crêpes the day before for easy assembly. Accompany these crêpes with a green salad. This dish is fantastic!

Serves 12 to 15

Filling
2 pounds fresh spinach, stems removed, or one and a half 10-ounce packages frozen spinach, thawed and squeezed dry
2 pounds whole-milk ricotta cheese
2 large eggs
1 cup grated Parmesan cheese, divided
2 tablespoons unsalted butter

2 tablespoons olive oil
2 medium shallots, minced

1 recipe Tomato Sauce, following
1 pound mozzarella cheese, coarsely shredded
2 recipes Classic Crêpes, with the crêpes made 6 to 7 inches in diameter
Additional Parmesan cheese, grated, for serving

1 · To make the filling: If you are using fresh spinach, bring a pot of salted water to a boil over high heat. Add half of the fresh spinach and stir until wilted. Remove with a slotted spoon to a colander to drain and cool. Repeat with the remaining spinach. When the spinach is cool, squeeze out the moisture with your hands. Place the ricotta, eggs, and

½ cup of the Parmesan cheese in a mixing bowl. Blend thoroughly. Chop the spinach and transfer it to the mixing bowl. Stir to combine all the ingredients.

2 · Melt the butter and oil in a small skillet over medium heat. Add the shallots and sauté until transparent. Cool and stir into the ricotta-spinach mixture. If you are not filling the crêpes right away, store the filling, covered, in the refrigerator for up to 6 hours.

3 · Preheat the oven to 375°F. Lightly grease a 15-by-12-inch deep casserole and cover the bottom with a layer of the Tomato Sauce. To assemble, lay a crêpe on a work surface and sprinkle it with a tablespoon of the mozzarella. Then spoon 2 heaping tablespoons of the ricotta-spinach filling down the center. Fold the top, bottom, and sides over the center to make

a package so that the filling is completely covered. Arrange the filled crêpes, seam side down, in the prepared pan. Repeat with the remaining crêpes (I place them slightly overlapping each other in rows). Cover with a layer of the Tomato Sauce (you will not use all of the Tomato Sauce; the remainder will be served with the crêpes) and sprinkle with any remaining mozzarella and the remaining ½ cup Parmesan cheese. Cover loosely with foil. (At this point the casserole may be frozen for up to 1 month.)

4 · Bake the manicotti, uncovered, in the preheated oven for about 60 minutes, until the sauce is bubbling and the cheese is slightly browned. Serve immediately, with extra Tomato Sauce reheated for ladling and a bowl of grated Parmesan on the side.

Tomato Sauce

This is a slow-cooking, thick marinara-type sauce, also perfect for ladling over pasta.

Makes 2 quarts sauce

3 tablespoons olive oil
1 large yellow onion, chopped
1 large red bell pepper, seeded and
  chopped
Three 35-ounce cans peeled Italian plum
  tomatoes, with their juice
½ cup dry red wine
2 cloves garlic, pressed
1½ tablespoons fresh chopped basil or
  2 teaspoons dried basil
1 tablespoon fresh chopped marjoram or
  oregano or 1 teaspoon dried herb
¼ teaspoon salt
½ teaspoon fresh-ground black pepper

1 · In a large nonreactive saucepan, heat the oil over medium heat. Add the onion and cook until translucent, 5 minutes. Add the bell pepper and cook a few minutes longer, until softened. Add the tomatoes with their juice and crush them lightly with a fork. Add the wine, garlic, and herbs. Bring to a boil, then reduce the heat to low and simmer, uncovered, for 2 to 3 hours hours, stirring occasionally. Add the salt and pepper halfway through cooking. I like to smooth out the sauce using an immersion blender; you can leave it chunky if you like. The sauce can be made up to 2 days ahead of time and refrigerated, or it may be frozen.

Buttermilk Crêpes

This is another of my favorite all-purpose crêpes. I love lowfat buttermilk, and it somehow finds its way into all my baking. If you are on a special diet, you can use commercial liquid egg substitutes here. These delightful crêpes will have a tangy flavor. They are good filled with a small pile of sautéed mushrooms. Top the uncooked side of the crêpe with cheese or cooked vegetables while still in the pan and fold in half. Serve with sour cream or a rich brown gravy left over from dinner.

Makes about eighteen 6-inch crêpes

2 large eggs
1 cup buttermilk
½ cup lowfat milk
1 tablespoon vegetable or nut oil

¾ cup unbleached all-purpose flour
¼ teaspoon salt
Pinch of sugar

1 · Place all the ingredients, in the order given, in a deep bowl, the canister of a blender, or the workbowl of a food processor. Using a large wire whisk, an immersion blender, canister blender, or food processor, beat the batter vigorously by hand or on high until the mixture is smooth, 30 seconds. Scrape down the sides and bottom of the bowl or container once. Beat or blend 15 seconds longer. The batter should be the consistency of smooth, heavy cream. Adjust the consistency of the batter, if necessary, adding more milk or more flour. Cover and refrigerate the batter for 1 to 3 hours, allowing the starch to absorb the liquid and swell. (The batter can be prepared up to 1 day in advance.) Bring the batter to room temperature and stir before using. If your batter is lumpy, strain it.

2 · Brush a 6-inch crêpe pan, skillet, or nonstick frying pan with some oil or spray it with cooking spray (if you want to use cooking spray for the oiling between crêpes, be sure to remove the pan from the heat source as you spray). You need only a thin layer of oil, just enough to keep the batter from sticking. Heat the pan over medium-high heat until hot but not smoking. Stir the batter a few times.

3 · Remove the pan from the heat and immediately ladle in 2 tablespoons of batter, tilting and rotating the pan quickly in all directions to coat the entire surface evenly. If the crêpes have holes, fill them in with a few drops of batter; this is a common problem that disappears when you master the art of tilting the pan. Return the pan to the heat. In about 1 to 1½ minutes, the edges of the crêpe will be lightly browned and will lift up slightly from the pan. The top will be set and almost dry. Slide the long spatula under the crêpe and turn it carefully, to prevent tearing. Cook the other side briefly, just until brown in spots but not crispy, 30 seconds. (When you fill the crêpes, keep the side that was cooked first on the outside; the second side is never as attractive.) The crêpes should remain soft, so do not overcook them. Invert the pan and release the crêpe onto a clean dish towel.

4 · Continue to make the crêpes in this manner, stirring the batter and greasing the pan lightly as needed before cooking each crêpe. If you will be using the crêpes within a few hours, cover them with another towel to keep them from drying out. Crêpes can also be refrigerated or frozen for longer storage.

Cornmeal Crêpes

I often use cornmeal crêpes in recipes that call for tortillas. They make a fantastic enchilada casserole. Or serve them as an appetizer, warm, with hot pepper jelly and a cold beer.

Makes about sixteen 7- to 8-inch crêpes

2 large eggs
½ cup cold milk or buttermilk
½ cup unbleached all-purpose flour
½ cup yellow, white, or blue cornmeal, or
  polenta

¼ teaspoon salt
2 tablespoons unsalted butter, melted
1 tablespoon vegetable or corn oil

1 · Place the eggs, milk or buttermilk, flour, cornmeal, and salt in a deep bowl or the workbowl of a food processor. Using a whisk, an immersion blender, or a food processor, beat until smooth. Stop once to scrape down the sides and bottom of the bowl or container. Do not overbeat, as you do not want to develop the gluten too much. Add the melted butter and oil. The batter should be the consistency of buttermilk. Adjust the consistency, if necessary—you may need to add a few tablespoons of water if you used thick buttermilk. Cover and refrigerate for 1 to 2 hours to overnight, allowing the starch to absorb the liquid and swell. (The batter can be prepared 1 day ahead without the butter and oil, and then refrigerated. Bring the batter back to room temperature and add the butter and oil just before using.)

2 · Brush a 6-inch crêpe pan, skillet, or nonstick frying pan with some oil or spray it with cooking spray (if you want to use cooking spray for the oiling between crêpes, be sure to remove the pan from the heat source as you spray). You need only a thin layer of oil, just enough to keep the batter from sticking. Heat the pan over medium-high heat until hot but not smoking. Stir the batter a few times.

3 · Remove the pan from the heat and immediately ladle in 3 tablespoons of batter, tilting and rotating the pan quickly in all directions to coat the entire surface evenly. If the crêpes have holes, fill them in with a few drops of

batter; this is a common problem that disappears when you master the art of tilting the pan. Return the pan to the heat. In about 1 to 1½ minutes, the edges will be lightly browned and will lift up slightly from the pan. The top will be set and almost dry. Slide the long spatula under the crêpe and turn it carefully, to prevent tearing. Cook the other side briefly, just until brown in spots but not crispy, 30 seconds. (When you fill the crêpes, keep the side that was cooked first on the outside; the second side is never as attractive.) The crêpes should remain soft, so do not overcook them. Invert the pan and release the crêpe onto a clean dish towel.

4 · Continue to make the crêpes in this manner, stirring the batter and greasing the pan lightly as needed before cooking each crêpe. If you will be using the crêpes within a few hours, cover them with another towel to keep them from drying out. Crêpes can also be refrigerated or frozen for longer storage.

Green Enchiladas

Enchiladas are the Mexican version of a filled pancake, usually made with tortillas. In this recipe, either yellow or blue cornmeal crêpes are filled with chicken and cream cheese, and served with a tangy cooked green tomatillo sauce called salsa de tomate verde. *Even if you have never made a Mexican sauce before, this one is very easy, and a delight to consume, so do try it. I first had* enchilada suissa, *which is what this dish is called, in the restaurant dining room of a hotel I stayed at in Mexico City. I was hooked, and ate there as often as I could during my stay.*

Serves 6 to 8

Chicken Filling

1 quart water seasoned with a pinch of salt, a few peppercorns, and 2 whole cloves garlic

1½ pounds skinless, boneless chicken breasts

2 tablespoons unsalted butter

1 large shallot, minced

1 pound cream cheese

2 cups shredded Monterey Jack cheese

Salsa Verde

1 pound (about 20) tomatillos, with their
  papery husks removed, rinsed
3 fresh serrano chiles or canned jalapeños
  (optional)
¾ cup chopped fresh cilantro
1 clove garlic, minced
1 small white boiling onion, chopped
2 tablespoons unsalted butter
½ teaspoon sugar
Salt

1 recipe Cornmeal Crêpes
2 cups (16 ounces) sour cream whisked
  with 2 tablespoons buttermilk or milk to
  thin slightly, or *crema Mexicana*

1 · Make the filling: Bring the seasoned water to a boil in a large
saucepan; reduce to a simmer.
Poach the chicken in the simmering liquid until cooked through,
about 20 minutes. Melt the butter
in a large skillet. Add the shallot
and sauté until soft; remove the
pan from the heat. Remove the
chicken from the cooking liquid
and, when it is cool enough to
handle, shred it. Toss the shredded
chicken with the cooked shallot.
Cut the cream cheese into 12
long, equal pieces.

2 · Make the sauce: Place the tomatillos and fresh serrano chiles, if
you are using them, in a saucepan
and cover with water. Bring to a
fast simmer and continue to cook,
uncovered, until the tomatillos are
soft but still whole, 10 minutes.
Remove the mixture from the
heat. Drain the tomatillos and
chiles, reserving the cooking
liquid. Place the whole tomatillos,
the boiled fresh chiles or the
canned jalapeños, the cilantro,
garlic, and onion in the workbowl
of a food processor. Ladle in about
¼ cup of the cooking water to thin
the mixture slightly. Process until
smooth, 15 seconds. Place the
butter in a nonstick skillet and
add the puree, sugar, and salt.
Bring to a boil and simmer for
10 minutes to thicken. You should
have about 2½ cups.

3 · Preheat the oven to 325°F. Grease
a 13-by-9-inch rectangular baking
dish and place a few tablespoons of
the sauce in the bottom. Moisten
the chicken mixture with a few
tablespoons of the sauce. To assemble the enchiladas, lay a crêpe
on a work surface and place a
spoonful of the sauce on top; use

the back of the spoon to spread the sauce around. Sprinkle with some Monterey Jack cheese (you will use it all up stuffing the enchiladas). Place a piece of cream cheese and some shredded chicken filling down the side. Roll up the crêpe and place it in the casserole dish, seam side down. Repeat with all the crêpes, laying the filled crêpes side by side. Cover them with all the sauce and pour the sour cream over the sauce, leaving a border all the way around the edge so you can see the sauce and crêpes.

4 · Bake, uncovered, for 30 to 35 minutes, until the sauce is bubbling. Serve immediately.

*M*y Favorite Buckwheat Crêpes

I adapted my first buckwheat crêpes from an old Chez Panisse recipe, and they have evolved from there. They are delightfully light flavored despite the addition of often intensely musky buckwheat. Buckwheat crêpes were once a staple in the diet of both the rich and the poor in the Brittany area of France, where they are traditional. The pancakes are cooked on a large round iron hotplate called a bilig. *A special batter ladle, called a* rozell, *and a long narrow wooden paddle designed for turning the crêpes, called a* spanell, *are traditionally used. These crêpes are good for dessert rolled with ice cream and topped with hot fudge or orange sauce; or just serve them plain, folded in quarters and dripping with maple butter or with butter and strawberry jam.*

Makes about sixteen 7- to 8-inch crêpes

1¾ cups milk
½ cup (1 stick) unsalted butter
1½ cups unbleached all-purpose flour
¾ cups light buckwheat flour

1 teaspoon salt
4 large eggs
2 tablespoons canola or walnut oil
1 cup flat beer, at room temperature

1 · Combine the milk and butter in a small saucepan to heat on the stovetop or in a glass bowl to heat in the microwave. Heat until the butter is melted.

2 · In a medium bowl, combine the flours, salt, eggs, oil, and beer. Beat hard with a whisk or immersion blender for 15 seconds. Add the warm milk mixture and beat for 1 minute, until very creamy. The batter may also be beaten by hand with the fingers of your outstretched hand for 10 minutes, in the old farmstead fashion. Or the batter may be mixed in a blender or food processor. The batter should be the consistency of smooth heavy cream. Cover the bowl with plastic wrap and place it in the refrigerator to rest for about 3 hours. (The batter can also be refrigerated for up to 1 day and brought to room temperature before making the crêpes.)

3 · Brush an 8-inch crêpe pan, skillet, or nonstick frying pan with some oil or spray it with cooking spray (if you want to use cooking spray for the oiling between crêpes, be sure to remove the pan from the heat source as you

spray). You need only a thin layer of oil, just enough to keep the batter from sticking. Heat the pan over medium-high heat until hot but not smoking. Stir the batter a few times.

4 · Remove the pan from the heat and immediately ladle in 3 tablespoons of batter, tilting and rotating the pan quickly in all directions to coat the entire surface evenly. If the crêpes have holes, fill them in with a few drops of batter; this is a common problem that disappears when you master the art of tilting the pan. Return the pan to the heat. In about 1 to 1½ minutes, the edges will be lightly browned and will lift up slightly from the pan. The top will be set and almost dry. Slide the long spatula under the crêpe and turn it carefully, to prevent tearing. Cook the other side briefly, just until brown in spots but not crispy, 30 seconds. (When you fill the crêpes, keep the side that was cooked first on the outside; the second side is never as attractive.) The crêpes should remain soft, so do not overcook. Invert the pan and release the crêpe onto a clean dish towel.

5 · Continue to make the crêpes in this manner, stirring the batter and greasing the pan lightly as needed before cooking each crêpe. If you will be using the crêpes within a few hours, cover them with another towel to keep them from drying out. Crêpes can also be refrigerated or frozen for longer storage.

Maple Butter Crêpes

I know these crêpes are decadent, but they are a unique sweet addition to a special occasion brunch menu. Fold the crêpes into quarters, heat them until the butter is dripping, and then eat them with a fork.

Serves 6 to 8

¾ cup (1½ sticks) lightly salted butter, at room temperature
⅔ cup pure maple syrup

1 recipe My Favorite Buckwheat Crêpes

1 · Prepare the crêpes and set them aside. Preheat the oven to 375°F. Butter a shallow 13-by-9-inch ceramic baking dish.

2 · Place the butter in the workbowl of a food processor or in a mixing bowl. With the food processor or an electric mixer running, cream the butter with the maple syrup by pouring in the syrup in a slow, steady stream. With a rubber spatula, spread each crêpe lightly with the maple butter. Fold it in half, spread with a bit more maple butter, then fold again into quarters. Arrange the folded crêpes in an overlapping fan pattern in the baking dish, dotting them with any leftover maple butter.

3 · Bake the crêpes, uncovered, until hot, about 15 minutes. Serve immediately.

$\mathcal{P}$alacsinta Crêpes

This is a great recipe that makes a light-textured crêpe; it contains no butter, except for what is used for greasing the pan, and calls for club soda, a classic trick for lightening the batter. Use these crêpes for wrapping savory fillings, or serve them for dessert filled with thick apricot preserves, rolled up and sprinkled with a combination of ground walnuts and powdered sugar.

Makes about twelve 8-inch crêpes

3 large eggs
1 cup unbleached all-purpose flour
¼ teaspoon salt

1 cup milk
½ cup club soda

1 · Place the eggs in a deep mixing bowl, blender canister, or the workbowl of a food processor. Using a large wire whisk, an immersion blender, a canister blender, or a food processor, beat the eggs vigorously by hand or on high until they are smooth, 10 seconds. Add half the flour and the salt; beat for 30 seconds. Add the remaining ½ cup flour and the milk; beat for 1 minute. Scrape down the sides and bottom of the bowl or container, and beat for 10 more seconds. Adjust the consistency of the batter, adding more flour or milk if necessary; the consistency should be like thick cream. Cover and refrigerate for 1 or 2 hours to overnight, allowing the starch to absorb the liquid and swell. (The batter can be prepared up to 24 hours ahead and refrigerated at this point.) After the batter has been refrigerated, allow it to come to room temperature, and stir in the club soda just before making the crêpes.

2 · Brush an 8-inch crêpe pan, skillet, or nonstick frying pan with some oil or spray it with cooking spray (if you want to use cooking spray for the oiling between crêpes, be sure to remove the pan from the heat source as you spray). You need only a thin layer of oil, just enough to keep the batter from sticking. Heat the pan over medium-high heat until hot but not smoking. Stir the batter a few times.

3 · Remove the pan from the heat and immediately ladle in 3 to 4 tablespoons of batter, tilting and rotating the pan quickly in all directions to coat the entire surface evenly. If the crêpes have holes, fill them in with a few drops of batter; this is a common problem that disappears when you master the art of tilting the pan. Return the pan to the heat. In about 1 to 1½ minutes, the edges will be lightly browned and will lift up slightly from the pan. The top will be set and almost dry. Slide the long spatula under the crêpe and turn it carefully, to prevent tearing. Cook the other side briefly, just until brown in spots but not crispy, 30 seconds. (When you fill the crêpes, keep the side that was cooked first on the outside; the second side is never as attractive.) The crêpes should remain soft, so do not overcook them. Invert the pan and release the crêpe onto a clean dish towel.

4 · Continue to make the crêpes in this manner, stirring the batter and greasing the pan lightly as needed before cooking each crêpe. If you will be using the crêpes within a few hours, cover them with another towel to keep them from drying out. Crêpes can also be refrigerated or frozen for longer storage.

Chantilly Dessert Crêpes

Chantilly crêpes are described as being as thin and delicate as handkerchiefs. These are made with cornstarch, but you can use a fine cake flour like Wondra in place of the cornstarch if you like. These crêpes are good for all types of desserts, such as crêpe suzettes, or filled with lemon curd and served with fresh strawberries.

Makes about twenty-two 6-inch crêpes

2 large eggs plus 2 egg yolks
¾ cup milk
¼ cup water
1 tablespoon rum, brandy, amaretto liqueur, Frangelico, or Grand Marnier
1 teaspoon vanilla extract

¾ cup cornstarch (increase to 1 cup cornstarch if you need a sturdier crêpe)
1 tablespoon sugar
Pinch of salt
3 tablespoons unsalted butter, melted

1 · Place the eggs and egg yolks, milk, water, liqueur, vanilla extract, cornstarch, sugar, and salt, in the order given, in a deep bowl, the canister of a blender, or the workbowl of a food processor. Using a large whisk, an immersion blender, a canister blender, or a food processor, beat vigorously by hand or on high until smooth, 30 seconds. Stop once to scrape down the sides and bottom of the bowl or container. Add the melted butter and blend for 15 seconds longer. The batter should be the consistency of buttermilk. Adjust the consistency of the batter, adding more milk or flour if necessary. Use the batter immediately or refrigerate it until needed. (The batter can be prepared 1 day ahead.) After the batter has been refrigerated, allow it to come to room temperature and stir before using.

2 · Brush a 6-inch crêpe pan, skillet, or nonstick frying pan with some oil or spray it with cooking spray (if you want to use cooking spray for the oiling between crêpes, be sure to remove the pan from the heat source as you spray). You need only a thin layer of oil, just enough to keep the batter from sticking. Heat the pan over medium-high heat until hot but not smoking. Stir the batter a few times.

3 · Remove the pan from the heat and immediately ladle in 2 tablespoons of batter, tilting and rotating the pan quickly in all directions to coat the entire surface evenly. If the crêpes have holes, fill them in with a few drops of batter; this is a common problem that disappears when you master the art of tilting the pan. Return the pan to the heat. In about 1 to 1½ minutes, the edges will be lightly browned and will lift up slightly from the pan. The top will be set and almost dry. Slide the long spatula under the crêpe and turn it carefully, to prevent tearing. Cook the other side briefly, just until brown in spots but not crispy, 30 seconds. (When you fill the crêpes, keep the side that was cooked first on the outside; the second side is never as attractive.) The crêpes should remain soft, so do not overcook them. Invert the pan and release the crêpe onto a clean dish towel.

4 · Continue to make the crêpes in this manner, stirring the batter and greasing the pan lightly as needed before cooking each crêpe. If you will be using the crêpes within a few hours, cover them with another towel to keep them from drying out. Crêpes can also be refrigerated or frozen for longer storage.

Fresh Lemon Dessert Crêpes

This recipe is pure Hungarian. Chantilly crêpes are served simply with fresh lemon wedges and sugar—a lovely and elegant ending to a heavy meal.

Serves 6

1 cup cold créme frâiche (page 339), for topping
1¼ cups sifted powdered sugar, for sprinkling
3 lemons, cut into large wedges, for squeezing
12 Chantilly Dessert Crêpes made with cognac or apricot brandy

1 · Prepare the Chantilly Dessert Crêpes and keep them warm in the oven until serving. Place the Créme Frâiche and powdered sugar each in a small serving bowl with spoons for serving. Place the lemon wedges in a small bowl.

2 · Remove the crêpes from the oven, fold each one into quarters, and arrange 2 each on individual dessert plates. Serve immediately, passing the bowls so that all the diners may top their crêpes with a sprinkling of powdered sugar, a dab of créme frâiche, and some lemon juice squeezed over all.

Crêpes Elizabeth

Take a gossamer dessert crêpe, faintly redolent of a bit of rum or amaretto, and fill it with fresh fruit. Here I use strawberries, but you can substitute sliced peaches or nectarines, fresh plums, or other berries.

Serves 5

2 pints ripe strawberries, hulled and sliced
2 tablespoons Grand Marnier or orange juice
2 tablespoons granulated sugar

White Chocolate Chantilly
2 cups cold heavy cream, divided
8 ounces white chocolate chips

10 Chantilly Dessert Crêpes
3 tablespoons unsalted butter, melted, for brushing
½ cup slivered blanched almonds

1 · Toss the strawberries with the orange liqueur or orange juice

and the sugar. Refrigerate for up to 4 hours.

2 · Make the White Chocolate Chantilly: Combine the white chocolate chips and ½ cup of the cream in the top of a double boiler or in a glass measuring cup. Melt the mixture over hot (not simmering) water on the stovetop or microwave the mixture in the glass measure for 1 minute. When the white chocolate is melted, stir to combine it with the cream. Let it cool a bit. In a chilled bowl using an electric mixer, whip the remaining 1½ cups cream until soft peaks form. Pour in the melted white chocolate and cream mixture and beat until soft peaks form. Cover and refrigerate for up to 4 hours.

3 · Butter a shallow ceramic or metal baking dish or casserole. Spoon 2 to 3 tablespoons of the strawberries down the center of each crêpe. Roll up to enclose the filling and place in the casserole. Repeat with all the crêpes, laying them side by side. Brush each with butter and sprinkle with almonds. Place 4 to 5 inches under the broiler and cook until the crêpes blister and the nuts brown slightly, about 2 minutes. Remove from the oven, place 2 crêpes on each individual dessert plate, and spoon some White Chocolate Chantilly on top. Serve immediately.

Orange Dessert Crêpes with Suzette Butter

Everyone loves crêpes suzette, but not too many bakers are eager to flambé. So here is a lovely variation, heated in the oven, without all the fanfare but with all the delightful flavors that make this one of the culinary world's most famous desserts. I stuff the crêpes with some mandarin oranges, too. You can serve these hot, right out of the pan.

Serves 6 to 8

Suzette Butter
¾ cup (1½ sticks) unsalted butter, at room temperature
1½ cups powdered sugar
Grated zest of 1 orange
¼ cup orange juice
2 tablespoons Grand Marnier

1 recipe Chantilly Dessert Crêpes
1½ cups canned mandarin oranges, drained

1 · Preheat the oven to 450°F.

2 · Make the Suzette Butter: In a mixing bowl, using an electric mixer, cream the butter with the powdered sugar and zest until fluffy. Slowly beat in the orange juice and liqueur. (The butter can be made ahead and refrigerated for up to 4 days. Bring it to room temperature before using it.)

3 · Spread a bit of the Suzette Butter in a shallow ceramic ovenproof baking dish that can withstand high heat. (If you will be serving the crêpes from the table, use a decorative ovenproof ceramic dish.) Place a crêpe on a work surface. With a rubber spatula, spread one side of the crêpe lightly with the Suzette Butter. Place a few mandarin orange segments over the butter. Fold the crêpe in half, spread with a bit more Suzette Butter, then fold again into quarters. You will use about a tablespoon of butter for each crêpe. Arrange the folded crêpes in an overlapping fan pattern in the baking dish, dotting them with any leftover Suzette Butter. Cover the baking dish with foil.

4 · Bake until bubbly hot, about 15 to 20 minutes. Serve immediately, right from the pan.

Apple Crêpes with Caramel Sauce

This combination is probably the most popular offering at crêperies that offer a choice of dessert fillings. Warm sautéed apples are stuffed inside a folded crêpe and bathed in the quickest-to-prepare rich butterscotch caramel sauce you've ever had. The caramel sauce is so easy that you can make it right before assembling the dessert.

Serves 4

3 tablespoons unsalted butter
3 large tart cooking apples, peeled, cored, and sliced ½ inch thick
2 tablespoons turbinado or raw sugar, or packed light brown sugar
½ teaspoon ground cinnamon or apple pie spice, or to taste
1 tablespoon Calvados or cognac (optional)

1 cup cold heavy cream

Caramel Sauce

1½ cups heavy cream

⅔ cup packed dark brown sugar

3 tablespoons light or dark corn syrup

2 tablespoons unsalted butter

2 teaspoons vanilla extract

8 Chantilly Dessert Crêpes or other crêpes

1 · In a large skillet, melt the butter over medium-high heat. Add the apples and sprinkle them with the sugar. Cook over medium heat until the sugar melts and begins to turn amber colored, 5 to 8 minutes, stirring occasionally. The apples will soften slightly, but still hold their shape. Sprinkle with the cinnamon and the liqueur, allowing the alcohol to evaporate before removing the pan from the stove.

2 · To make the whipped cream: In a chilled bowl using an electric mixer, whip the cream (I leave it unsweetened) until soft peaks form. Cover and refrigerate for up to 4 hours.

3 · Make the Caramel Sauce: Place the cream in a deep saucepan. Over medium heat, just warm the cream. Mix in the brown sugar, corn syrup, and butter with a whisk. Stir until the sugar is dissolved, about 3 to 4 minutes. Remove from the heat and stir in the vanilla extract. Keep warm in a hot-water bath until serving. You should have about 2 cups.

4 · To serve, place a crêpe on a work surface and spoon some apple filling on one quarter of it. Fold the crêpe into quarters. Place 2 crêpes on an individual dessert plate and ladle on some Caramel Sauce and a small dollop of whipped cream. Repeat with the remaining crêpes. Serve immediately.

Chocolate Dessert Crêpes

Yes, crêpes can be made with chocolate! I love these rolled up with vanilla ice cream inside with cold raspberry sauce on the side, or with coffee ice cream and hot fudge sauce. You can fill the crêpes with ice cream a day or two ahead, separating the layers with parchment or waxed paper, and store them in the freezer in airtight plastic containers until you are ready to serve them. These are great for parties!

Makes about fifteen 7- to 8-inch crêpes

3 large eggs

⅔ cup water

½ cup milk

½ teaspoon vanilla extract

1 cup unbleached all-purpose flour

3 tablespoons sugar

3 tablespoons unsweetened cocoa powder

¼ teaspoon salt

3 tablespoons unsalted butter, melted, or walnut oil

1 · Using a whisk, an immersion blender, or a food processor, combine the eggs, water, milk, vanilla extract, flour, sugar, cocoa, and salt. Beat until smooth. Scrape down the sides and bottom of the bowl or container. Incorporate the melted butter. The batter should be the consistency of buttermilk; adjust the consistency, adding more milk or flour, if necessary. Cover and chill the batter for 1 or 2 hours to overnight, allowing the starch to absorb the liquid and swell. (If you are preparing the batter 1 day ahead, don't add the melted butter to the butter before refrigerating. Bring the batter back to room temperature and add the butter just before cooking.)

2 · Brush an 8-inch crêpe pan, skillet, or nonstick frying pan with some oil or spray it with cooking spray (if you want to use cooking spray for the oiling between crêpes, be sure to remove the pan from the heat source as you spray). You need only a thin layer of oil, just enough to keep the batter from sticking. Heat the pan over medium-high heat until hot but not smoking. Stir the batter a few times.

3 · Remove the pan from the heat and immediately ladle in 3 tablespoons of batter, tilting and rotating the pan quickly in all directions to coat the entire

surface evenly. If the crêpes have holes, fill them in with a few drops of batter; this is a common problem that disappears when you master the art of tilting the pan. Return the pan to the heat. In about 1 to 1½ minutes, the edges of the crêpe will be lightly browned and will lift up slightly from the pan. The top will be set and almost dry. Slide the long spatula under the crêpe and turn it carefully, to prevent tearing. Cook the other side briefly, just until brown in spots but not crispy, 30 seconds. (When you fill the crêpes, keep the side that was cooked first on the outside; the second side is never as attractive.) The crêpes should remain soft, so do not overcook them. Invert the pan and release the crêpe onto a clean dish towel.

4 · Continue to make the crêpes in this manner, stirring the batter and greasing the pan lightly as needed before cooking each crêpe. If you will be using the crêpes within a few hours, cover them with another towel to keep them from drying out. Crêpes can also be refrigerated or frozen for longer storage.

Swedish Pancakes

Swedish pancakes sound really out of the ordinary, but they are just ordinary pancakes made from thinner-than-usual pancake batter, 3 parts liquid to 1 part flour, and cooked like an oversized crêpe. They are much beloved by diners of Scandinavian descent, and part of the traditional Thursday night split pea soup and pancake dinner so many of my friends remember from their childhood. This recipe, translated from Vär Kokbok, the most widely owned cookbook in the Swedish language, is the specialty of Michael Horvath, the brother of my editor. He makes them regularly for his children, who are wild for them. The recipe came with "rules of the table for the six-and-under crowd": you may not have a dessert pancake unless you have eaten at least two dinner pancakes first. He serves a creamy spinach sauce (recipe follows) with the pancakes for dinner, and lingonberry preserves (made from a tart red berry, related to the cranberry, that grows profusely in mountainous Scandinavia) or fresh fruit and whipped cream with the pancakes for dessert. (To feed six people both dinner and dessert crêpes, you will need to make a double batch of the batter.) The traditional plättpan, a pan about 10 inches in diameter with 7 shallow 3-inch-diameter depressions, is great for making small pancakes. It is readily available from a well-stocked kitchen store like Williams-Sonoma or Sur La Table. If you do not have a plättpan, you can use a nonstick omelette pan or crêpe pan.

Makes eight to ten 9- to 10-inch pancakes,
fifteen 5- to 6-inch pancakes, or twenty-five *plättar*

1 cup unbleached all-purpose flour
½ teaspoon salt
2½ cups milk

3 large eggs, beaten until smooth
1 tablespoon unsalted butter or margarine,
    melted, or vegetable oil

1 · Combine the flour and salt in a mixing bowl or deep pitcher (the pitcher is easier). Add half the milk and mix with a whisk or immersion blender until smooth. Add the remaining milk and mix for 15 seconds. Add the eggs and butter or oil and mix for another 15 seconds. Do not overmix. The batter will be thin and easy to pour. (At this point, the batter can be refrigerated for from 1 hour to overnight.)

2 · Heat a 10- to 12-inch nonstick skillet to make large pancakes, or a 6- to 8-inch nonstick skillet to make small pancakes, over high heat until a drop of water skates over the surface, and lightly grease the pan with a piece of paper towel moistened with vegetable oil. Reduce the heat to medium. Using a 2- to 4-tablespoon measure for each pancake, ladle in enough batter to cover the entire bottom of the pan. Cook until bubbles form on the surface, the edges are dry, and the bottoms are golden brown, about 1 minute. Turn once, cooking the opposite side until golden, about 30 seconds. The second side of the pancake will take half the amount of time to cook as the first side does. Place the finished pancake on a platter in a warm oven and continue to make pancakes until the batter is used up. Serve the pancakes rolled up with Michael's Creamy Spinach Sauce or with a berry syrup for dessert, if you like.

NOTE: *To make the pancakes in a* plättpan, *grease the pan the same way and spoon 2 tablespoons batter into each of the depressions in the griddle. You will be able to make 7 pancakes at once.*

Michael's Creamy Spinach Sauce

Makes enough sauce to fill 8 to 10 Swedish pancakes

6 strips bacon, cut into small pieces
1 large yellow onion, finely chopped
Two 10½-ounce packages frozen spinach, thawed and squeezed to remove excess water
½ cup grated Parmesan cheese
3 tablespoons heavy cream or half-and-half
Salt
Fresh-ground black pepper

Fry the bacon in a skillet on medium-high heat until the fat is just rendered. Add the onion and cook until the onion is translucent and soft. Reduce the heat to medium-low and add the spinach. Cook until the spinach is just heated through, about 10 minutes, adding a tablespoon or two of water if the mixture looks too dry. Add the cheese and cream, stirring constantly, until the cheese is melted and the sauce is thick and creamy. Season with salt and pepper to taste.

Waffles

Waffles

Bringing out the honeycombed waffle iron is a sure sign that a meal is going to be a special occasion. A homey comfort food that has gone in and out of style, waffles have withstood the tests of time and fashion. The classic waffle, with its decorative grid pattern, is ready-made to hold dark amber pools of maple syrup and melted butter. Although waffles are certainly not categorized as fancy food, they dress up well. With the addition of a number of savory ingredients, morning waffles are ready for supper. With a dusting of powdered sugar, sweet topping or spirit-spiked sauce, ice cream or flavored whipped cream, they make an unusual dessert.

Waffles have a rich and illustrious history. The original European waffle irons, with handles attached for baking over an open fire, date back to the twelfth century, when they were used to shape and bake religious sacramental wafers. Chaucer wrote of English "wafers," and crisp French *gaufres* have been enjoyed as a dessert for centuries. La Varrene's culinary bible, *La Cuisinier Franfais*, published in 1651, featured waffle recipes. In the seventeenth century, German *waffelen* were cooked between hinged cast-iron disks, which created a waffle with intricately embossed landscapes and patterns worthy of the Dutch masters. In the late 1700s Thomas Jefferson brought a long-handled French open-fire waffle iron home to Virginia from one of his forays to Europe and created the first *gaufres* party supper for his friends. The traditional Dutch wedding gift in early New Amsterdam was a waffle iron carved with the bride's initials, and the butter-rich recipe for *wafels* is credited with most influencing the modern American waffle. Belgian waffle makers, with their exaggerated deep grids, were introduced at the New York World Fair in 1964 and are still popular in many homes.

Waffle batters are similar to those for muffins and pancakes, with the wet and dry ingredients first mixed separately, then, just before baking, combined with a minimum of strokes to form a soft, thick, pourable batter. Cake flour makes a more tender waffle than all-purpose flour, but it is an optional variation depending on your preference. To provide the crispness characteristic of waffles, there is usually a bit more fat in waffle recipes as compared to pancake batters. Although many recipes suggest beating egg whites until fluffy and then folding them into the batter, which is supposed to result in a lighter batter and a crisper waffle, this step is not required. One exception is for batters that are very low in fat, for which the additional leavening power of the stiffly beaten egg whites is essential. As with all quick breads, beat the batter just until blended (there will be a few lumps), because overmixing produces a tough, dense waffle.

Bake waffles on a lightly greased and heated iron, whether it is a pre-heated countertop electric waffle iron with reversible grids; a hinged, stove-top model, which is heated on both sides and flipped once during baking; the delicate "Five of Hearts" circular-shaped models; a curly edged waffle iron embossed with carousel figures; a thick Belgian waffle iron; or even an exotic European model picked up while traveling. Unless you have a nonstick model, a waffle iron needs to be seasoned before its first use (see page 352 for specific instructions). For the best results, always follow the manufacturer's instructions for your model. Spray-on cooking oil is the most efficient way to grease all the little corners, even on a nonstick surface (*always* spray the surface before preheating it).

Heat the waffle iron until the indicator light says the surface is hot. Depending on the recipe, ladle in about ½ cup to 1 cup of batter, covering the surface one-half to two-thirds full, depending on the size of the iron, and gently close the top. The batter will spread out when the iron is closed, making a full-sized waffle. After a try or two, you will know exactly how much batter to pour onto your iron.

Timing is crucial to a waffle's color and texture. As with all culinary techniques, it is a skill best learned by experience. The general rule is about 4 to 5 minutes cooking time in a standard electric model, or until steam stops escaping from the waffle iron. A high temperature tends to make a crisp waffle, while a lower temperature bakes a waffle that is more moist and tender. When the lid is lifted, the waffle should not stick. If it does, close the iron and wait another minute. Remove the waffle with a fork and touch only the handles of the iron to prevent burns.

Waffle irons should never be submerged in water for cleaning; instead wipe the inside with a damp cloth or scrub gently with a kitchen brush (a clean toothbrush also works well), protecting the electrical element from dampness. The manufacturer's instructions will provide the best method of cleaning your specific model, whether electric or stovetop.

As with all griddlecakes, waffles are best eaten as soon as they are baked. Leftover batter can be stored in the refrigerator for a day. To refresh the batter, combine ½ teaspoon of baking powder with 2 tablespoons of milk per 2 cups of flour in the batter, and stir into the batter before baking. Fully baked waffles can be frozen for up to 2 months. To freeze, cool waffles completely before wrapping each waffle separately in plastic wrap or freezer bags. To serve, for an impromptu meal or snack, reheat frozen waffles on a clean baking sheet in a 350°F oven for 10 to 15 minutes, or pop the frozen waffle into the toaster, where it will emerge as hot and crisp as freshly made.

Buttermilk Waffles

Today's recipes for waffles are remarkably similar to their predecessors, and they have nourished a steadfast group of waffle eaters over the centuries. Waffles are at home with sweet breakfast toppings as well as savory dinner accompaniments throughout the seasons. These waffles only get better when a handful of toasted pecans or chopped fresh herbs from the garden are added to create an array of sweet or savory crisp honeycombs. If you love waffles, do not miss the variations listed here, each one creating a very different flavor. Serve with sweet butter and pure maple syrup or delightful Fresh Strawberry–Spumante Sauce (following) for special summer brunches.

Makes 6 to 8 large waffles, depending on the size of the waffle iron

2 cups unbleached all-purpose flour
1 teaspoon baking soda
½ teaspoon baking powder
¼ teaspoon salt
4 large eggs, separated

¼ cup vegetable oil
2 cups buttermilk
Fresh Strawberry–Spumante Sauce
  (optional), following

1 · In a large bowl, combine the flour, baking soda, baking powder, and salt. In another bowl, beat the egg yolks, oil, and buttermilk with a whisk until foamy.

2 · With an electric mixer, beat the egg whites in a separate bowl until soft peaks form. Pour the buttermilk and egg yolk mixture into the dry ingredients, stirring just until moistened. Fold in the whites until no streaks are visible.

3 · Heat the waffle iron to medium-high or according to the manufacturer's instructions. Brush the waffle iron grids with oil or melted butter. For each waffle, pour about 1 cup of the batter onto the grid. Close the lid and bake until the waffle is crisp and well browned, about 4 to 5 minutes. Remove the waffle from the iron with a fork, to protect your fingers. Serve immediately with Fresh Strawberry–Spumante Sauce, if desired, or cool completely on racks, store in plastic bags, and freeze for up to 2 months.

Fresh Strawberry–Spumante Sauce

Makes about 3 cups sauce

2 pints fresh strawberries, rinsed and hulled
½ cup Asti Spumante sparkling wine
3 tablespoons superfine sugar

In a blender or food processor, combine all the ingredients and process until smooth. Cover and chill for several hours to overnight. Pour or ladle onto any of the hot Buttermilk Waffles.

VARIATIONS:

Super Whole-Grain–Buttermilk Waffles

Substitute ¾ cup whole wheat flour, 3 tablespoons *each* oat bran and wheat germ, 2 tablespoons cornmeal or buckwheat flour, and 1 tablespoon packed brown sugar in place of 1 cup of the unbleached all-purpose flour, and add to the dry ingredients in Step 1. Continue to mix and bake as directed.

Lemon Buttermilk Waffles

Substitute the zest and juice of 2 large lemons and 2 tablespoons sugar for ¼ cup of the buttermilk, and 5 tablespoons melted unsalted butter for the oil, when combining the liquid ingredients in Step 1. Continue to mix and bake as directed.

Rice Buttermilk Waffles

Add ¾ cup cold, cooked short- or long-grain white or brown rice (try imported white basmati or domestic brown basmati for a real treat) when combining the liquid ingredients in Step 1. Continue to mix and bake as directed.

Sour Cream Buttermilk Waffles

Add ⅔ cup sour cream and 2 tablespoons melted unsalted butter when combining the liquid ingredients in Step 1. Continue to mix and bake as directed.

Seven-Grain Buttermilk Waffles

Substitute ½ cup seven-grain cereal (a flavorful combination of cracked wheat, oats, bran, rye, cornmeal, millet, and flaxseed) for an equal amount of flour. Combine the seven-grain cereal and 1 cup of the buttermilk in a bowl, cover, and refrigerate for 2 hours to overnight to soften the grains. Add the soaked grains and 2 tablespoons of maple syrup to the liquid ingredients in Step 1. Continue to mix and bake as directed.

Homemade Buttermilk Griddle Mix Waffles

An alternative to commercial mixes, Homemade Buttermilk Griddle Mix is a nutritious mixture of dry ingredients that are combined ahead of time and stored in an airtight container. Having this mix on hand allows the busy baker to quickly mix in the eggs, butter, and milk or water to create a batter that makes crisp and tasty waffles with a minimal amount of time and effort in the kitchen.

Makes 6 to 8 large waffles, depending on the size of the waffle iron

3 large eggs, separated
6 tablespoons (¾ stick) unsalted butter or margarine, melted

1½ cups water or milk
2¼ cups Homemade Buttermilk Griddle Mix (page 141)

1 · In a clean bowl, beat the egg whites until stiff, but not dry, peaks form. In another bowl, whisk the egg yolks, butter or margarine, and water or milk until foamy.

2 · Place the griddle mix in a large bowl, add the egg yolk mixture, and combine with a few strokes. Fold in the beaten whites until no white streaks are visible. The batter will be just evenly moistened. Do not overmix.

3 · Heat the waffle iron to medium-high or according to the manufacturer's instructions. Brush the waffle iron grids with oil or melted butter. For each waffle, pour about 1 cup of the batter onto the grid. Close the lid and bake until the waffle is crisp and well browned, about 4 to 5 minutes. Remove the waffle from the iron with a fork, to protect your fingers. Serve immediately, or cool completely on racks, store in plastic bags, and freeze for up to 2 months.

*B*anana Waffles

Waffles are a great way to start the day because they can provide a quarter of the day's calories and a boost of complex carbohydrates in one meal. Add a few tablespoons of honey-crunch wheat germ to these banana-enriched waffles for more fiber. Serve with spicy turkey sausage and fresh juice, and top with vanilla yogurt and sliced fresh bananas or maple syrup.

Makes 6 to 8 large waffles, depending on the size of the waffle iron

1¼ cups unbleached all-purpose flour
1 teaspoon baking powder
1 teaspoon baking soda
Pinch of salt
Pinch of ground cinnamon
2 large eggs, separated

5 tablespoons unsalted butter, melted, or
  nut oil
2 large bananas, mashed (about 1 cup)
¾ cup milk, coconut milk (page 334), or
  papaya or passion fruit juice

1 · In a large bowl, combine the flour, baking powder, baking soda, salt, and cinnamon. In another bowl, beat the egg yolks, melted butter or oil, mashed banana, and milk with a whisk until foamy.

2 · With an electric mixer, beat the egg whites in a separate bowl until soft peaks form. Pour the banana mixture into the dry ingredients and combine with a few strokes. Fold in the beaten whites until no white streaks are visible. The batter will be just evenly moistened. Do not overmix.

3 · Preheat the waffle iron to medium-high or according to the manufacturer's instructions. Brush the waffle iron grids with oil or melted butter. For each waffle, pour about 1 cup of the batter onto the grid. Close the lid and bake until the waffle is crisp and well browned, about 4 to 5 minutes. Remove the waffle from the iron with a fork, to protect your fingers. Serve immediately, or cool completely on racks, store in plastic bags, and freeze for up to 2 months.

$\mathcal{P}$ecan Waffles

I was invited to a friend's house for brunch, and she prepared these waffles right before my eyes. The buttery nuts add a dramatic dimension of flavor that melds perfectly with maple syrup, one of pecans' natural partners. The waffles end up tasting as if they contain far more exotic ingredients than they really do. Spiced Honey-Maple Syrup (following) is a delightful, and very quickly prepared, special syrup to serve with your Pecan Waffles. It is sweet, buttery, and spicy at the same time.

Makes about 4 large waffles, depending on the size of the waffle iron

1 cup unbleached all-purpose flour
2 tablespoons medium-grind yellow
  cornmeal
1 tablespoon whole wheat or buckwheat
  flour
1 tablespoon packed light brown sugar
1 teaspoon baking powder

Pinch of salt
2 large eggs
2 tablespoons vegetable or pecan oil
⅔ cup milk
½ cup chopped pecans
Spiced Honey-Maple Syrup (optional),
  following

1 · Place all of the ingredients, except the pecans, in a blender or food processor. Blend well, 1 minute, until smooth. Add the pecans and pulse a few times to distribute.

2 · Preheat the waffle iron to medium-high or according to the manufacturer's instructions. Brush the waffle iron grids with oil or melted butter. For each waffle, pour about ¾ cup of the batter onto the grid. Close the lid and bake until the waffle is crisp and well browned, about 4 to 5 minutes. Remove the waffle from the iron with a fork, to protect your fingers. Serve immediately, drizzled with Honey-Maple Syrup, if you wish, or cool completely on racks, store in plastic bags, and freeze for up to 2 months.

Spiced Honey–Maple Syrup

Makes about 1 cup syrup

½ cup light honey
½ cup pure maple syrup
3 tablespoons unsalted butter
1 teaspoon apple pie spice

Combine all the ingredients in a small saucepan or microwave-proof bowl. Warm over low heat or microwave for 2 minutes at a time to melt the butter and gently warm the honey and syrup. Serve warm, drizzled over waffles.

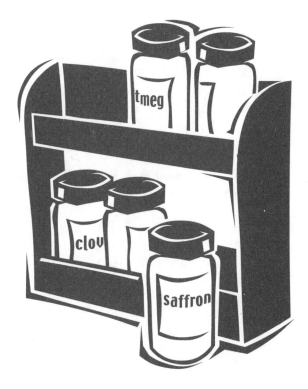

Pumpkin–Sour Cream Waffles

This is a perfect waffle recipe that I adapted only slightly from a recipe that was taught in a great Los Angeles cooking school, Ma Cuisine, in the 1980s. It is richly flavored with pumpkin and sour cream, and great to serve at fall holiday brunches. Serve these fabulous waffles topped simply with maple syrup and butter, alongside fresh fruit and juice. I especially like them made in a heart-shaped waffle iron.

Makes about 8 large waffles, depending on the size of the waffle iron

1¾ cups unbleached all-purpose flour

2¼ teaspoons baking powder

½ teaspoon baking soda

1½ teaspoons apple pie spice or a combination of ¾ teaspoon ground cinnamon and ¾ teaspoon fresh-ground nutmeg

½ teaspoon salt

4 large eggs, separated

½ cup vegetable oil or pecan oil

¼ cup packed dark brown sugar

1 cup buttermilk

1 cup sour cream

1 cup canned pumpkin puree (or homemade, page 351)

1 · In a large bowl, combine the flour, baking powder, baking soda, spices, and salt. In another bowl, beat the egg yolks, oil, brown sugar, buttermilk, sour cream, and pumpkin puree with a whisk until smooth, 1 minute.

2 · With an electric mixer, beat the egg whites in a separate bowl until soft peaks form. Pour the pumpkin–sour cream mixture into the dry ingredients, and stir just until moistened. With a large spatula, fold in the whites until no white streaks are visible.

3 · Heat the waffle iron to medium-high or according to the manufacturer's instructions. Brush the waffle iron grids with oil or melted butter. For each waffle, pour 1 heaping cup of the batter onto the grid. Close the lid and bake until the waffle is crisp and well browned, about 4 to 5 minutes. Remove the waffle from the iron with a fork, to protect your fingers. Serve immediately, or cool completely on racks, store in plastic bags, and freeze for up to 2 months.

Whole Wheat Waffles with Cherry Sauce

I was first served these waffles in a rustic restaurant below Bucks Lake in the California Sierras, north of Lake Tahoe. They were hot and crunchy, served with cut-glass pitchers of pure maple syrup, and I couldn't stop eating them. When I returned home, I successfully re-created the recipe. For variety, sprinkle the batter with sesame or sunflower seeds just before closing the lid to bake the waffles. If you would like to make these with buttermilk, be sure to substitute ½ teaspoon baking soda for an equal amount of baking powder to achieve the best leavening action. The Cherry Sauce (following) may be used on any breakfast waffle in place of maple syrup.

Makes 6 to 8 large waffles, depending on the size of the waffle iron

1 cup unbleached all-purpose flour
1 cup whole wheat flour
2½ teaspoons baking powder
¼ teaspoon salt
3 large eggs, separated

⅓ cup vegetable oil or 6 tablespoons
  (¾ stick) unsalted butter, melted
1¼ cups milk
Cherry Sauce, following

1 · In a large bowl, combine the flours, baking powder, and salt. In another bowl, beat the egg yolks, oil or melted butter, and milk with a whisk until foamy.

2 · With an electric mixer, beat the egg whites in a separate bowl until soft peaks form. Pour the milk mixture into the dry ingredients, stirring just until moistened. With a large spatula, fold in the whites until no white streaks are visible.

3 · Preheat the waffle iron to medium-high heat or according to the manufacturer's instructions. Brush the waffle iron grids with oil or melted butter. For each waffle, pour about 1 cup of the batter onto the grid. Close the lid and bake until the waffle is crisp and well browned, about 4 to 5 minutes. Remove the waffle from the iron with a fork, to protect your fingers. Serve immediately topped with Cherry Sauce, or cool completely on racks, store in plastic bags, and freeze for up to 2 months.

Cherry Sauce
Makes about 2 cups sauce

2 tablespoons cornstarch
2 tablespoons orange or lemon juice
2 tablespoons sugar
1 cup unsweetened apple juice or water
One 12-ounce package frozen unsweetened
  dark sweet cherries

In a saucepan, combine the corn-starch, orange or lemon juice, sugar, and apple juice or water with a whisk. Bring to a boil, then reduce the heat to a simmer. Cook until slightly thick-ened, stirring occasionally, about 2 minutes. Add the cherries and cook until hot. Remove from the heat; serve warm. Store, covered, in the refrigerator for up to 1 week. Reheat before serving.

VARIATION:

Whole Wheat–
Hazelnut Waffles

Add ½ cup ground toasted hazelnuts to the dry ingredients in Step 1. Continue to mix and bake as directed.

*O*at-Cornmeal Waffles with Dried Fruit Syrup

This is an old-fashioned, hearty, whole-grain waffle with a crunchy texture. Cornmeal, oats, and wheat are a particularly harmonious combination of grains that creates a robust flavor. Serve these waffles with warm, homemade Dried Fruit Syrup (following) and sweet butter, or with equal amounts of whipped crème fraîche and plain yogurt folded together to make an ethereal topping, accompanied by lots of sliced fresh fruit on the side.

Makes 6 to 8 large waffles, depending on the size of the waffle iron

1¼ cups unbleached all-purpose flour
1 cup fine-grind yellow cornmeal, preferably stone-ground
⅓ cup rolled oats
3 tablespoons packed light brown sugar
1 teaspoon baking powder
1 teaspoon baking soda

¼ teaspoon salt
2 large eggs
2½ cups buttermilk
6 tablespoons (¾ stick) unsalted butter, melted
Dried Fruit Syrup, following

1 · In a large bowl, combine the flour, cornmeal, rolled oats, brown sugar, baking powder, baking soda, and salt. In another bowl, beat the eggs and the buttermilk with a whisk until foamy.

2 · Pour the buttermilk and egg mixture into the dry ingredients and combine with a few strokes. Drizzle the surface with the melted butter and fold in. The batter will be just evenly moistened. Do not overmix.

3 · Preheat the waffle iron to medium-high or according to the manufacturer's instructions. Brush the waffle iron grids with oil or melted butter. For each waffle, pour about 1 cup of the batter onto the grid. Close the lid and bake until the waffle is crisp and well browned, about 4 to 5 minutes. Remove the waffle from the iron with a fork, to protect your fingers. Serve immediately with Dried Fruit Syrup, or cool completely on racks, store in plastic bags, and freeze for up to 2 months.

Dried Fruit Syrup

Makes about 1 cup syrup

½ cup pure maple syrup
¼ cup dried cranberries
¼ cup finely chopped dried apricots or figs

Combine the ingredients in a small saucepan. Simmer over low heat for a few minutes until the mixture is warmed and the dried fruit is plumped. Transfer to a pitcher and serve warm.

Rice Waffles

I always seem to have cold leftover rice in the refrigerator, and these waffles are an excellent way to put it to good use. Use any type of rice, from the floral basmati or jasmine to pecan rice or brown rice. I like to have a stash of these waffles in the freezer; they reheat nicely in the toaster. Serve them with sweet butter and a commercial or homemade (page 354) fruit syrup, such as raspberry or blueberry.

Makes about 6 large waffles, depending on the size of the waffle iron

1 cup unbleached all-purpose flour

2 teaspoons baking powder

¼ teaspoon salt

2 large eggs, separated

3 tablespoons vegetable or canola oil

2 tablespoons honey

1 cup milk

1 cup cold or room temperature cooked rice

1 · In a large bowl, combine the flour, baking powder, and salt. In another bowl, beat the egg yolks, oil, honey, and milk with a whisk until foamy.

2 · With an electric mixer, beat the egg whites in a separate bowl until soft peaks form. Pour the milk mixture into the dry ingredients, stirring just until moistened. With a large spatula, fold in the whites and rice until no white streaks are visible.

3 · Preheat the waffle iron to medium-high or according to the manufacturer's instructions. Brush the waffle iron grids with oil or melted butter. For each waffle, pour about 1 cup of the batter onto the grid. Close the lid and bake until the waffle is crisp and well browned, about 4 to 5 minutes. Remove the waffle from the iron with a fork, to protect your fingers. Serve immediately, or cool completely on racks, store in plastic bags, and freeze for up to 2 months.

Wild Rice Buttermilk Waffles

Wild rice is often referred to as the "gourmet grain," and some brands are still harvested by hand in the Great Lakes region by Native Americans. Wild rice has a husky flavor that mellows considerably when added to a batter. These waffles may well become a staple in your repertoire; if so, keep extra cooked rice on hand in the freezer so you can make these waffles anytime. For an exceptional flavor combination, substitute ½ cup of chopped toasted pecans for an equal amount of the wild rice. Serve these waffles with pure maple syrup or Apple Cider Syrup (following) for breakfast. For a substantial supper, these waffles are excellent topped with creamed mushrooms or poultry, served along with a leafy green salad.

Makes 6 to 8 large waffles, depending on the size of the waffle iron

2 cups unbleached all-purpose flour
2 teaspoons baking powder
½ teaspoon baking soda
¼ teaspoon salt
1½ cups buttermilk

4 large eggs, separated
⅓ cup hazelnut or other flavorful nut oil
1½ cups cooked wild rice (page 355)
Apple Cider Syrup (optional), following

1 · In a bowl, combine the flour, baking powder, baking soda, and salt. In another bowl, whisk together the buttermilk, egg yolks, nut oil, and wild rice.

2 · With an electric mixer, beat the egg whites in a separate bowl until soft peaks form. Pour the buttermilk and wild rice mixture into the dry ingredients, stirring just until moistened. Fold in the whites until no white streaks are visible.

3 · Preheat the waffle iron to medium-high heat or according to the manufacturer's instructions. Brush the waffle iron grids with oil or melted butter. For each waffle, pour about 1 cup of the batter onto the grid. Close the lid and bake until the waffle is crisp and well browned, about 4 to 5 minutes. Remove the waffle from the iron with a fork, to protect your fingers. Serve immediately, drizzled with Apple Cider Syrup, if desired, or cool completely on racks, store in plastic bags, and freeze for up to 2 months.

Apple Cider Syrup

Makes about 1¼ cups syrup

1 cup fresh unfiltered apple cider or apple
 juice
2 tablespoons packed light brown sugar
2 tablespoons light corn syrup
Juice of ½ lemon
2 cinnamon sticks
3 tablespoons unsalted butter

Combine the cider or apple juice, brown sugar, corn syrup, lemon juice, and cinnamon sticks in a small, heavy saucepan. Bring to a boil and reduce the liquid by one third, about 10 minutes. Remove from the heat, discard the cinnamon sticks, add the butter, and swirl to melt. Serve the syrup warm from a pitcher. Keeps for one week, covered, in the refrigerator. Rewarm before serving.

Spiced Gingerbread Waffles with Pan-Glazed Apples

These waffles are delightfully spiced and molasses-laced, and very popular with waffle lovers. Serve them for brunch with yogurt or for a Mardi Gras dessert, with ice cream and the warm, spicy Pan-Glazed Apples (following).

Makes 6 to 8 large waffles, depending on the size of the waffle iron

2 cups unbleached all-purpose flour
½ cup whole wheat flour
¼ cup packed light or dark brown sugar
4 teaspoons baking powder
1 teaspoon baking soda
1 tablespoon instant espresso powder
1 tablespoon ground ginger
1 teaspoon ground cinnamon
1 teaspoon ground allspice

¼ teaspoon salt
2 large eggs
1½ cups buttermilk
½ cup light molasses, slightly warmed for easy mixing
6 tablespoons (¾ stick) unsalted butter, melted
¾ cup golden raisins
Pan-Glazed Apples, following

1 · In a large bowl, combine the flours, brown sugar, baking powder, baking soda, espresso powder, spices, and salt. In another bowl, beat the eggs, buttermilk, and molasses with a whisk until foamy.

2 · Pour the buttermilk-molasses mixture into the dry ingredients and combine with a few strokes. Drizzle the surface with the melted butter and fold in along with the golden raisins. The batter will be just evenly moistened. Do not overmix.

3 · Preheat the waffle iron to medium-high or according to the manufacturer's instructions. Brush the waffle iron grids with oil or melted butter. For each waffle, pour about 1 cup of the batter onto the grid. Close the lid and bake until the waffle is crisp and well browned, about 4 to 5 minutes. Remove the waffle from the iron with a fork, to protect your fingers. Serve immediately, topped with warm Pan-Glazed Apples, or cool completely on racks, store in plastic bags, and freeze for up to 2 months.

Pan–Glazed Apples

Makes enough apples to top one batch of Spiced Gingerbread Waffles

4 tablespoons (½ stick) unsalted butter
3 large tart apples, peeled, cored, and cut
  into ¼-inch-thick slices
3 tablespoons sugar, or to taste
1 teaspoon ground cinnamon, or to taste

Melt the butter in a 12-inch sauté pan over medium heat and add the apples. Sprinkle with sugar and cinnamon to taste and cook until tender, stirring occasionally, about 8 to 10 minutes. Serve immediately.

Vanilla Belgian Waffles

Belgian waffles have a larger, more exaggerated honeycombed grid than do standard waffles, which makes for a dramatic pooling of sweet syrups or sauces. Although any waffle recipe can be made in a Belgian waffle maker, this is a quick recipe to begin your experimentation. This batter is wonderful with a cup of fresh blueberries or pitted cherries gently folded in just before baking, and the finished waffles served with pure Vermont maple syrup. You may also substitute whole wheat pastry flour for the unbleached flour. I've included a couple of variations too. The chocolate version is especially nice with a warm Brandied Orange Syrup (following) that is really special for after-theater or after-movie dessert gatherings. Belgian waffles are also spectacular topped with a thin wedge of Brie or Bel Paese soft cheese, then heated in a 350°F oven for about 4 minutes just to melt the cheese. Serve hot, ladled with defrosted frozen strawberries or raspberries in syrup—perfect on a rainy night in the dead of winter.

Makes 6 to 8 large waffles, depending on the size of the waffle iron

2 cups unbleached all-purpose flour
1 tablespoon baking powder
1 tablespoon sugar
Pinch of salt
3 large eggs

½ cup (1 stick) unsalted butter, melted
1¼ cups milk
1 tablespoon vanilla extract
Brandied Orange Syrup, following

1 · In a bowl, combine the flour, baking powder, sugar, and salt.

2 · In another bowl, beat the eggs with a whisk or electric mixer until thick and foamy, about 2 minutes. Add the melted butter, milk, and vanilla extract. Add the dry ingredients and beat until smooth. Do not overmix.

3 · Preheat the Belgian waffle iron to medium-high or according to the manufacturer's instructions. Brush the waffle iron grids with oil or melted butter. For each waffle, pour about ⅔ to 1 cup of the batter onto the grid, depending on the size of your waffle iron. Close the lid and bake until the waffle is crisp and well browned, about 4 to 5 minutes. Remove the waffle from the iron with a fork, to protect your fingers. Serve immediately, or cool completely on racks, store in plastic bags, and freeze for up to 2 months.

Brandied Orange Syrup

Makes about 2 cups syrup

1 cup sugar
½ cup orange juice concentrate
¼ cup water
¼ cup brandy or cognac
½ cup (1 stick) unsalted butter

In a medium saucepan, combine all the ingredients and bring to a boil, stirring with a whisk. Reduce for 1 to 2 minutes, or until thickened. (This syrup can also be made in the microwave oven.) Remove from heat. Serve warm or chilled. For a more pronounced brandy flavor, stir in an extra tablespoon of brandy before serving.

Breakfast Raspberry Puree

Uncooked berry sauces are a tart and colorful addition to a breakfast waffle. I keep bags of frozen raspberries in the freezer to be able to make this sauce year-round, although you can make the sauce and keep it in the freezer as well.

Makes about 2 cups

Two 10-ounce bags frozen raspberries or 1 generous pint fresh raspberries, picked over and rinsed
⅓ cup sugar, or to taste
2 tablespoons crème de cassis, or to taste

1 · Place the frozen raspberries in a small bowl. Sprinkle with the sugar. Let the berries stand for 1 to 2 hours at room temperature (you don't need to cover them) to defrost the berries. They will exude lots of juice.

2 · Push the berries through a sieve to remove the seeds and puree. Stir in the crème de cassis. Refrigerate until serving.

VARIATIONS:

Belgian Waffles with Nuts

Add ½ cup ground pecans, hazelnuts, walnuts, or almonds and 1 additional tablespoon sugar to the dry ingredients in Step 1. Mix and bake as directed. Serve with 1 cup of homemade Yogurt Cheese (page 339), Homemade Mascarpone (page 339), or unsweetened whipped cream mixed with 3 tablespoons of hazelnut or other nut liqueur and fresh fruit.

Chocolate Belgian Waffles

Add ½ cup unsweetened Dutch-process cocoa powder and 5 additional tablespoons sugar to the dry ingredients in Step 1. Mix and bake as directed. These waffles are good served with Brandied Orange Syrup (following), or with Breakfast Raspberry Puree (following).

Popovers and Oven Pancakes

Popovers and Oven Pancakes

From crusty deep golden to ruddy brown, puffed and airy popovers, also known as puffovers and mahogany cakes, are the miracles of the quick-bread world. Aerated solely by the power of beaten eggs and high baking temperatures, the thin crêpe-like batter with a high proportion of liquid must go into the pan *cold* and then be baked at a high temperature so that the outer surface of the popover will set properly. The moisture in the batter creates enough steam in its short time in the oven to create a dramatic doming and an almost hollow interior. Despite legions of recipes calling for preheated hot pans and preset oven temperatures as high as for baking pizza, popovers can bake just as successfully by placing them in a cold oven and then setting the temperature to medium-high, an easy alternative to juggling scalding equipment.

Making popovers is as simple as making oatmeal, but to ensure success it is essential that all instructions be followed precisely. The batter must have the correct proportions of liquid to flour to fat, although the recipes can be doubled or tripled with no problem. Popovers with added ingredients such as vegetables, herbs, or whole-grain flours will not rise quite as high as plain ones, so there is a limit to the variations.

Ingredients are mixed with a whisk, rotary beater, or electric beater and refrigerated for from one hour to overnight, if possible. Individual cups should be placed on a baking sheet for easiest handling and must be well greased with butter, oil, or a nonstick cooking spray such as Pam. Timing is quite crucial to produce a crisp crust and moist interior. Bake the popovers on the center rack of a cold oven set at 375°F. Overbaked popovers are very rigid, underbaked ones tend to collapse, and if the pan is not greased enough, they will stick mercilessly. To test for doneness, take one popover out of its pan. It should feel feather-light, be dry to the touch, and be golden brown.

There are many popover pans available, but I favor the heavy-duty black steel Yorkshire pudding pans, with six deep 4-inch oval cups suspended from a wire frame, available in gourmet cookware shops. These pans are also available in a commercial tinned steel family size popover frame with 20 cups, made by Chicago Metallic and available in restaurant supply stores. All these frames make the classically shaped popover. If you use the black steel pans, reduce the oven temperature by 25°F to prevent overbaking. The other excellent alternative for small popovers are heavy-gauge aluminum baba molds. They are tapered and measure approximately 3 by 2 inches. Other pans that can be used for popovers are individual 3½-by-2-inch heat-proof porcelain soufflé dishes, cast-iron gem pans, standard 2¾-inch muffin cups, or individual 6-ounce Pyrex cups. Do not use thin aluminum equipment. Whatever receptacles are used, the cups should be deeper than wide to create that traditional popover shape, and should be filled no more than two-thirds full, containing about ⅓ cup batter each. Although wider popovers will not dome as high as smaller popovers made in deep cups (as in the baba molds), they are just as delicious. Miniature popovers, which are great for serving with cocktails, can be made in 1¾-inch miniature or tattler muffin pans. Oversized popovers can be made in 4½-inch fluted porcelain quiche dishes or 10-ounce Pyrex custard cups. Adjust the amount of batter, greasing, and baking time for small or oversized popovers, always filling whatever size mold no more than two-thirds full. Some bakers make one large popover using a ceramic gratin dish or an 8-by-8-inch square Pyrex baking dish, filling it with all of the batter. After baking, the pudding is cut into wedges or squares at the table.

Serve popovers instead of bread at any meal. They are as at home alongside roasted meats for dinner as with eggs and jam for breakfast, but whatever the meal, they must be made fresh and eaten immediately. Consider using a sweet popover as you would a cream-puff pastry: remove the top dome, fill with ice cream, and serve with a hot fudge sauce. Fill split savory popovers with creamed poultry, seafood, or vegetables for brunch. And, of course, the most famous of all popovers is a stalwart holiday addition: Yorkshire pudding, in which roasted meat fat is usually substituted for the melted butter.

The recipes for oven pancakes use batters that are basically similar to popovers or crêpes, but are a lot less fussy. The baked pancake is the popular *Pfankuchen* of German ancestry and rightly claims to be one of the easiest, yet most delicate of breakfast foods. The ingredients are pantry staples, and the assembly time is minimal. Oven pancakes make a spectacular savory light meal for a group, along with a salad and fruit; a mildly sweet brunch entrée; or a European-style dessert served with a sweet wine.

Mile-High Popovers

My girlfriend Julie loves dining in the casually elegant ambiance of the Thunderbird Bookstore and Cafe in Carmel Valley, where entrées are served in front of a cozy fireplace, accompanied by fresh-baked, hot popovers as the bread offering. Here is my attempt to re-create a recipe worthy of her description. I've included lots of variations, including the addition of whole grains, cheese, vegetables, herbs, or sweet spices. For a version with less fat, substitute 8 egg whites for the 6 whole eggs. If you want extra protection against sticking, line the bottom of the popover cups with parchment paper.

Makes 1 dozen popovers

6 large eggs
2 cups whole milk
2 cups unbleached all-purpose flour

4 tablespoons (½ stick) unsalted butter,
    melted, or vegetable oil
¼ teaspoon salt

1 · In a 1-quart measuring cup with a pouring spout, using a whisk or a hand rotary beater, or in an electric blender, beat the eggs until foamy. Add the milk, flour, melted butter or oil, and salt. Beat just until smooth. Do not overmix. Cover and refrigerate for from 1 hour to overnight.

2 · Generously grease 12 popover or muffin cups, individual Pyrex or soufflé dishes, or baba molds with cooking spray, butter, or oil. Place the individual dishes on a baking sheet so they are not touching. Pour the batter into each cup until two-thirds full.

3 · Place the pans in the center of a cold oven and immediately set the temperature to 375°F. Bake for 30 minutes *without opening the oven door*. Then open the oven door and pierce the side of each popover to allow steam to escape during the last phase of baking. Bake the popovers for 10 to 15 minutes more, until they are firm and golden brown. Let the popovers cool for 1 to 2 minutes before pricking each one again to allow the steam to escape. Remove the popovers from the molds by running a knife around the rim and inverting. Serve *immediately* while hot and puffy.

NOTE: *Popovers can be made a day ahead and reheated. After baking, cool completely on a rack and place in an airtight plastic storage bag at room temperature for up to 24 hours. To heat and recrisp, arrange the popovers spaced apart on a flat baking sheet and bake in a preheated 375°F oven until warm, about 5 to 7 minutes.*

VARIATIONS:

Bran Popovers

Add ¼ cup miller's wheat, oat, or rice bran with the flour in Step 1. Proceed to mix and bake as directed.

Cornmeal Popovers

Substitute ½ cup cornmeal or *masa harina* (tortilla flour) for an equal amount of unbleached flour and add with the flour in Step 1. Proceed to mix and bake as directed.

Buckwheat Popovers

Substitute ⅓ cup light or dark buckwheat flour for an equal amount of unbleached flour and add with the flour in Step 1. Proceed to mix and bake as directed.

Spinach Popovers

Stir ½ cup fresh chopped spinach leaves and ¼ teaspoon fresh-ground nutmeg into the batter in Step 1. Proceed to mix and bake as directed.

Sun-Dried Tomato and Bacon Popovers

Stir ⅓ cup crumbled cooked bacon and 3 tablespoons drained, minced, oil-packed sun-dried tomatoes into the batter in Step 1. Proceed to mix and bake as directed.

Roasted Garlic and Cheddar Popovers

Substitute olive oil for the butter in Step 1. Stir ½ cup shredded cheddar cheese and about 6 large cloves roasted garlic (page 351) into the batter in Step 1. Proceed to mix and bake as directed. These popovers work best if the pans have been lined with parchment paper to prevent sticking.

Parmesan-Herb Popovers

Stir ½ cup shredded or grated Parmesan cheese and 2 tablespoons chopped fresh basil, dill, tarragon, or thyme into the batter in Step 1. Proceed to mix and bake as directed.

Yorkshire Pudding with Wild Rice

Stir 1 cup cooled, cooked wild rice (page 355) into the popover batter in Step 1. Place 6 tablespoons unsalted butter (you may substitute roasted meat drippings, if available, for all or part of the butter) in a 13-by-9-inch casserole or oval gratin dish and place in a preheated 425°F oven until melted and hot. Remove the dish from the oven when sizzling and pour in the wild rice batter. Return the dish to the center of the oven to bake until the pudding is golden and puffed, about 25 to 30 minutes. Serve immediately, cut into squares.

Sweet Cinnamon Popovers

Add 2½ teaspoons ground cinnamon and 2 tablespoons packed brown sugar to the flour in Step 1. Proceed to mix and bake as directed.

Orange-Nut Popovers

Add 2 tablespoons ground walnuts, hazelnuts, pecans, or almonds, 2 tablespoons sugar, and the grated zest of 1 orange to the flour in Step 1. Proceed to mix and bake as directed.

Sweet Tangerine Popovers

Tangerine juice is a perfect ingredient in sweet breakfast or dessert popovers. I think tangerines are too underused in baking. Their tart-sweet flavor is a bit more assertive than that of regular oranges. The fact that popovers are placed in a cold oven is a great time saver. Make this batter the night before and bake these in the morning. Serve them for breakfast or brunch with butter and jam. Hard-core popover lovers use a sweet popover like this one instead of a biscuit when making strawberry and cream shortcakes.

Makes 1 dozen popovers

6 large eggs
1 cup whole milk
1 cup tangerine juice
½ teaspoon vanilla extract
2 cups unbleached all-purpose flour

1 tablespoon sugar
2 tablespoons unsalted butter, melted, or
 walnut oil
½ teaspoon salt

1 · In a 1-quart measuring cup with a pouring spout or in a bowl, using a whisk, hand rotary beater, or hand-held immersion blender, or in a food processor, beat the eggs until foamy. Add the milk, tangerine juice, vanilla extract, flour, sugar, melted butter or oil, and salt. Beat just until smooth. Do not overmix. Cover the batter and refrigerate for from 1 hour to overnight.

2 · Generously grease 12 popover or muffin cups, individual Pyrex or soufflé dishes, or baba molds with cooking spray, butter, or oil. Place the individual dishes on a baking sheet so they are not touching. Pour the batter into each cup until two-thirds full.

3 · Place the pans in the center of a cold oven and immediately set the temperature to 375°F. Bake the popovers for 30 minutes *without opening the oven door*. Open the door and pierce the side of each popover to allow steam to escape during the last phase of baking. Bake for 10 to 15 minutes more, until the popovers are firm and golden brown. Let the popovers cool for 1 to 2 minutes before pricking each one again to allow the steam to escape. Remove the popovers from the molds by running a knife around the rim and inverting. Serve *immediately* while hot and puffy.

Graham Popovers

A beloved type of whole wheat flour that is popular with home bakers, graham flour is worth searching out, as it has a much nuttier flavor than regular whole wheat flour. One bite of these popovers and you will always have a stash of graham flour in the refrigerator. These popovers are delightful served hot with scrambled eggs or creamed seafood spooned inside.

Makes 1 dozen popovers

6 large eggs
2 cups whole milk
1 cup unbleached all-purpose flour
1 cup graham flour or whole wheat flour

4 tablespoons (½ stick) unsalted butter, melted, or nut oil
½ teaspoon salt

1 · In a 1-quart measuring cup with a pouring spout or in a bowl, using a whisk, hand rotary beater, or hand-held immersion blender, or in a food processor, beat the eggs until foamy. Add the milk, flours, melted butter or oil, and salt. Beat just until smooth. Do not overmix. Cover the batter and refrigerate for from 1 hour to overnight.

2 · Generously grease 12 popover or muffin cups, individual Pyrex or soufflé dishes, or baba molds with cooking spray, butter, or oil. Place the individual dishes on a baking sheet so they are not touching. Pour the batter into each cup until two-thirds full.

3 · Place the pans in the center of a cold oven and immediately set the temperature to 375°F. Bake the popovers for 30 minutes *without opening the oven door.* Open the oven door and pierce the side of each popover to allow steam to escape during the last phase of baking. Bake for 10 to 15 minutes more, until the popovers are firm and golden brown. Let the popovers cool for 1 to 2 minutes before pricking each one to allow the steam to escape. Remove the popovers from the molds by running a knife around the rim and inverting. Serve *immediately* while hot and puffy.

Yorkshire Pudding with Chives

I got this recipe for Yorkshire pudding from my mother. It originally came from the wonderful cookbook written by the late actor, artist, and home chef Vincent Price. I add fresh chives and use different types of flour. To make the puffiest Yorkshire pudding ever, do not double or triple the recipe; make separate batches instead. My mom would make 2 or 3 separate batches, then pour them all into the roasting pan with the correct measure of fat left in the pan. Serve these for special holiday roast beef dinners.

Makes 4 servings

⅞ cup whole wheat pastry flour, unbleached all-purpose flour, or white spelt flour
¼ teaspoon salt
½ cup milk
2 large eggs

½ cup water
About ⅓ cup melted unsalted butter, margarine, or roast beef fat
3 tablespoons minced fresh chives

1 · In a 4-cup glass measuring cup with a pouring spout or in a bowl, using a whisk, hand rotary beater, or hand-held immersion blender, or in a food processor, beat the flour, salt, and milk together until smooth. Add the eggs and beat until the batter is pale yellow and fluffy, 2 minutes. Pour in the water, then beat on high speed until bubbly. Let stand at room temperature for 1 hour.

2 · Half an hour before baking, preheat the oven to 400°F. Place a 9-inch square baking dish, ceramic oval gratin dish, or popover mold pan with 6 cups in the oven. Heat until hot, 5 to 8 minutes. Using heavy oven mitts, carefully remove the pan from the oven and pour in melted butter or beef fat to cover the bottom of the dish or each cup to a depth of ¼ inch. Return the dish or pan to the oven and heat until smoking, another 5 minutes; watch carefully to prevent burning or splattering.

3 · Beat the batter again with a whisk until bubbly. Stir in the chives. Wearing heavy oven mitts, carefully remove the hot pan from the oven and pour the

batter into the baking dish, or each cup, until two-thirds full (the pudding will double in height during baking). Bake the pudding for 20 minutes *without opening the oven door*. Open the oven door and pierce the Yorkshire pudding to allow steam to escape during the last phase of baking. Reduce the oven temperature to 350°F and bake for an additional 10 to 15 minutes, until the pudding is firm and golden brown. Turn the pudding out of the cups and place in a serving basket or cut into squares while hot and puffy and serve at the table. Serve immediately.

Baked Pancake with Cucumber Salsa

A baked pancake is one big, puffy round, baked in the oven rather than on top of the stove. Also known as a "Dutch Baby," it looks and tastes like a delicate, oversized popover. This savory version is very popular because it is easy and fast to assemble and ready to serve in 20 minutes, giving the cook time to brew the coffee and set the table. Make the vegetable-laden Cucumber Salsa (following) the night before to develop its flavor.

Makes 4 servings

4 tablespoons (½ stick) unsalted butter
3 large eggs
¾ cup milk
⅔ cup unbleached all-purpose flour
3 tablespoons whole wheat flour

½ cup grated Monterey Jack or crumbled goat cheese, such as Montrachet or Chabis
Cucumber Salsa, following

1 · Preheat the oven to 400°F. Place the butter in 1 large or 4 individual gratin dishes, or in a 10-inch cast-iron skillet or deep pie plate. Place the pan on the center rack of the oven to melt the butter.

2 · Meanwhile, in a small bowl, using a whisk, or in a blender or food processor, beat the eggs until foamy, about 1 minute. Add the milk and flours. Beat hard or blend just until smooth.

3 · Remove the hot pan from the oven and carefully pour in the batter. The pan will be less than half full. Bake the pancake for 15 minutes, until puffy and golden. Sprinkle with the cheese and bake 5 minutes longer to melt the cheese. Serve immediately, cut into wedges and topped with spoonfuls of Cucumber Salsa.

Cucumber Salsa

Makes about 1½ cups salsa

1 English cucumber, seeded and chopped
1 slightly underripe medium tomato, peeled, seeded, and chopped
1 fresh mild poblano, New Mexico, or Anaheim green chile, roasted, peeled, and minced (page 352)
3 tablespoons finely chopped fresh cilantro
2 tablespoons olive oil

1 tablespoon red wine or apple cider vinegar
¼ teaspoon red pepper flakes, or to taste
1 small clove garlic, minced

Mix all the ingredients together in a small bowl. Refrigerate, covered, for from 2 hours to overnight to meld the flavors.

Mushroom Oven Pancake with Chive Sauce

This oven pancake is a heavenly brunch or light supper dish, and considering that medieval cooks believed that mushrooms sprang from bolts of lightning that hit the earth, this dish is heavenly in more than one sense. Sautéed cultivated or wild mushrooms are covered with a thin batter, baked in the oven until brown and puffy, and served with chilled Chive Sauce (following). This recipe is inspired by a recipe of Elizabeth Schneider, one of my favorite food writers and an earthy gourmand.

Makes 4 servings

6 tablespoons (¾ stick) unsalted butter, divided
1 pound fresh domestic or wild mushrooms, such as morel, shiitake, or oyster, stems removed and tops sliced
2 shallots, minced

Salt
Fresh-ground pepper
4 large eggs
1¼ cups milk
1 cup unbleached all-purpose flour
Chive Sauce, following

1 · Preheat the oven to 400°F. In a heavy skillet over high heat, melt 4 tablespoons of the butter. When sizzling, add the sliced mushrooms and the shallots. Sauté until the mushrooms are just cooked and slightly browned and the liquid has evaporated, about 3 minutes. Season with salt and pepper. Remove from the heat and set aside.

2 · Place the remaining 2 tablespoons of butter in 1 large or 4 individual gratin dishes, or in a 10-inch cast-iron skillet or deep pie plate. Place the pan on the center rack of the oven to melt the butter.

3 · Meanwhile, in a small bowl, using a whisk, or in a blender or food processor, beat the eggs until foamy, about 30 seconds. Add the milk and flour. Beat hard just until smooth.

4 · Remove the hot pan from the oven and spread the sautéed mushrooms over the bottom. Carefully pour the batter over the mushrooms. The pan will be about half full. Bake the pancake for 20 to 25 minutes, until puffy and golden. Serve immediately, cut into wedges, with spoonfuls of Chive Sauce on the side.

Chive Sauce

Makes about ¾ cup sauce

⅓ cup plain yogurt
⅓ cup sour cream or crème fraîche (page 339)
2 tablespoons minced fresh chives
1 tablespoon olive oil
1 tablespoon Dijon mustard

In a small bowl, combine the yogurt, sour cream or crème fraîche, chives, olive oil, and mustard with a whisk until blended. Decorate the top with a few chive blossoms, cover, and refrigerate until serving.

Toad-in-the-Hole

What a humorous name for this traditional British country casserole. I always imagine it served for lunch at Mr. Toad's mansion in the children's story The Wind in the Willows. *Here the popover batter is poured over hunks of cooked plain or smoked sausages. As the casserole bakes, the sausage pieces peek out the top of the golden puff, hence the name. If you are having company for brunch, make a double batch and use a paella pan; it looks beautiful.*

Serves 5

1 cup milk

½ cup water

3 large eggs

1½ cups unbleached all-purpose flour

¼ teaspoon salt

1½ pounds fresh or smoked sausages, such as pork sausages, breakfast sausages, turkey Italian sausages, chicken apple sausages, or bangers

5 tablespoons unsalted butter or margarine, cut into 5 pieces

¼ teaspoon dried thyme leaves

¼ teaspoon cayenne or fresh-ground white pepper

Few splashes Worcestershire sauce

1 · In a deep bowl, using a whisk, hand rotary beater, or hand-held immersion blender, or in a food processor, beat the milk, water, eggs, flour, and salt together until smooth. Beat on high speed until bubbly, 2 minutes. Cover the batter with plastic wrap and refrigerate for 1 hour.

2 · Preheat the oven to 425°F. Butter a 13-by-9-inch baking dish or shallow ceramic casserole. You can also cook this dish in a 12-inch cast-iron frying pan.

3 · Pierce each sausage with a fork, and place it in a heavy frying pan. Over medium-high heat, brown the sausages on all sides, about 10 minutes. Make sure they are cooked through but not dried out. Remove the sausages from the pan and cut into 2-inch pieces. Reserve any fat in the pan.

4 · Arrange the pieces of butter in the baking dish or casserole dish and place the pan in the oven to melt the butter, about 3 minutes. Stir the thyme, cayenne, and Worcestershire sauce into the cold batter with a whisk. Remove the pan from the oven with heavy oven mitts and pour in any reserved fat from the sausages. Arrange the sausage pieces over the bottom of the pan and pour the batter over them. Bake the casserole for 10 minutes, then reduce the oven temperature to 375°F and bake for an additional 18 to 25 minutes, until golden brown and puffy. Serve at once, cut into big squares or wedges.

Baked Apple and Pear Oven Pancake

Serve this sweet pfankuchen *hot from the oven sprinkled with a mist of powdered sugar and with lemon wedges. Or go for the gold by napping it with an elegant Berry Coulis (following).*

Serves 6

6 tablespoons (¾ stick) unsalted butter
2 medium tart apples, such as Granny Smith, peeled, cored, and sliced
2 medium firm pears, such as Red Bartlett or Comice, peeled, cored, and sliced
⅓ cup packed light brown sugar
1½ teaspoons ground cinnamon

Juice of 1 lemon
6 large eggs
1½ cups milk
1½ cups unbleached all-purpose flour
1 teaspoon vanilla extract
½ teaspoon salt
Berry Coulis (optional), following

1 · Preheat oven to 425°F. Melt the butter in a skillet and sauté the apple and pear slices over medium-high heat just until tender, but still firm. Sprinkle with the brown sugar, cinnamon, and lemon juice. Stir to combine. Place a 12-inch round or a 13-by-9-inch rectangular glass baking dish in the oven to heat for 2 minutes. Remove the baking dish with oven mitts and scrape the sautéed fruit into it. If the skillet used to sauté the fruit is ovenproof, it may be used to bake the pancake. Arrange the fruit evenly over the bottom of the pan.

2 · In a bowl, using a whisk, or in a blender or food processor, mix together the eggs, milk, flour, vanilla extract, and salt until well blended and smooth. Pour the batter over the hot fruit. Immediately place the pancake in the oven and bake for about 20 minutes, until puffed and brown. Let stand for 5 minutes before cutting into wedges. Serve immediately, topped with Berry Coulis, if desired.

Berry Coulis

Makes about 1½ cups sauce

One 16-ounce package unsweetened frozen
  raspberries, strawberries, or boysenberries
1 to 2 tablespoons sugar
⅛ cup Chambord or orange liqueur

Place the berries in a small bowl and sprinkle with the sugar to taste. Let stand for 30 minutes, or until defrosted. Add the liqueur and stir to combine. Cover and refrigerate for from 4 hours to overnight. Serve chilled.

Frying Pan Breakfast Clafouti

Food writer John Thorne adapted the clafouti into a less rich and sweet version for a unique lowfat breakfast food. It is a favorite vehicle for summer fruits: apricot halves, delicate peaches, nectarine slices, fresh pitted cherries, plum halves, blueberries, and raspberries are all good choices. When winter comes, use chunks of canned or fresh pineapple, frozen blueberries, halved cranberries, kiwis, or pieces of pear. I love canned sour cherries and peaches packed in pear juice. Whatever you use, the prepared fruit should measure about 1½ cups (any canned fruit should be drained before measuring). Any leftovers should be refrigerated. Heap oversized spoonfuls of this light-textured clafouti into shallow soup bowls, sprinkle with powdered sugar, and serve with coffee and thick slices of toasted baguette.

Serves 2 to 4

1 cup lowfat milk	½ cup unbleached all-purpose flour or
⅓ cup granulated or raw sugar, divided	whole wheat pastry flour
2 large eggs	1 tablespoon unsalted butter
Dash of salt	1½ cups fresh, frozen, or canned fruit (see
Zest of 1 lemon	headnote)

1 · Preheat the oven to 425°F. Combine the milk, ¼ cup of the sugar, eggs, salt, lemon zest, and flour in a small bowl. Beat with a whisk or hand-held immersion blender until frothy, at least 30 seconds. Set aside.

2 · In a 10-inch ovenproof nonstick or cast-iron skillet, melt the butter over medium heat. Add the fruit and shake until soft and evenly coated, 2 minutes. Sprinkle with the remaining 2 tablespoons of sugar, and cook just until the sugar is dissolved and a syrup is formed. Immediately pour the batter over the warm fruit.

3 · Bake the *claflouti* for 20 minutes, or until puffed, brown, and a knife inserted into the center comes out clean. Serve immediately.

My Favorite Fresh Apricot Clafouti

Coming out of the oven, this dish looks like a dappled brown puffy oven pancake, yet in a short time it collapses into a firm custard pudding. The fancy-named clafouti is a rustic peasant dessert originally hailing from the Limousin region of France, where it is traditionally made with stemmed, unpitted fresh cherries. It is a real hallmark of French country baking, and all classic French cookbooks carry a recipe for it. But the dish is a delight made with any seasonal fruit, even canned fruit. The batter consists of very few ingredients and is handled just like a popover batter, only it is poured over fresh fruit before baking. The dessert is served warm from the oven or at room temperature, dusted with powdered sugar. Clafouti is one-pan heaven. This version of the classic is adapted from a recipe by food writer and gardener Georgeanne Brennan. Clafouti is traditionally baked in its own straight-sided scalloped ceramic dish; you can also bake it in a 9-inch pie pan. I dare you to serve it with vanilla ice cream.

Serves 2 to 4

1 cup milk

¼ cup heavy cream or fat-free half-and-half

¼ cup packed light brown sugar

3 large eggs

2 teaspoons almond or vanilla extract

Dash of salt

⅔ cup unbleached all-purpose flour

18 fresh apricots, halved and pitted

1 · Preheat the oven to 350°F. Butter a shallow fluted *claufouti* baking dish or 9-inch pie pan.

2 · Combine the milk, heavy cream or half-and-half, brown sugar, eggs, almond or vanilla extract, salt, and flour in a small bowl. Beat with a whisk or hand-held immersion blender until frothy, about 2 minutes. Pour a quarter of the batter into the baking dish and place it in the oven for 2 minutes to set.

3 · Remove the baking dish from the oven and arrange the fruit cut side down on top of the warm batter. Pour the remaining batter over the fruit. Return the dish to the oven and bake for 30 to 35 minutes, or until puffed, brown, and a knife inserted into the center comes out clean. Serve immediately.

Dumplings

Dumplings

I like to remind bakers about dumplings. They are easy to make and loved by everyone. Large or small, sweet or savory, quick bread dumplings are little round balls, spheres, or small fat sausage shapes of dough made from flour, potatoes, semolina, or breadcrumbs. They go into soups, stews, or a pot of boiling water to be cooked, and then are eaten as part of the soup or stew, or like noodles with butter or gravy. Leftover dumplings are often sliced and fried in butter.

There are hundreds of regional recipes in German, Italian, and Hungarian cookbooks (most cities in these countries have a traditional dumpling), and as many names for them all rooted in the Latin word *nodulus*, or "little knot." Since dumplings are such basic everyday fare, recipes for them are notoriously sketchy. It was assumed that all cooks knew how to make a wide variety of dumplings. Once a skill that every good cook inherited with her family's culinary history, dumplings are often neglected today.

Potato dumplings are a traditional culinary art in Germany and Austria; *gnocchi* are their Italian cousin. These dumplings are made from a thick mixture that holds together on its own, and then they are submerged in boiling liquid to cook. Other dumplings are composed of a meat, vegetable, cheese, or fruit mixture that is wrapped in a dough and then boiled. Kasha *varenikes* (buckwheat groat dumplings known affectionately in the Midwest as "prairie ravioli"), even ravioli, agnolotti (little filled half-moons), boiled *pierogi*, and the Chinese meat-filled won ton dumpling, are all related. Bread dumplings are served throughout Eastern Europe. Cubed leftover bread is mixed with onion, herbs, or spices, even bacon, liver, or marrow, and moistened with milk and boiled. Often some farina is also added. In Czech countries, dumplings are served with roast goose, duck, or venison and rich, meaty gravy. Bread dumplings work well as a side dish with meals of braised meats and cabbage. Considered peasant food, dumplings are rich with family tradition. You can always spot old-fashioned cooks—they love dumplings.

American dumplings are basically a drop biscuit dough. They are dropped on top of a bubbling stew and cook by steaming into a fluffy, soft bread you can eat with a spoon. Spaetzle dumplings are also made from a soft dough, shaped by being pushed through the holes of a grater or colander with large holes. Spaetzle is served as a side dish like noodles or rice. *Knaidlach* is a word that probably won't be familiar to a baker unless you are Jewish; this is the name for a matzoh ball dumpling, made from matzoh meal, eggs, and melted butter or chicken fat. Knaidlach are a must with chicken soup, and I have fond memories of the first bowl of soup I ate with these heart-warming little dumplings. Try to eat just a few.

Dumpling connoisseurs agree that the secret to good dumplings is to slide them carefully into the gently boiling water, since they shouldn't be jostled or overcrowded; otherwise even the toughest dumpling will disintegrate or collect in clumps on the bottom of the pot. If it is a drop dumpling you are making, be sure to drop the dough on top of something solid in the pot of stew, like a chunk of meat or vegetable, so it can steam on top of the bubbling stew.

*B*uttermilk Drop Dumplings

One of the best old-fashioned, soul-satisfying dinners is lamb stew, beef stew, or stewed chicken with drop dumplings. The dumplings are made just like a moist drop biscuit dough and plopped on top of the stew to steam until done. If you can find a soft white pastry flour, such as White Lily, use it to make these. I combine unbleached all-purpose flour with cake flour to imitate a nice pastry flour. These dumplings are best eaten right after they are made; otherwise they get soggy.

Serves 6

1 cup unbleached all-purpose flour	1 teaspoon salt
1 cup cake flour	1½ tablespoons margarine or solid
1½ teaspoons baking powder	vegetable shortening
1 teaspoon baking soda	1 cup cold buttermilk

1 · In a medium bowl, combine the flours, baking powder, baking soda, and salt. Cut in the margarine or shortening with a fork until the mixture is crumbly. Stir in the buttermilk and blend until a soft dough is formed. Do not overmix.

2 · Using an oversized spoon, scoop out some dough and drop it immediately on top of the simmering stew, taking care to place the dumpling on top of something solid rather than directly into the liquid. You should be able to cook all the dumplings at once; it is okay if they touch each other. Cover and steam the dumplings for 12 to 15 minutes, until they are cooked through.

Spaetzle

My Hungarian relatives gave my mother a spaetzle press as a gift, a tool that looks like a hand grater. Mastering the traditional alternative method of making spaetzle, the grating and slicing of dough off a cutting board dipped in boiling water, is an art few can master, so the hand tool to make the dumplings is really nice to have. You spoon the batter into the top hopper, then push and pull it across the grater above a kettle of boiling water. The spaetzle drop right in and come out perfect every time. You can also make these quite easily using a standard grater. Soft spaetzle (meaning "little sparrows") dumplings are a specialty in Hungary (where, known as galuska, they are a must served with chicken paprikash) and southern Germany. They are said to have originated in medieval monastery kitchens for meatless Friday meals. This is the recipe my mother makes, serving the fat little egg dough ribbons with beef stew.

Serves 4

1⅓ cups unbleached all-purpose flour or
  semolina pasta flour
¾ teaspoon salt
2 large eggs

½ cup warm milk
1 tablespoon unsalted butter, for serving
Sour cream or light sour cream, for serving

1 · In a medium bowl, combine the flour and salt. Make a well and add the egg and milk into the center. Blend well with a wooden spoon until ingredients are evenly moistened; dough will be stiff like a soft pasta dough. Cover with plastic wrap and let rest at room temperature for 15 minutes.

2 · In a large stockpot, bring salted water to a rapid boil. Place the spaetzle maker, if you are using one, over the boiling water; it will rest on the rim of the pot. Place the dough in the hopper and slide the carriage back and forth, dropping pear-shaped bits of dough into the water. Alternately, you can push the dough through the large holes of a hand grater. There should be a little space in between the spaetzle as they cook. Simmer, uncovered, until they float back up to the surface, about 5 minutes. Remove with a slotted spoon and rinse quickly with some cold water. If you are serving the spaetzle right away, place them in a shallow bowl and toss them with a

tablespoon of unsalted butter and dab of light sour cream to keep them from sticking. Serve the spaetzle immediately, or keep them warm in a 325°F oven. If you wish, you can cool the spaetzle on a baking sheet instead, and reheat them in a 325°F oven. Then toss them with the butter and sour cream before serving.

Fluffy Knaidlach

What is real chicken soup without Jewish matzoh balls, also known as knaidlach, made from matzoh meal? According to a certain brand of kitchen humor, the question to ask upon being served these dumplings is "Are they matzoh balls or cannonballs?!" This is how knaidlach eaters traditionally assess whether the cook is good at her trade—and the dumplings are as light and fluffy as they should be. This recipe comes from Elaine Freedman, wife of the first baker I worked for, in 1970, and makes the best matzoh balls.

Makes 10 dumplings, serves 4

3 tablespoons unsalted butter, melted and
  cooled, or vegetable oil
3 large eggs, slightly beaten
¾ cup matzoh meal

1 teaspoon salt
1 tablespoon finely minced fresh parsley
  (optional)

1 · In a medium bowl, combine the melted butter or oil and the eggs. Add the matzoh meal, salt, and parsley, if you are using it. Blend well with a fork until the ingredients are evenly moistened. Cover with plastic wrap and refrigerate the dough for 1 hour.

2 · In a large stockpot, bring salted water to a rapid boil. Divide the dough into 10 equal portions. Using your hands, roll each portion into a ball, moistening your hands if necessary. Drop the dumplings into the boiling water; there should be 1 to 2 inches between them as they cook. Lower the heat to a simmer and cover. Cook for 45 minutes. Remove with a slotted spoon and drop into the soup.

Gnocchi Verdi

Gnocchi, *the Italian word for "dumplings," sounds a lot like* knödel, *the German word for "dumpling." The Romans first made* gnocchi *with soaked bread and eggs, then, with the culinary advancements during the Italian Renaissance, the recipe became more sophisticated, using potatoes and semolina. A substantial, filling comfort food like pasta,* gnocchi *are made throughout Italy. Here is a favorite spinach version. Because the dumplings look so plain, if you are called a* gnocco (*the singular of* gnocchi) *in Italy, it is like being called a "puddinghead." Of course,* gnocchi *may look plain, but they taste great and have a delicate texture. Serve these with a bolognese or marinara sauce of your choice and more Parmesan passed in a separate bowl.*

Serves 3 to 4

One 10-ounce package frozen chopped
  spinach, thawed and squeezed dry
1 cup ricotta cheese
½ cup grated Parmesan cheese
1 cup dry breadcrumbs
¼ cup minced green onions, white parts
  only

3 tablespoons minced fresh basil
¼ teaspoon fresh-ground nutmeg
2 large eggs
About ½ cup unbleached all-purpose flour

1 · In a medium bowl, combine the spinach, ricotta, Parmesan, breadcrumbs, green onion, basil, nutmeg, and eggs; stir until smooth. Divide into 16 portions and form each into a 3-inch log. Place the flour on a large plate and roll each log in the flour to coat lightly. Place the *gnocchi* on a baking sheet. (At this point the *gnocchi* can be covered with plastic wrap and refrigerated overnight.)

2 · In a large stockpot, bring 4 inches of salted water to a rapid boil. Slide the *gnocchi* into the simmering water, with about 1 inch space between the *gnocchi,* and cook, uncovered, for about 8 minutes. When cooked, the *gnocchi* should be dry in the center when cut in half. Remove them from the pot with a slotted spoon to a shallow buttered casserole (in which they can be kept warm in the oven before serving) or directly to individual plates to be topped with sauce.

Butternut Squash Gnocchi with Sage Butter

This is a lovely variation on plain gnocchi, *using cooked butternut or winter squash as an ingredient. Considering how good these* gnocchi *are, they should be served as often as pasta. Serve as a side dish to roasted meats and chicken or for a light meal with a green salad.*

Serves 3 to 4

1 medium butternut squash (about 1½ pounds)

1 pound whole-milk ricotta cheese

⅓ cup grated Parmesan cheese

½ teaspoon salt

¼ teaspoon fresh-ground nutmeg

¼ teaspoon fresh-ground black pepper, plus more to taste

1 large egg, lightly beaten

1⅔ cups unbleached all-purpose flour, or a few tablespoons more as needed

4 tablespoons (½ stick) unsalted butter, melted

1 tablespoon chopped fresh sage

1 · Cut the unpeeled winter squash in half lengthwise and place the halves cut side down in a baking dish. Cover and microwave for 12 minutes on high, uncovering halfway through cooking, and cook until the flesh is soft when pierced with a knife. Alternately, bake the squash halves in a 350°F oven, cut side down in 1 inch of water, for about 1 hour. Let cool, scrape out the seeds, and peel. Mash the pulp well. If the flesh is very watery, drain the squash through a mesh strainer. A 1½-pound butternut squash should yield about 1½ cups of cooked, mashed flesh.

2 · In a large bowl, mix the ricotta, Parmesan, salt, nutmeg, pepper, and egg. Add 1¼ cups squash flesh (save the rest for another purpose or discard), then add 1⅔ cups of flour, about ¼ cup at a time, until the dough comes together and forms a soft, pliable dough. You may need a few tablespoons more flour, since the density of the squash can vary. Knead the dough lightly a few times to form a smooth ball, adding more flour as needed. The dough should be soft, but firm enough to shape.

3 · To make the *gnocchi*, turn the dough out onto a lightly floured surface and divide it into 4 equal portions. With the palms of your hands, roll each portion into a small cylinder about ¾ inch in diameter. With a small sharp knife, cut each cylinder into 1½-inch-long pieces and pinch the ends of each piece together to make a teardrop shape. Cover the shaped *gnocchi* with a clean tea towel while you shape the rest of the dough.

4 · Bring 3 quarts of water with 1 tablespoon of salt to a rolling boil. Preheat the oven to 350°F and butter a 13-by-9-inch baking dish, an oval gratin dish, or 3 to 4 individual gratin dishes.

5 · Gently drop about one quarter of the *gnocchi* into the boiling water and cook until they rise to the surface, about 5 minutes. Do not add too many at one time, or they will stick together. Remove the *gnocchi* from the pot with a slotted spoon, drain them, and transfer them to the prepared dish or dishes. Repeat until all the *gnocchi* are cooked.

6 · Drizzle the *gnocchi* with the melted butter, toss with the chopped sage, and add a few more grindings of black pepper. Bake for 10 minutes, just until heated through. Serve the *gnocchi* immediately.

Ricotta-Parsley Dumplings for Soup

This is a variation on a plain gnocchi *that is dropped directly into soup broth and cooked; you choose the soup. These are delightfully delicate* gnocchi.

Makes about 18 dumplings; serves 4 to 5

2 cups unbleached all-purpose flour
1 tablespoon baking powder
2½ tablespoons minced fresh Italian parsley
1 teaspoon salt

2 large eggs
½ cup part-skim or whole-milk ricotta
  cheese
¼ cup milk

1 · In a medium bowl, combine the flour, baking powder, parsley, and salt. Make a well and add the eggs, ricotta, and milk to the center. Blend well with a wooden spoon until the dough is evenly moistened and just holds together. Cover with plastic wrap and let rest at room temperature for 10 minutes.

2 · Using a large tablespoon, scoop out some dough. Roll the dough into a ball with your hands, moistening them with some water if necessary. Repeat the process until the dough is used up. Drop the *gnocchi* into the boiling soup broth. You should be able to cook all the gnocchi at once; it is okay if they are touching. Lower the heat to a simmer and cover. Cook for 15 minutes, ladle the soup and *gnocchi* into bowls, and serve.

Tamale Dumplings for Soup

This is a twist on old-fashioned cornmeal dumplings that uses masa harina, *the dried ground cornmeal used for making tortillas and tamales. When making these dumplings, you can use either the fine grind, which is used for tortillas, or the coarse grind (*masa harina para tamales*), which is used especially for tamales.* Masa harina *adds a lovely homespun, smokey quality to the dumpling, since the cornmeal is treated with lime. Make the dumplings miniature, as in Mexican wedding soup, rather than in big portions, like the other dumplings in this chapter. These dumplings are a great addition to Mexican and Southwestern-style chicken and vegetable soups.*

Makes about 16 dumplings; serves 3 to 4

⅔ cup water
2½ tablespoons canola oil
¼ teaspoon ground cumin
¼ teaspoon salt
⅔ cup *masa harina*
⅓ teaspoon ground chili powder (page 331), or to taste

1 large egg
1 large egg white, beaten slightly
¼ cup cooked fresh yellow or white corn kernels, or thawed frozen baby corn kernels

1 · In a medium saucepan, combine the water, oil, cumin, and salt. Bring to a boil. Add the *masa harina* in a stream and cook, stirring constantly with a wooden spoon, until the mixture pulls away from the sides of the pan, about 4 minutes. Remove the pan from the heat and quickly beat in the chili powder, egg, and egg white. Stir in the corn kernels.

2 · Using a teaspoon, scoop out some dough. Shape the dough into a small ball using your hands, moistening them with some water if necessary. Drop the dumplings into the boiling soup broth as they are formed. You should be able to cook all of them at once; it is okay if they are touching. Lower the heat to a simmer and cover. Cook for 5 minutes before ladling the soup and dumplings into bowls, and serve.

Silky Potato Dumplings

Potato dumplings are the largest in the family, usually about the size of a woman's fist. They are often served at weddings and have all sorts of wonderful nicknames like little thieves, heart squeezers, clods, hairy buttons, and belly-pokers. This excellent recipe for authentic knödel *is from my friend, the late Mary Anne McCready. Potato dumplings are good with all types of roasted meats and game, sauced with rich gravies, or with bratwurst and sauerkraut. Traditionally a large cube of day-old bread or a Kaiser roll is sautéed in butter or oil and placed in the center of each dumpling before boiling as a special treat. Plan on serving 1 to 2 of these large dumplings per person; they will be devoured.*

Makes about 14 dumplings; serves 8

2½ pounds russet potatoes (about 6 large)

9 ounces potato flour (not potato starch flour)

2 cups boiling water or boiling potato water

1 teaspoon salt

1 · Cut the potatoes into large chunks and place in a 2-quart saucepan; cover with water. Bring to a boil, reduce to a simmer, and cook until just soft. Drain the potatoes (you can reserve the potato liquid for use in this recipe or another; refrigerated, it will keep for a day) and cool to room temperature. Refrigerate the potatoes, covered, overnight.

2 · Peel the potatoes. Rice or grate the potatoes into a mixing bowl. Add the potato flour, salt, and boiling water (if using the potato water, add enough water to make 2 cups). Knead the mixture in the bowl to form a soft dough ball. Pull off large pieces of dough and shape into 4-inch-diameter round balls (the size of a tennis ball); place the dumplings on a baking sheet to transport them to the stove.

3 · Fill a large deep saucepan about 6 inches deep with water, lightly salt it, and bring the water to a boil over high heat. Preheat the oven to the lowest setting, and place a large shallow baking dish in it to warm.

4 · With a slotted spoon, slip the dumplings into the boiling water. You should be able to cook about 3 at a time. Keeping the water at a gentle rolling boil, simmer the dumplings for 15 minutes, uncovered. The dumplings will float and be compact looking; they will shrink to 3 inches in diameter when cooked through. Remove each one with a slotted spoon to drain and place in the warmed baking dish. Cover the dish with a foil tent and return the baking dish to the oven. Continue to shape and cook the remaining dumplings. The dumplings may be kept warm in the oven for up to 2 hours before serving. If there are any leftovers, they can be reheated the next day in the microwave.

Scones and Soda Breads

Scones and Soda Breads

With a few tips, scones are an easily made and satisfying addition to breakfast, tea, and hors d'oeuvres and the base for unusual sandwiches. They are at once tender, rich, flaky, and versatile. They are excellent plain or can be easily embellished with nuts, herbs, or even chocolate chips for flavor variations. They can be cut into endless shapes: wedges, squares, stars, hearts, or half-moons. Even better, they are fast to make. The entire preparation time for assembling, mixing, forming, and baking scones is about 45 minutes.

Use fresh ingredients such as aluminum-free baking powder, sweet butter, eggs, and all-purpose and pastry flours for the best flavor. All types of flour, such as barley, oats, corn, rye, and bran, make beautiful scones. Liquids commonly used for moistening the dry ingredients include buttermilk, milk, yogurt, or cream.

Use the following techniques for perfect results: Quickly mix the dry ingredients with the cold fat to make big coarse crumbs, and when stirring in the cold liquid, a quick hand is again needed so the air is not forced out of the dough. This is especially important when the scones do not contain eggs, which help with the leavening. Measure the liquids carefully to make a soft, pliable dough. Too much liquid makes a heavy scone that is hard to shape.

Gently knead the dough just until it holds together, since overhandling will produce a very tough and chewy scone. The kneading is not a vigorous technique as called for in yeast-bread making to activate the gluten, but a very gentle working just to form a cohesive ball.

When rolling out the scone, keep it thicker than ½ inch to achieve the best shape. For even browning, bake only one sheet at a time in the center of a preheated oven. The scones will rise to double their raw size in the oven. Pay close attention to baking times. Always remember that after they are out of the oven, quick breads continue to cook during the cooling process, and overbaking makes them dry, a disaster for the texture of the scone.

After baking and cooling, scones and soda breads can be frozen in heavy-duty plastic freezer bags for up to a month and reheated in a warm oven for 5 to 8 minutes. The shaped raw dough can also be frozen on a parchment-lined baking sheet and placed in freezer bags when frozen. To bake frozen scones, remove them from the freezer, place on a parchment-lined baking sheet, and immediately bake in a preheated oven about 5 minutes longer than specified in the recipe.

Serve sweet scones with sweet butter, jams and preserves, fruit curds, honeys, yogurt cheese, homemade herb butters, or clotted cream and Devonshire cream. Savory scones are good served with such diverse foods as seafood salads with avocado mayonnaise, sliced meats with cornichons and honey mustard, and hard cheeses spread with chutney.

Also in this quick dough family are soda breads, the legendary homemade Celtic country hearth loaves that have been popular in the bastions of Celtic culture since Roman times: Ireland, Wales, Cornwall, the Scottish Highlands, and Brittany. These breads are still very much alive, made today throughout the British Isles using the same techniques as for scones. They have a thick, rather chunky-crisp crust that when bitten into reveals a moist-textured interior. They are made with a variety of flours, but the very best are made with a proportion of Irish wheat, which is renowned for its wholesome flavor. In the United States, use a good-quality, very fresh, stone-ground whole wheat flour as a substitute. Traditionally, soda breads were baked over banked peat fires in a suspended cast-iron pot, on a bakestone or griddle, or in clay ovens. Now baked in modern conventional ovens, soda breads are still a beloved staple. If you own a baking stone, soda breads will bake nicely on one.

Recipes for authentic loaves made in centuries past contain no baking powder or yeast; the sole leavening was bicarbonate of potash, or saleratus, an early form of modern baking soda, which gave the breads a unique tangy flavor. Baking soda and small amounts of baking powder are the leavenings used exclusively today. These breads are low in sugar and fat, yet high in fiber, so the flavors of the whole grains and fresh buttermilk speak for themselves. When you are making these ancient Celtic breads, I suggest that you beat the doughs in a "sunwise" (clockwise) direction, as per Druidic recipe instructions from the Middle Ages, to come as close to the authentic results as possible.

Old-Fashioned Lemon Cream Scones

One bite of this warm, homemade scone and you'll be transformed into a lover of these exquisitely simple tea breads. The crust should be a thin, slightly crunchy exterior band over a dense, yet moist and fluffy, interior. The cream is important in producing the crumb, but substitute milk if you must. This basic recipe is the springboard for many variations, but I always come back to the plain scones. Served with butter and homemade Fresh Strawberry or Peach Jam (following), they cannot be beat. If you desire scones made with fresh summer berries, rather than mixing them into the dough, incorporate them by gently sandwiching them between two rounds of the dough and pinching the outer edges before cutting the dough into wedges. This technique keeps the berries from being squashed, losing their shape, and bleeding heavily into the dough.

Makes 8 scones

2 cups unbleached all-purpose flour
2 tablespoons sugar
1 tablespoon baking powder
Grated zest of 2 lemons
¼ teaspoon salt
4 tablespoons (½ stick) cold unsalted butter, cut into pieces

2 large eggs
½ cup heavy cream
½ teaspoon ground cinnamon mixed with 2 tablespoons sugar (optional), for sprinkling
Fresh Strawberry Jam (optional), following
Fresh Peach Jam (optional), following

1 · Preheat the oven to 400°F. Grease a baking sheet or line it with parchment paper. In a medium bowl, combine the flour, sugar, baking powder, lemon zest, and salt. Cut in the butter with a fork or a heavy-duty electric mixer until the mixture resembles coarse crumbs. In a small bowl or 1-cup measure, whisk together the eggs and cream. Add to the dry mixture and stir until a sticky dough is formed.

2 · Turn out the shaggy dough onto a lightly floured work surface and knead gently just until the dough holds together, about 6 times. Divide into 3 equal portions and pat each into a 1-inch-thick round about 6 inches in diameter. With a knife or straightedge, cut each round into quarters, creating 4 wedges. The scones can also be formed by cutting the dough using a 3-inch biscuit cutter to make 10 to 12 smaller scones.

3 · Place the scones about 1 inch apart on the prepared baking sheet. Sprinkle the tops with the cinnamon sugar, if desired. Bake in the center of the oven until crusty and golden brown, 15 to 20 minutes. Serve immediately with butter and homemade jam, or cool on a rack and freeze in heavy-duty freezer bags for up to a month.

Fresh Strawberry Jam

Exceptional, chunky, fresh-fruit jams are easily made within half an hour. Homemade jams are less sweet than commercial jams and much more exciting in both flavor and color.

Using this recipe, you may substitute raspberries, blackberries, ollalaberries, or blueberries for the strawberries, but definitely taste the berries while adding the sugar to adjust for differing tartness. For sophisticated palates, add ¼ cup cognac, port, or orange liqueur as the jam finishes cooking in Step 3. Use over- as well as underripe berries. Because they absorb water quickly, never float berries in water to clean them; just rinse them under running water.

A microwave oven is excellent for jam making because the sugar will not easily scorch, as it tends to do on the stovetop, although recipe instructions are included for both methods. The following recipes are geared to a 700-watt microwave oven, so adjust the times accordingly if your oven has a different wattage. Pectin is important for thickening microwaved jams, as the liquid does not evaporate during cooking,

resulting in a greater yield per batch than in the stovetop method. If you decide to make the jam on the stovetop, expect less yield and more stirring. Store your homemade jams in a covered container in the refrigerator for up to 2 months; freeze in plastic containers; or, more traditionally, process, pack, and seal in sterilized jars.

Makes about 4 cups (four ½-pint jars)

2 quarts (8 cups) fresh strawberries, washed, drained, and hulled
⅓ cup fresh lemon juice
One 1.75- or 2-ounce box powdered pectin
4 cups sugar, or to taste

1 · Coarsely crush the berries by hand or in the food processor, leaving a few whole berries or chunks, as desired. Place in a deep stainless steel or enamel saucepan or deep straight-sided microwaveproof glass or porcelain casserole dish

about three times the volume of the fruit, preferably with a pouring spout. Sprinkle with the lemon juice and the pectin. Let stand for 10 minutes.

2 · Over medium-high heat on the stovetop, or on high power in the microwave oven, bring the mixture to a rolling boil that cannot be stirred down. Boil for about 8 minutes, uncovered. Add the sugar and stir well.

3 · Bring the mixture back to a rolling boil over medium-high heat, or on high power in the microwave oven for about 10 minutes, stirring twice. Boil for exactly 1 minute. Remove from the heat and skim off the white foam with a large metal spoon. Stir occasionally for 10 minutes before ladling into storage jars such as French *confiture* glass jars with plastic lids, quilted jelly jars, or glass-topped jars with wire closures. Let stand until cool. Store, covered, in the refrigerator for up to 2 months.

Fresh Peach Jam

Stone fruits, and all overripe fruits, are low in natural pectin and acid, so both powdered pectin and lemon juice need to be added to create a jam with substance and proper flavor balance. Please note that the cooking time for this recipe may vary, and the yield may be different each time you make it, depending on the juiciness and seasonal variations of the fruit.

Makes about 6 cups (six ½-pint jars)

4 cups peeled, pitted, and finely chopped fresh peaches
2 tablespoons fresh lemon juice
One 1.75- or 2-ounce box powdered pectin
3 to 3½ cups sugar, or to taste

Follow directions for Fresh Strawberry Jam, adding the lemon juice to the fruit in Step 1. This recipe can also be used for unpeeled apricots, plums, and nectarines.

VARIATIONS:

Currant Lemon Cream Scones

Add ⅔ cup dried currants to the dry ingredients in Step 1. Mix, shape, and bake as directed. Dried blueberries, cranberries, or cherries may also be substituted.

Fresh Rosemary Lemon Cream Scones

Add 1 tablespoon fresh chopped rosemary to the dry ingredients in Step 1. Mix, shape, and bake as directed.

Cornmeal Lemon Cream Scones

Substitute ¾ cup fine-grind yellow, white, or blue cornmeal for an equal amount of flour in Step 1. Mix, shape, and bake as directed.

Dark and White Chocolate Lemon Cream Scones

Add ¼ cup each bittersweet and white chocolate chips to the dry ingredients in Step 1. Mix, shape, and bake as directed.

Honey Lemon Cream Scones

Substitute an equal amount of honey for the sugar and reduce the cream by 1 tablespoon in Step 1. Mix, shape, and bake as directed. Brush the hot scones with additional warmed honey before serving.

Crème Fraîche Scones

These are especially tender, unique scones with no extra added fat or eggs, apart from the crème fraîche. This recipe is adapted from the Crème Fraiche Cookbook *by Sadie Kendall (Ridgeview Press, 1989). Sadie serves them with Homemade Mascarpone (page 339) and a Seville orange marmalade or a sublime rose-hip jelly. I like these scones coated with slivered blanched almonds before baking. They are especially good with a tablespoon of freshly grated nutmeg or vanilla extract added to the crème fraîche the night before mixing the dough.*

Makes 8 scones

2 cups white cake flour or whole wheat
  pastry flour
1 tablespoon sugar
2¼ teaspoons baking powder

¼ teaspoon salt
1¼ cups crème fraîche
1 to 3 tablespoons buttermilk

1 · Preheat the oven to 425°F. Grease a baking sheet or line it with parchment paper. In a medium bowl, combine the flour, sugar, baking powder, and salt. Cut in the crème fraîche with a fork or a heavy-duty electric mixer until the mixture makes a sticky, yet cohesive dough. Add a few tablespoons of the buttermilk if the dough seems too stiff.

2 · Turn the dough out onto a lightly floured work surface and knead gently just until the dough holds together, about 6 times. Divide the dough into 2 equal portions and pat each into a 1-inch-thick round about 6 inches in diameter. With a knife or straightedge, cut each round into quarters, making wedges. The scones can also be formed by cutting the dough with a 2-inch biscuit cutter to make 12 to 14 smaller scones.

3 · Place the scones about 1 inch apart on the prepared baking sheet. Bake in the center of the oven until crusty and golden brown, about 15 to 18 minutes. Serve immediately, or cool on a rack and freeze in heavy-duty freezer bags for up to a month.

Orange-Raisin Scones

Serve Orange-Raisin Scones with tea or Mexican hot chocolate for breakfast. An equal amount of plumped dried cherries or shelled pistachios may be substituted for the raisins in winter, or chopped fresh firm plums in the summertime.

Makes 12 scones

1¾ cups unbleached all-purpose flour
3 tablespoons sugar
2½ teaspoons baking powder
Grated zest of 2 oranges
½ teaspoon salt
5 tablespoons cold unsalted butter, cut into
  pieces

⅔ cup dark or golden raisins
1 large egg
½ cup cold half-and-half (can be half
  orange juice)

1 · Preheat the oven to 400°. Line a baking sheet with parchment paper. In a medium bowl, combine the flour, sugar, baking powder, orange zest, and salt. Cut in the butter with a fork or a heavy-duty electric mixer until the mixture resembles coarse crumbs. Add the raisins.

2 · In a small bowl or 1-cup measure, beat together the egg and half-and-half, and orange juice, if you are using it. Add to the dry mixture and stir just until a sticky dough is formed. Turn the shaggy dough out onto a lightly floured work surface and knead gently just until the dough holds together, about 8 times. Divide the dough into 3 equal portions and pat each into a 1-inch-thick round about 6 inches in diameter. With a knife or straightedge, cut each round into quarters, making wedges.

3 · Place the scones about 1 inch apart on the prepared baking sheet. Bake in the center of the oven until crusty and golden brown, 15 to 20 minutes. Serve immediately, or cool on a rack and freeze in heavy-duty freezer bags for up to a month.

Fig-Walnut Scones

California is the home of beautiful black, amber, and violet figs: the Mission (or Franciscana), the Kadota (or Italian Dottato), and the Calimyrna (or Smyrna). Figs survived the Ice Age along with the olive, and I certainly am glad they did. A lover of temperate weather, the fig is a prolific and succulent summer fruit with deeply lobed green leaves, which I often use as decoration. The dried fruit is intensely sweet and naturally deeply nourishing. If you love buttermilk scones, as I do, this combination of nuts and fruit will give you a good reason to make them more often.

Makes 12 scones

3 cups unbleached all-purpose flour
⅓ cup sugar
1 tablespoon baking powder
½ teaspoon baking soda
½ teaspoon salt
Grated zest of 1 orange
¾ cup (1½ sticks) cold unsalted butter, cut
  into small pieces

¾ cup coarsely chopped dried figs
½ cup chopped walnuts
1 cup cold buttermilk
2 tablespoons sugar mixed with ¼ teaspoon
  each ground cinnamon, allspice, and
  mace, for sprinkling

1 · Preheat the oven to 400°F. Grease a baking sheet or line it with parchment paper. In a medium bowl, combine the flour, sugar, baking powder, baking soda, salt, and orange zest. Cut in the butter with a fork or a heavy-duty electric mixer until the mixture resembles coarse crumbs. Stir in the figs and walnuts. Add the buttermilk to the dry mixture and stir until a sticky dough is formed.

2 · Turn out the shaggy dough onto a lightly floured work surface and knead gently just until the dough holds together, about 6 times. Divide the dough into 3 equal portions and pat each into a 1-inch-thick round about 6 inches in diameter. With a knife or straightedge, cut each round into quarters, making wedges. The scones can also be formed by cutting the dough with a 2-inch biscuit cutter to make 12 to 14 smaller scones. Sprinkle the tops lightly with the spiced-sugar mixture.

3 · Place the scones about 1 inch apart on the prepared baking sheet. Bake in the center of the oven until crusty and golden brown, 15 to 20 minutes. Serve immediately, or cool on a rack and freeze in heavy-duty freezer bags for up to a month.

VARIATION:

Fresh Cranberry–Walnut Scones

Substitute 1½ cups whole fresh or frozen unthawed cranberries or 1 cup dried cranberries for the dried figs in Step 1. Mix, shape, and bake as directed.

Buttermilk Cherry Scones

One bite of these warm, homemade scones and you'll be transformed into a lover of these exquisitely simple tea breads, if you aren't already. The crust should be a thin, slightly crunchy exterior band over a dense, yet moist and fluffy, interior. These scones are great with butter and jam.

Makes 12 scones

2½ cups unbleached all-purpose flour
¼ cup rolled oats
¼ cup packed light brown sugar
1½ teaspoons baking powder
1 teaspoon cream of tartar
¼ teaspoon baking soda
½ teaspoon salt

5 tablespoons cold unsalted butter, cut into pieces
3 ounces (⅔ cup) tart dried cherries
1 large egg
¾ cup cold buttermilk
1¼ teaspoons vanilla extract

1 · Preheat the oven to 400°F. Line a baking sheet with parchment paper. In a medium bowl, combine the flour, oats, brown sugar, baking powder, cream of tartar, baking soda, and salt. Cut in the butter with a fork or a heavy-duty electric mixer until the mixture resembles coarse crumbs. Add the cherries.

2 · In a small bowl or a 2-cup measure, beat together the egg, buttermilk, and vanilla extract. Add to the dry mixture and stir until a sticky, just moistened dough is formed. Turn out the shaggy dough onto a lightly floured work surface and knead gently just until the dough holds together, about 6 times. Divide the dough into 2 equal portions and pat each into a 1-inch-thick round about 7 inches in diameter. With a knife or straightedge, cut each round into 6 wedges.

3 · Place the scones about 1 inch apart on the prepared baking sheet. Bake in the center of the oven until crusty and golden brown, 15 to 20 minutes. Serve immediately, or cool on a rack and freeze in heavy-duty freezer bags for up to a month.

Maple Tea Scones with Homemade Devonshire Cream

Essentially this is a plain scone; the delicate undercurrent of maple flavor is subtle and barely sweet. I like these cut with a heart-shaped cutter and served barely cool, piled on a flat basket lined with giant fresh fig leaves for a dramatic presentation. They are an undisputed star on a brunch table, but you'll probably make them often as they also satisfy cravings for a little "something special" bread. The cool, creamy Homemade Devonshire Cream spread (following) complements the hot scones with a bit of tang.

Makes 12 scones

3 cups unbleached all-purpose flour
1 tablespoon baking powder
½ teaspoon baking soda
¼ teaspoon salt
¾ cup (1½ sticks) cold unsalted butter, cut
  into pieces

½ cup milk
½ cup pure maple syrup
1½ teaspoons vanilla extract
Homemade Devonshire Cream, following

1 · Preheat the oven to 375°F. Grease a baking pan or line it with parchment paper. In a medium bowl, combine the flour, baking powder, baking soda, and salt. Cut in the butter with a fork or a heavy-duty electric mixer until the mixture resembles coarse crumbs. In a small bowl or a 1-cup measure, combine the milk, maple syrup, and vanilla extract. Add to the dry mixture and stir until a sticky dough is formed, adding a few more tablespoons of milk, 1 tablespoon at a time, if the dough is too stiff.

2 · Turn out the shaggy dough onto a lightly floured work surface and knead gently just until the dough holds together, about 6 times. Divide the dough into 3 equal portions and pat each into a 1-inch-thick round about 6 inches in diameter. With a knife or straightedge, cut each round into quarters, creating wedges. The scones can also be formed by cutting the dough with a 3-inch biscuit cutter (if you are using a cutter, you may wish to pat the dough into one large 1-inch-thick round).

3 · Place the scones about 1 inch apart on the prepared baking sheet. Bake in the center of the oven until crusty and golden brown, 16 to 20 minutes. Serve immediately with jam and Homemade Devonshire Cream, or cool on a rack and freeze in heavy-duty freezer bags for up to a month.

Homemade Devonshire Cream

Makes 1½ cups spread

½ cup heavy cream
1 tablespoon powdered sugar
¾ cup cultured sour cream

In a clean mixing bowl, whip the heavy cream with the powdered sugar until soft peaks form. Add the sour cream and beat until just fluffy and well combined. Scrape into a covered container and refrigerate until serving.

Pumpkin Scones with Maple Butter

When you use pumpkin in baked goods, you are rewarded with a much-loved treat. The pumpkin puree ends up being part of the liquid ingredients. I love these scones with Maple Butter (following) and tea.

Makes 8 scones

1½ cups unbleached all-purpose flour
½ cup whole wheat pastry flour
3 tablespoons packed dark brown sugar
2 teaspoons baking powder
½ teaspoon baking soda
½ teaspoon salt
1½ teaspoons apple pie spice
6 tablespoons (¾ stick) cold unsalted butter, cut into pieces
⅓ cup finely chopped dried apples

⅓ cup currants
1 large egg
¼ cup cold buttermilk
½ cup pumpkin puree, canned or homemade (page 351)
2 tablespoons half-and-half or milk, for brushing
2 tablespoons raw or granulated sugar, for sprinkling
Maple Butter (optional), following

1 · Preheat the oven to 400°F. Line a baking sheet with parchment paper. In a medium bowl, combine the unbleached flour, whole wheat flour, brown sugar, baking powder, baking soda, salt, and apple pie spice. Cut in the butter with a fork or a heavy-duty electric mixer until the mixture resembles coarse crumbs. Add the currants and the dried apples.

2 · In a small bowl or 1-cup measure, whisk together the egg, buttermilk, and the pumpkin puree. Add to the dry mixture and stir until a sticky dough is formed. Turn the dough out onto a lightly floured work surface and knead gently just until the dough holds together, about 8 times. Divide it into 2 equal portions and pat each into a 1-inch-thick round about 6 inches in diameter. With a knife or straightedge, cut each round into quarters, creating wedges.

3 · Place the scones about 1 inch apart on the prepared baking sheet. Brush the tops with the half-and-half or milk and sprinkle with the sugar. Bake in the center of the oven until crusty and golden brown, 15 to 20 minutes. Serve immediately with Maple Butter, or cool on a rack and freeze in heavy-duty freezer bags for up to a month.

Maple Butter

Makes ½ cup

½ cup (1 stick) unsalted butter, at room
   temperature
3 tablespoons pure maple syrup

In a small bowl using the back of a spoon, or in a blender or food pro- cessor, cream the butter and maple syrup until fluffy and well combined. Store, covered, in the refrigerator for up to 3 days. Bring to room tempera- ture before serving.

Oat Scones with Apple-Pear Butter

Oat scones are a crumbly and tender relative of Scottish scones. They can be dressed up for a special breakfast or tea by adding ½ cup chopped moist, pitted dates to the batter and serving the scones spread with Apple-Pear Butter (following). Substitute an equal amount of barley flour for the rolled oats to create another traditionally flavored scone. Since the time my friend Zelda left a pot of cinnamon basil on my porch for a gift, I have become quite taken with the intensely scented basils, including the anise, lemon, and opal varieties. For a subtle summer scone, bring the cream to a boil with half a dozen fresh-scented basil leaves and chill overnight before removing the leaves and using the infusion in the following recipe.

Makes 12 scones

1 cup unbleached all-purpose flour or whole wheat pastry flour

1 cup rolled oats

3 tablespoons packed light brown sugar

2 teaspoons baking powder

¼ teaspoon salt

6 tablespoons (¾ stick) cold unsalted butter, cut into pieces

1 large egg

½ cup half-and-half or light cream

Apple-Pear Butter, following

1 · Preheat the oven to 375°F. Grease a baking sheet or line it with parchment paper. Combine the flour and oats in the workbowl of a food processor and process until the oats are ground. In a medium bowl, combine the flour-oat mixture, brown sugar, baking powder, and salt. Cut in the butter with a fork or a heavy-duty electric mixer until the mixture resembles coarse crumbs. In a small bowl or 1-cup measure, whisk together the egg and half-and-half. Add to the dry mixture and stir until a sticky dough is formed.

2 · Turn the dough out onto a lightly floured work surface and knead gently just until the dough holds together, about 6 times. Pat the dough into a ¾-inch-thick round about 8 inches in diameter. Cut out the scones with a 2-inch biscuit cutter to make 12 to 14 small scones.

3 · Place the scones about 1 inch apart on the prepared baking sheet. Bake in the center of the oven until crusty and golden brown, about 15 to 18 min-

utes. Serve immediately, split in half and spread with Apple-Pear Butter, or cool on a rack and freeze in heavy-duty freezer bags for up to a month.

Apple-Pear Butter

Makes about 2 cups butter

¼ pound (2 cups) dried unsulphured apple slices
2 ounces (1 cup) dried pears
2 cups unsweetened apple or pear juice
2 teaspoons ground cinnamon
1 teaspoon ground allspice
½ teaspoon ground cloves
2 tablespoons unsalted butter

Combine all the ingredients except the butter in a heavy saucepan and bring to a boil. Reduce heat to a simmer and cook, uncovered, for 30 minutes, stirring occasionally. Remove from the heat, stir in the butter, and cool. Puree the Apple-Pear Butter in a blender or food processor until smooth. Scrape into a springtop glass jar and refrigerate until needed. It will keep for about 2 months.

Oat Bran Scones with Dried Apricots

Oat bran is milder in flavor than wheat bran and seems to have found a permanent home in the whole-grain pantry for bakers. It has a natural sweet flavor that is inherent to the oat family, and it combines with dried fruits and other grains to create baked goods with a unique hearty texture. Tuck these, spread with luscious Apricot-Orange Curd (following), alongside a plate of scrambled eggs for breakfast.

Makes 12 small scones

⅔ cup chopped dried apricots
⅓ cup rolled oats, for sprinkling on baking pan
1½ cups unbleached all-purpose flour
½ cup oat bran, ground to a powder in a blender or food processor
2 tablespoons packed light brown sugar

1 tablespoon baking powder
¼ teaspoon salt
5 tablespoons cold unsalted butter, cut into pieces
¾ cup cold buttermilk
Apricot-Orange Curd (optional), following

1 · In a small bowl, cover the dried apricots with boiling water and let stand for 10 minutes.

2 · Preheat the oven to 400°F. Grease a baking sheet or line it with parchment paper. Sprinkle the baking sheet with ⅓ cup rolled oats. In a medium bowl, combine the flour, oat bran, brown sugar, baking powder, and salt. Cut in the butter with a fork or a heavy-duty electric mixer until the mixture resembles coarse crumbs. Drain the plumped apricots and add them to the dry mixture along with the buttermilk. Stir until a sticky dough is formed.

3 · Turn the dough out onto a lightly floured work surface and knead gently just until the dough holds together, about 6 times. Divide the dough into 3 equal portions and pat each into a 1-inch-thick round about 4 inches in diameter. With a knife or straightedge, cut each round into quarters, creating wedges. The scones can also be formed by cutting the dough with a 2-inch biscuit cutter to make 12 to 14 smaller scones.

4 · Place the scones about 1 inch apart on the prepared baking sheet. Bake in the center of the oven until crusty and golden brown, about 15 to 18 minutes. Serve immediately with Apricot-Orange Curd, if desired, or cool on a rack and freeze in heavy-duty freezer bags for up to a month.

Apricot-Orange Curd

An age-old spread for toasted English muffins, waffles, and fresh scones is this thick jam made with eggs and citrus. Heat the whole lime in the microwave for 30 seconds first to yield more juice when squeezing.

Makes about 2 cups spread

½ cup (1 stick) unsalted butter
6 dried apricot halves, soaked in boiling
  water for 20 minutes and drained
⅔ cup frozen orange juice concentrate,
  thawed
Grated zest of 2 oranges
Juice of 1 lime
⅔ cup sugar
4 large eggs
2 large egg yolks

Melt the butter in the top section of a double boiler. In a blender or food processor, puree the apricots with the orange juice concentrate. Add the remaining ingredients except the butter and blend until well combined. With the water at a simmer, slowly add the apricot-egg mixture to the butter, stirring constantly with a whisk. Cook over medium heat, stirring constantly, until thickened, a full 10 minutes. Pour into a jar and let cool slightly before storing in the refrigerator, covered, for up to 3 weeks.

VARIATION:

Wheat Bran Scones with Dried Cranberries

Substitute an equal amount of dried cranberries for the dried apricots in

Step 1. Substitute an equal amount of All-Bran commercial whole-grain cereal for the oat bran in Step 2. Continue to mix, shape, and bake as directed.

Graham Scones with Pine Nuts and Golden Raisins

These days we all know the virtues of whole-grain flour: the fiber, the carbohydrates, the vitamins and minerals—good nutrition in every bite. But beyond these virtues is the gloriously nutty flavor that is totally unique to graham flour, a special grind of whole wheat. Although fresh whole wheat flour is perfectly acceptable, please search out coarse-textured graham flour for these scones, and savor the taste. For more information on whole-grain flours, please refer to pages 342-343.

Makes 12 scones

2¼ cups graham flour or finely ground whole wheat flour
3 tablespoons packed light brown sugar
2 teaspoons baking powder
½ teaspoon baking soda
¼ teaspoon salt

½ cup (1 stick) cold unsalted butter, cut into pieces
½ cup pine nuts
½ cup golden raisins
2 large eggs
⅔ cup buttermilk

1 · Preheat the oven to 400°F. Grease a baking pan or line it with parchment paper. In a medium bowl, combine the flour, brown sugar, baking powder, baking soda, and salt. Cut in the butter with a fork or a heavy-duty electric mixer until the mixture resembles coarse crumbs. Add the pine nuts and the golden raisins. Toss to combine. In a small bowl or 1-cup measure, whisk together the eggs and buttermilk. Add to the dry mixture and stir until a sticky dough is formed.

2 · Turn out the shaggy dough onto a lightly floured work surface and knead gently just until the dough holds together, about 6 times. Divide the dough into 3 equal portions and pat each into a 1-inch-thick round about 6 inches in diameter. With a knife or straightedge, cut each round into quarters, creating wedges. The scones can also be formed by cutting the dough with a 2-inch biscuit cutter to make 12 to 14 smaller scones.

3 · Place the scones about 1 inch apart on the prepared baking sheet. Bake in the center of the oven until crusty and golden brown, 15 to 20 minutes. Serve immediately, or cool on a rack and freeze in heavy-duty freezer bags for up to a month.

Santa Fe Scones

The flavors of the Southwest have leapt into Middle America's kitchens with a passion. Creamy mild Monterey Jack cheese, pungent red chili powder, sweet cornmeal, and crunchy fresh red bell peppers make a savory scone that is good with egg dishes for brunch or alongside supper entrées.

Makes 8 scones

2 cups unbleached all-purpose flour

½ cup fine-grind yellow, white, or blue cornmeal, preferably stone-ground

1 tablespoon baking powder

1 teaspoon commercial or homemade (page 331) chili powder

¼ teaspoon ground cumin

¼ teaspoon salt

½ cup (1 stick) cold unsalted butter, cut into pieces

2 ounces (½ cup) Monterey Jack cheese, cut into small cubes

½ cup seeded and minced red bell pepper, drained on a paper towel

2 large eggs

¾ cup cold buttermilk

1 · Preheat the oven to 400°F. Grease a baking pan or line it with parchment paper. In a medium bowl, combine the flour, cornmeal, baking powder, chili powder, cumin, and salt. Cut in the butter with a fork or a heavy-duty electric mixer until the mixture resembles coarse crumbs. Add the cheese and red pepper. Toss to combine. In a small bowl or 1-cup measure, whisk together the eggs and buttermilk. Add to the dry mixture and stir until a sticky dough is formed.

2 · Turn out the shaggy dough onto a lightly floured work surface and knead gently just until the dough holds together, about 6 times. Divide the dough into 2 equal portions and pat each into a 1-inch-thick round about 6 inches in diameter. With a knife or straightedge, cut each round into quarters, creating wedges. The scones can also be formed by cutting the dough with a 2-inch biscuit cutter to make 12 to 14 smaller scones.

3 · Place the scones on the prepared baking sheet about 1 inch apart. Bake in the center of the oven until crusty and golden brown, about 15 to 18 minutes. Serve immediately, or cool on a rack and freeze in heavy-duty freezer bags for up to a month.

Irish Soda Bread

My three great aunts, Nellie, Mamie, and Annie, were born in County Cork, southern Ireland, and immigrated to this country at the turn of the century, entering through Ellis Island. Nellie was known for the excellent baked goods she made in her iron wood-burning stove in their old Victorian home on Redmond Street in New Brunswick, New Jersey. One of her favorites, this crusty white bread, also known affectionately in Ireland as spotted dog, is great warm from the oven, or toasted and spread with soft goat cheese and jam after it has come to room temperature.

Makes 2 round loaves

4 cups unbleached all-purpose flour
¼ cup raw or granulated sugar
1 tablespoon baking powder
1 teaspoon baking soda
1 teaspoon cream of tartar
1½ teaspoons salt
1½ cups dried currants, rinsed in hot water
 and patted dry

3 tablespoons minced candied orange peel
 or dried pineapple
1½ cups cold buttermilk
4 tablespoons (½ stick) butter or margarine,
 melted
1 large egg

1 · Preheat the oven to 400°F. Line a baking sheet with parchment paper or grease two 8-inch round metal cake pans. In a large bowl, combine the flour, the sugar, if you are using it, the baking powder, baking soda, cream of tartar, salt, currants, and candied peel.

2 · In another bowl, combine the buttermilk, melted butter or margarine, and egg with a whisk. Add the wet ingredients to the dry, and stir with a wooden spoon just to moisten. Turn out onto a lightly floured surface and knead gently until the sticky dough just comes together, about 5 times, dusting with flour, if needed. Divide the dough into 2 equal portions and shape each into an 8-inch round. Sprinkle all over with flour.

3 · Place the rounds on the prepared baking sheet or in the cake pans. With a sharp knife, slash the tops with an X about ½ inch deep. Bake the loaves in the middle of the oven for 10 minutes, then reduce the oven temperature to 375°F and bake for an additional 20 to 25 minutes, or until the loaves are brown and crusty. Cool the loaves on the baking sheet. Serve them warm or at room temperature on the day they are baked.

Oat and Herb Brown Soda Bread

Every hotel and restaurant in Ireland has some type of house recipe for soda bread. The traditional bread is always round with a deep X marked into the top, and contains a combination of baking soda and buttermilk. Not only do soda breads sometimes include dried fruit; they are also made with seeds, spices, and, as here, herbs. The combination of whole wheat flour, oats, and wheat germ in this loaf is an attempt to approximate the texture of Irish whole-meal flour, which is not available in the United States.

Makes 2 round loaves

2 cups unbleached all-purpose flour
1 cup whole wheat flour
½ cup quick-cooking Irish oats
¼ cup toasted wheat germ
¼ cup packed light brown sugar
2½ teaspoons baking soda
1 teaspoon crumbled dried basil
1 teaspoon crumbled dried marjoram
½ teaspoon crumbled dried rosemary

½ teaspoon dried thyme
Pinch of caraway seeds
1 teaspoon salt
1 cup golden raisins
1¼ cups cold buttermilk
5 tablespoons unsalted butter or margarine, melted
1 large egg

1 · Preheat the oven to 375°F. Line a baking sheet with parchment paper or grease two 8-inch round metal cake pans. In a large bowl, combine the flours, oats, wheat germ, brown sugar, baking soda, herbs, caraway seeds, salt, and raisins.

2 · In another bowl, combine the buttermilk, melted butter or margarine, and egg with a whisk. Add the wet ingredients to the dry and stir with a wooden spoon just to moisten. Turn the dough out onto a lightly floured surface and knead gently until it just comes together, about 5 times, dusting with flour if needed. Divide the dough into 2 equal portions and shape each into a 7-inch round. Sprinkle all over with flour.

3 · Place the rounds on the prepared baking sheet or in the cake pans. With a sharp knife, slash the tops with an X about ½ inch deep. Bake in the middle of the oven for 35 to 40 minutes, or until the loaves are brown and crusty. Cool the loaves on the baking sheet. Serve warm or at room temperature, on the day they are baked.

Soda Bread with Caraway and Drambuie

Soda breads are Celtic country hearth breads made throughout the British Isles and originally baked in the wood-fired clay ovens built into home chimneys. This bread is easily mixed and baked, ready to serve to hungry diners in less than an hour. Drambuie is a romantic, Gaelic liqueur made of good Scotch malt whiskey, heather honey, and a secret collection of spices. Soda breads beg to be eaten crusty and warm, spread with butter or served with cheeses.

Makes 2 medium round loaves

1½ cups golden raisins
6 tablespoons Drambuie
2 cups unbleached all-purpose flour
2 cups whole wheat flour, preferably
  stone-ground
¼ cup packed light brown sugar
2 teaspoons baking powder

1 teaspoon baking soda
1 teaspoon salt
1 tablespoon caraway seeds
1½ cups buttermilk
2 large eggs
2 tablespoons unsalted butter, melted

1 · Combine the raisins and liqueur in a small bowl. Let stand at room temperature to macerate for 30 minutes.

2 · Preheat oven to 375°F. Grease a baking sheet or two 8-inch round metal cake pans or line them with parchment paper. In a large bowl, combine the flours, brown sugar, baking powder, baking soda, salt, and caraway seeds. In another bowl, combine the buttermilk, eggs, and butter and beat slightly with a whisk. Add the macerated raisins.

3 · Make a well in the dry ingredients and pour in the buttermilk-raisin mixture. Stir with a wooden spoon just to moisten. The dough will not be as stiff as yeast bread dough. Turn out onto a lightly floured work surface and knead gently until the dough comes together, about 5 times. Form by hand into 2 free-form round loaves and place on the prepared baking sheet or in the cake pans. With a serrated knife, make an X no more than ¼ inch deep on the top of each loaf to allow for expansion and even baking.

4 · Bake the loaves in the center of the oven until they sound hollow when tapped and are brown and crusty, about 40 to 50 minutes. Cool the loaves on the baking sheet. Serve warm or at room temperature on the same day they are made.

Whole Wheat Yogurt Bread with Dried Cherries

Whole Wheat Yogurt Bread is low in fat, because the recipe contains no butter or eggs in the manner of a traditional soda bread. I have been making this versatile loaf in one form or another for twenty years, serving it for lunch alongside a fresh green salad and a piece of good cheese. This loaf is especially good toasted and spread with homemade Yogurt Cheese (page 339). Mixed dried fruit or dark or golden raisins may be substituted for the dried cherries, if desired. Please do not forget to slash the X on top to keep the loaf from cracking open during baking.

Makes 2 small round loaves

2 cups whole wheat flour, preferably
  stone-ground
¾ cup unbleached all-purpose flour
¼ cup wheat bran flakes
2 teaspoons baking soda

½ teaspoon salt
2 cups plain yogurt
⅓ cup light molasses
1 cup dried cherries, soaked in hot water
  for 10 minutes and drained

1 · Preheat the oven to 350°F. Grease a baking sheet or two 8-inch round metal cake pans or line them with parchment paper. In a medium bowl, combine the flours, bran flakes, baking soda, and salt. In another bowl, combine the yogurt, molasses, and cherries and beat slightly with a whisk.

2 · Make a well in the dry ingredients and pour in the wet ingredients. Stir just until moistened. The dough will be very soft, even slightly sticky, and just able to hold its own shape. Divide the dough by hand into 2 free-form round loaves and place on the prepared baking sheet or in the cake pans. The loaves will be rough and cracked-looking with some flour on the surface. With a serrated knife, make an X no more than ¼ inch deep on the top of each loaf to allow for expansion and even baking.

3 · Bake the loaves in the center of the oven until the they sound hollow when tapped and are brown and crusty, about 55 to 60 minutes. Turn them out of the pans to cool on a rack. Serve warm or at room temperature on the same day they are made.

Wild Rice–Whole Wheat Soda Bread with Goat Cheese Butter

This is a connoisseur's soda bread—pure American ingredients in a traditional setting. Wholesome and sweet, whole wheat soda breads are certainly not unusual, but the wild rice in this version gives the loaves a moist and complex earthy character that I find inspiring. I can almost believe a soul lies within each grain, as the Chinese say. With this bread I serve my favorite mellow goat cheese spread, its flavor tempered with the addition of a mild cream cheese.

Makes 2 small free-form round loaves

2 cups whole wheat flour, preferably stone-ground
1 cup unbleached all-purpose flour
½ cup rolled oats
2 tablespoons packed light brown sugar
1 teaspoon baking soda

½ teaspoon salt
½ cup cooked wild rice (page 355)
1¼ cups buttermilk
2 tablespoons unsalted butter, melted
1 large egg
Goat Cheese Butter (optional), following

1 · Preheat the oven to 350°F. Grease a baking sheet or two 8-inch round metal cake pans or line them with parchment paper. In a medium bowl, combine the flours, oats, brown sugar, baking soda, and salt. In another bowl, combine the wild rice, buttermilk, melted butter, and egg and beat slightly with a whisk.

2 · Make a well in the dry ingredients and pour in the wet ingredients. Stir the batter just until moistened. Turn out onto a lightly floured work surface and knead gently until the dough comes together, about 5 times. Form by hand into 2 free-form round loaves and place on the prepared baking sheet or in the cake pans. With a serrated knife, make an X no more than ¼ inch deep on the top of each loaf to allow for expansion and even baking.

3 · Bake the loaves in the center of the oven until they sound hollow when tapped and are brown and crusty, about 40 to 50 minutes. Turn out of the pans to cool on a rack. Serve warm or at room temperature the same day they are made, with Goat Cheese Butter, if desired.

Goat Cheese Butter

Makes about 1½ cups butter

4 ounces fresh cream cheese, at room
 temperature
4 ounces fresh goat cheese, such as
 Montrachet or Chabis
½ cup (1 stick) unsalted butter, at room
 temperature
Grated zest of ½ orange (optional)

By hand in a bowl, or in a food
processor, combine the cream cheese,
goat cheese, and butter and beat just
until smooth, fluffy, and evenly combined. Transfer to a small serving
dish or decorative mold and sprinkle
the top with the orange zest, if you
are using it. Chill, covered, for from 1
hour to overnight. Let stand at room
temperature for 30 minutes before
serving.

Biscuits and Shortcakes

Biscuits and Shortcakes

In some households, biscuits are still *the* bread. Whether served for breakfast with jam, hot with cool salads, cold as a small sandwich, or even as a shortcake for dessert, biscuits can grace the most sophisticated dinner table with pride. The most memorable shortcakes I have ever eaten were served to me at the grand opening of Fetzer Vineyards' Valley Oaks Food and Wine Center in Hopland, California. Under a beautiful outdoor arbor, Chef Ralph Tingle served traditional strawberry shortcake in charming individual bite-sized portions. I will never take a berry shortcake for granted again.

Historically known as "saleratus biscuits" because of the type of leavening used in making them, the satisfying little breads had a quick-to-make and quick-to-bake reputation. Whether baked in old northeast and Appalachian cookstoves, on Southern plantations, in outdoor Dutch ovens, or for New York tea rooms, the biscuit quickly became a daily staple. They were firmly adopted by the male-centered cuisine of cowboys, lumberjacks, sea cooks, and Alaskan fishing camps. The simple bread could be made without expensive eggs, unreliable yeasts, and long baking times.

Southern cooks claim the honor of being the best biscuit makers. To achieve their superior results they use smoky-tasting homemade lard (*not* the same as super-processed commercial brands), the softest wheat pastry flour, and a good, strong 30-minute beating to tenderize the dough. Making perfect biscuits is possible for any baker who sets his or her mind to searching out a good recipe and fresh ingredients, and to following instructions carefully. A warm biscuit fresh from the oven is worth the time invested, even if you live above the Mason-Dixon line and have never heard of a biscuit brake (which is used for folding the beaten biscuit dough).

Many biscuit bakers swear by sifting the flour. If your goal is the most tender biscuits ever, then do it, but you can use your own judgment. The South boasts pure flours milled to a delicate lightness specifically for biscuits, such as White Lily, but all-purpose flour is also used. The War Eagle Grist Mill in Arkansas packages its own whole-grain biscuit mix, as do many small local mills. Another secret is *fresh* baking powder; less than four months old is best. Aside from the basic ingredients, biscuits can be further enhanced with the addition of whole grains, chopped fruits, nuts, and citrus rinds for truly endless variations. For shortcakes, sugar is added.

The techniques for making biscuits and shortcakes are very simple. Some type of ice-cold vegetable shortening, salted or unsalted butter, margarine, lard, even bear fat, (yes, they are all interchangeable; it is the flavor that will vary) is cut into a mixture of flour, baking powder, and salt. Generally, 2 to 3 tablespoons of fat per cup of flour is the ratio to look for. The swift motion of the fingers, a pastry blender, fork, or two knives may be used to break up the fat to form coarse crumbs. (An electric mixer or food processor makes good biscuits, but it is important that you not overmix.) It is this step that gives biscuits their unique flaky texture and makes them different from other types of quick breads. The moisture that evaporates when the cold fat comes in contact with the hot temperature during the baking creates a fine-grained layering effect similar to that of French puff pastry.

Cold liquid, usually heavy cream, buttermilk, or milk, is added all at once and stirred to create a soft dough that just holds together. Any other wet ingredients, such as pure extracts, juices, or eggs, are added at this time. Always hold back and reserve about 2 tablespoons of the liquid called for, and add it after mixing if the dough is too dry. To form drop biscuits, add at least ¼ cup more liquid. Dropped biscuits are not as delicate as their rolled cousins, but they are very good indeed. The secret to delicate biscuits is to handle the dough gently and to use just enough flour to make the dough manageable. Use a light touch to knead the very soft dough a few times with the heel of the hand and to distribute the moisture gently with a soft folding and rolling action. This step is necessary to create tender biscuits, but too much kneading makes them tough. Flour is used very sparingly for dusting, just to keep the delicate dough from sticking to the work surface, your hands, and the biscuit cutters. Keep a collection of cutters in a range of sizes and shapes, from the practical fluted round to the whimsical half-moon, for the greatest variety in shaping biscuits. The average biscuit is 2 inches in diameter. Unless otherwise specified, the yields listed in the following recipes are for standard-sized biscuits.

Roll or pat the dough to a thickness half the size you want the finished biscuit to be. Press a sharp cutter straight down into the dough with one push.

No twisting or the biscuit will bake un-evenly. Biscuits cut from the first roll-ing are more tender than those cut from subsequent rollings. Square bis-cuits can be made by cutting the dough into a grid with a chef's knife. After they are cut, for even greater height, you can place the dough upside down on the prepared baking sheet. To reroll the remaining dough, press the scraps together rather than kneading again, keeping the top surface as level as possible for an even biscuit.

For crisp-sided biscuits, place the shaped dough pieces ½ inch to 2 inches apart to allow for expansion, on an ungreased or parchment-lined baking sheet. For soft sides, let the raw shapes touch slightly. The tops can be brushed with milk or melted butter to yield shiny, soft crusts. A super-hot oven is imperative, so watch cooking times carefully. Smaller biscuits will bake to a golden brown faster than larger ones. Although bis-cuits can be eaten hot from the oven, it is best to let them rest for a few minutes after baking to allow excess moisture to evaporate. Every so often there is a stray leftover, so wrap the day-olds in foil and reheat them at 325°F for 10 to 12 minutes. Biscuits can also be frozen in plastic freezer bags for up to 2 months.

To Make Biscuits and Shortcakes in a Food Processor:

This method may be used with any of the biscuit or shortcake recipes that follow. Place the dry ingredients in the workbowl fitted with the steel blade. Process a few seconds just to aerate and mix. Place the butter in pieces on top of the flour mixture and replace the top. Process by puls-ing *just* until the butter is the size of small peas. Do not completely incor-porate the butter with the flour, or the biscuits will be tough. Add the cold liquid through the feed tube and pulse *just* until a wet mass is formed. Remove the dough from the work-bowl and continue to form and bake as directed in the recipe.

Classic Buttermilk Biscuits

This classic buttermilk biscuit has a proportion of three parts dry ingredients to one part tangy liquid to create a dough that will bake high and crisp crusted. These biscuits sit as easily, fresh and hot, at a regal dinner as they do rewarmed and slightly chewy, spread with jam the next morning. This recipe is a springboard to infinite flavor possibilities, the variations on the original recipe ranging from Pecan to Jalapeño to Blueberry, all superb. Please try them.

Makes about 1 dozen 2-inch dinner biscuits, or 2 dozen 1¼-inch cocktail biscuits

2 tablespoons unbleached all-purpose flour,
 for sprinkling on baking pan
2 tablespoons cornmeal, for sprinkling on
 baking pan
2 cups unbleached all-purpose flour
2 teaspoons baking powder
¼ teaspoon baking soda

¼ teaspoon salt
6 tablespoons (¾ stick) cold unsalted butter,
 margarine, or solid vegetable shortening,
 cut into pieces
1 large egg
¾ cup cold buttermilk

1 · Preheat the oven to 425°F. Grease a baking sheet or line it with parchment paper then sprinkle it with 2 tablespoons each of flour and cornmeal. In a bowl, combine the flour, baking powder, baking soda, and salt.

2 · Cut the butter into the dry ingredients with a pastry blender or two knives. The mixture should resemble coarse crumbs, with no large chunks of butter remaining. If the butter gets very soft at this point, refrigerate the mixture for 20 minutes to rechill. Add the egg and buttermilk, stirring just to moisten all the ingredients. The dough will be moist, then stiffen while stirring. It should be slightly shaggy, but not sticky.

3 · Turn the dough out onto a lightly floured work surface and knead gently about 10 times, or just until the dough holds together. Roll or pat out the dough into a rectangle ¾ inch thick. Take care not to add too much flour at this point or the biscuits will be tough. Cut the dough using a floured 2½-inch biscuit cutter, pushing straight down without twisting. Cut the biscuits

as close together as possible so there will be a minimum of scraps. Pack together and reroll the scraps to cut out additional biscuits.

4 · Place the shaped biscuits ½ inch apart on the prepared baking sheet. Bake immediately in the center of the oven for 15 to 18 minutes, or until golden brown. Let rest a few minutes and serve hot.

VARIATIONS:

Pecan Biscuits

Add ⅓ cup coarsely chopped toasted or raw pecans to the dry ingredients in Step 1. Proceed to mix, form, and bake as directed. For tea biscuits, add 3 tablespoons of sugar.

Wild Rice Biscuits

Add ⅔ cup cooled cooked wild rice (page 355) to the dry ingredients in Step 1. Proceed to mix, form, and bake as directed.

Jalapeño Biscuits

Add ¼ cup coarsely chopped fresh or canned jalapeños to the liquid ingredients in Step 2. Proceed to mix, form, and bake as directed.

Blueberry Biscuits

Add ¼ cup sugar to the dry ingredients in Step 1. Add ½ cup fresh or unthawed, frozen, blueberries and the grated zest of 1 orange to the liquid ingredients in Step 2. Proceed to mix, form, and bake as directed.

Whole Wheat Biscuits

Substitute ¾ cup whole wheat flour or 2 cups whole wheat pastry flour for an equal amount of unbleached flour and add to the dry ingredients in Step 1. Proceed to mix, form, and bake as directed.

Old-Fashioned Cream Biscuits

Cream Biscuits are as special as they are simple. They are made with heavy cream, which provides both the liquid and the fat, to create a creamy-colored, moist-textured little bread. If you love biscuits, these old-fashioned gems are the apex of the genre.

Makes about 14 biscuits

1¾ cups unbleached all-purpose flour
¼ cup whole wheat pastry flour
1 tablespoon baking powder

½ teaspoon salt
1 to 1¼ cups cold heavy cream

1 · Preheat the oven to 425°F. Grease a baking sheet or line it with parchment paper. In a mixing bowl, combine the flours, baking powder, and salt. Stir in 1 cup of heavy cream, then add additional cream, 1 tablespoon at a time, until a soft dough is formed.

2 · Turn the dough out onto a lightly floured work surface and knead gently about 10 times, or just until the dough holds together. Roll or pat out the dough into a rectangle ¾ inch thick. Take care not to add too much flour at this point or the biscuits will be tough. Cut the dough using a sharp knife or pastry wheel to form 14 squares. Alternatively, cut out biscuits using a floured 2½-inch biscuit cutter (I like the half-moon shape for these), pushing straight down without twisting, and rerolling the scraps to cut out additional biscuits.

3 · Place the shaped biscuits on the prepared baking sheet. Let stand for 20 minutes at room temperature. Bake in the center of the oven 15 to 18 minutes, or until golden brown. Let rest a few minutes and serve hot.

VARIATIONS:

Summer Cream Biscuits

Add ¼ cup total combined loosely packed coarsely chopped fresh watercress leaves, Italian parsley, and basil to the dry ingredients in Step 1. Proceed to mix, form, and bake as directed.

Breakfast Orange Cream Biscuits

Substitute ½ cup orange juice for an equal amount of the heavy cream in Step 1 and add the grated zest of 1 large orange. Proceed to mix, form, and bake as directed.

Cornmeal-Orange Biscuits

Enjoy Cornmeal-Orange Biscuits made with the juice of fresh oranges, picked from your back-yard tree, if possible. Otherwise, search out juicy California or Florida orbs. The nubby texture of cornmeal mingling with the orange undertones makes a mouth-watering dinner or brunch biscuit that will find its way into your cache of best recipes.

Makes 16 square biscuits

2 tablespoons unbleached all-purpose flour, for sprinkling on baking pan

2 tablespoons cornmeal, for sprinkling on baking pan

3 cups unbleached all-purpose flour

1 cup fine-grind yellow cornmeal, preferably stone-ground

2 tablespoons baking powder

2 tablespoons sugar

1 teaspoon cream of tartar

½ teaspoon salt

Grated zest of 1 large orange

¾ cup (1½ sticks) cold unsalted butter, cut into pieces

1 cup cold buttermilk

½ cup orange juice

1 · Preheat the oven to 425°F. Grease a baking sheet or line it with parchment paper, and sprinkle it with the 2 tablespoons of flour and the 2 tablespoons of cornmeal. In a bowl, combine the flour, cornmeal, baking powder, sugar, cream of tartar, salt, and orange zest.

2 · Cut the butter into the dry ingredients with a pastry blender or two knives. The mixture should resemble coarse crumbs, with no large chunks of butter remaining. Add the buttermilk and orange juice and stir just to moisten all the ingredients. The dough will be moist, then stiffen while stirring. It should be slightly shaggy, but not sticky.

3 · Turn the dough out onto a lightly floured work surface and knead gently about 10 times, or just until the dough holds together. Roll or pat out the dough into a ¾-inch-thick rectangle. Take care not to add too much flour at this point or the biscuits will be tough. Cut the dough using a sharp knife or pastry wheel to form 16 small squares.

4 · Place the squares ½ inch apart on the prepared baking sheet. Bake immediately in the center of the oven for 15 to 18 minutes, or until golden brown. Let rest a few minutes and serve hot.

Sweet-Potato Biscuits

I have been making these biscuits every fall for years, and I still adore them. The sweet potato makes them dense, sweet, and moist. They are as excellent served with roasted and grilled meats as they are with butter and honey. Sweet-Potato Biscuits are a must for winter holiday tables. For a filling hors d'oeuvre, use them to sandwich slices of smoked turkey.

Makes about 1 dozen biscuits

1 large sweet potato or yam (about 10 ounces), baked and peeled
1⅔ cups unbleached all-purpose flour
1 tablespoon packed light brown sugar
2½ teaspoons baking powder

½ teaspoon salt
6 tablespoons (¾ stick) cold unsalted butter, cut into pieces
¼ cup cold milk or half-and-half

1 · Mash or puree the sweet potato pulp by hand, in a blender, or in a food processor until smooth. You should have about ¾ cup. Preheat the oven to 425°F. Grease a baking sheet or line it with parchment paper. In a bowl, combine the flour, sugar, baking powder, and salt.

2 · Cut the butter into the dry ingredients with a pastry blender or two knives. The mixture should resemble coarse crumbs, with no large chunks of butter remaining. Add the sweet potato pulp and milk or cream and stir just to moisten all the ingredients. The dough will be moist, then stiffen while stirring. It should be slightly shaggy, but not sticky.

3 · Turn the dough out onto a lightly floured work surface and knead gently about 10 times, or just until the dough holds together. Roll or pat out the dough into a ¾-inch-thick rectangle. Take care not to add too much flour at this point or the biscuits will be tough. Cut the dough using a floured 2-inch biscuit cutter, pushing straight down without twisting. Reroll the scraps to cut out additional biscuits.

4 · Place the shaped biscuits ½ inch apart on the prepared baking sheet. Bake immediately in the center of the oven for 15 to 18 minutes, or until golden brown. Let rest a few minutes and serve hot.

Banana–Whole Wheat Biscuits

Bananas are the original forbidden fruit of the Hindus, and for centuries the "Tree of Paradise" was cultivated only in Southeast Asian monasteries to provide shade and sustenance for the holy wise men. Luckily, we mortals can now easily enjoy the nurturing quality and tropical flavor of the banana. These unusual biscuits are luscious for brunch with sweet butter and jam and are a perfect snack for children. For serving with cocktails, use the biscuits to sandwich thin slices of Black Forest ham and honey mustard.

Makes about 18 biscuits

1½ cups whole wheat pastry flour
¾ cup unbleached all-purpose flour
1 tablespoon baking powder
¼ teaspoon baking soda
½ teaspoon salt
6 tablespoons (¾ stick) cold unsalted butter,
  cut into pieces

½ cup sour cream
1 medium ripe banana, mashed
¼ cup cold milk or fresh coconut milk
  (page 334)

1 · Preheat the oven to 425°F. Grease a baking sheet or line it with parchment paper. In a bowl, combine the flours, baking powder, baking soda, and salt.

2 · Cut the butter into the dry ingredients with a pastry blender or two knives. The mixture should resemble coarse crumbs, with no large chunks of butter remaining. Add the sour cream, mashed banana, and milk and stir just to moisten all the ingredients. The dough will be moist, then stiffen while stirring. It should be slightly shaggy, but not sticky.

3 · Turn the dough out onto a lightly floured work surface and knead gently about 10 times, or just until the dough holds together. Roll or pat out the dough into a ¾-inch-thick rectangle. Take care not to add too much flour at this point or the biscuits will be tough. Cut the dough using a floured 2-inch biscuit cutter, pushing straight down without twisting. Reroll the scraps to cut out additional biscuits.

4 · Place the shaped biscuits ½ inch apart on the prepared baking sheet. Bake immediately in the center of the oven for 15 to 18 minutes, or until golden brown. Let rest a few minutes and serve hot.

Whole Wheat Dinner Biscuits

I am a lover of biscuits for dinner, and this is the recipe I make the most often. The combination of whole wheat flour and cake flour makes for one light, tender biscuit! Serve these biscuits with butter when they are still hot, and with cream cheese and jelly when cold for a snack with tea.

Makes 9 to 10 biscuits

1 cup whole wheat flour
1 cup cake flour
1 tablespoon baking powder
½ teaspoon baking soda
½ teaspoon salt
6 tablespoons (¾ stick) cold unsalted butter
  or margarine, cut into pieces

1 large egg yolk
¾ cup cold buttermilk
2 tablespoons unsalted butter or margarine,
  melted, for brushing
1½ tablespoons sesame seeds or poppy
  seeds, for sprinkling

1 · Preheat the oven to 425°F. Grease a 9-inch round metal cake pan. In a bowl, combine the flours, baking powder, baking soda, and salt.

2 · Cut the butter or margarine into the dry ingredients with a pastry blender or two knives. The mixture should resemble coarse crumbs, with no large chunks of butter or margarine remaining. If the butter or margarine gets very soft at this point, refrigerate the mixture for 20 minutes to rechill. Add the egg yolk and buttermilk, stirring just to moisten all the ingredients. The dough will be moist, then stiffen while stirring. It should be slightly shaggy, but not sticky.

3 · Turn the dough out onto a lightly floured work surface and knead gently about 10 times, or just until the dough holds together. Roll or pat out the dough into a ¾-inch-thick rectangle. Take care not to use too much flour on the work surface or the biscuits will be tough. Cut the dough using a floured 2½- to 3-inch biscuit cutter, pushing straight down without twisting. Cut the biscuits as close together as possible so there will be a minimum of scraps. Pack together and reroll the scraps to cut out additional biscuits.

4 · Place the shaped biscuits with their sides just touching in the prepared cake pan. Brush the tops with the melted butter or margarine and sprinkle with the sesame or poppy seeds. Bake in the center of the oven for 20 to 25 minutes, or until golden brown and firm to the touch. Let rest for 5 minutes in the pan and slide out into a basket. Pull apart and serve hot.

Poppy Seed–Cheese Biscuits

Here is a dinner biscuit with a crisp crust, tender texture, golden color, and lofty sides that give a tempting glimpse into a multitude of flaky layers. The cheese is so good with the poppy seed topping, you'll be glad to have made a big batch. Poppy Seed–Cheese Biscuits put to shame the premade commercial types that come from pop-open cans. For before-dinner snacks, cut the biscuits into smaller squares to make about 40 to 48 hot appetizers.

Makes about 24 biscuits

2 tablespoons unbleached all-purpose flour, for sprinkling on baking sheet

2 tablespoons wheat germ, for sprinkling on baking sheet

3 cups unbleached all-purpose flour

½ cup nonfat dry milk powder

⅓ cup grated mozzarella cheese

⅓ cup grated sharp New York cheddar cheese

¼ cup toasted wheat germ

4 teaspoons baking powder

¾ teaspoon cream of tartar

½ teaspoon salt

¾ cup (1½ sticks) cold unsalted butter, cut into pieces

1 large egg

1¼ cups cold water

1 large egg beaten with 1 teaspoon water, for glaze

3 tablespoons poppy seeds, for sprinkling

1 · Preheat the oven to 375°F. Grease a baking sheet or line it with parchment paper; sprinkle the baking sheet with 2 tablespoons of flour and 2 tablespoons of wheat germ. In a bowl, combine the flour, milk powder, cheeses, wheat germ, baking powder, cream of tartar, and salt.

2 · Cut the butter into the dry ingredients with a pastry blender or two knives. The mixture should resemble coarse crumbs, with no large chunks of butter remaining. Add the egg and cold water and stir just to moisten all the ingredients. The dough will be moist, then stiffen while stirring. It should be slightly shaggy, but not sticky.

3 · Turn the dough out onto a lightly floured work surface and knead gently about 10 times, or just until the dough holds together. Roll or pat out the dough into a 1-inch-thick rectangle. Take care not to add too much flour at

this point or the biscuits will be tough. Cut the dough using a sharp knife or pastry wheel to form 24 squares.

4 · Place the squares ½ inch apart on the prepared baking sheet. Beat the egg glaze in a small bowl until foamy and brush over the tops of the biscuits to glaze. Sprinkle each biscuit with poppy seeds. Bake immediately in the center of the oven for 15 to 20 minutes, or until golden brown. Let rest a few minutes and serve hot.

Old-Fashioned Shortcake Biscuits with Grand Marnier Strawberries and Crème Chantilly

Genuine fruit shortcakes are an American summer passion. It is the balance of sweet, juicy fruit, fluffy whipped cream, and crumby, rich biscuits that make them irresistible. This version serves them up with Grand Marnier Strawberries and Crème Chantilly (following), the brain-child of my baker-friend Janet Gentes for the Country Gourmet restaurant. Start with ripe berries, then whip the cream with just a dash of sugar and a splash of liqueur for a hint of flavoring. If whipped cream is not part of your diet, substitute crème fraîche, plain yogurt, or frozen yogurt. The biscuit must be impeccably fresh, crisp on the outside and soft on the inside.

Makes 8 shortcakes

2 cups unbleached all-purpose flour
2 tablespoons sugar
1 tablespoon baking powder
½ teaspoon salt
½ cup (1 stick) cold unsalted butter, cut into pieces

1 large egg
⅓ to ½ cup cold milk, buttermilk, or heavy cream, plus more if necessary
Grand Marnier Strawberries and Crème Chantilly, following

1 · Preheat the oven to 400°F. Take out a baking sheet and line it with parchment paper or leave it ungreased. In a mixing bowl, combine the flour, sugar, baking powder, and salt. Cut the butter pieces into the dry ingredients using a pastry blender or two knives until the mixture resembles coarse cornmeal laced with small chunks of butter. Combine the egg and the milk, buttermilk, or heavy cream in a measuring cup or small bowl. Add to the dry ingredients and stir just until moistened. If the mixture seems too dry, add additional milk, buttermilk, or heavy cream 1 tablespoon at a time.

2 · Turn the dough out onto a clean work surface and gently knead a few times just until the dough comes together. The dough will not be totally smooth. Roll out to a thickness of 1 inch and cut into 4-inch circles, squares, or hearts. Individual shortcakes can be made as small as 1½ inches (the dough can also be formed into 1 large biscuit that can be filled then cut into wedges to serve). Place the individual shortcakes about 1 inch apart on the prepared

baking sheet. Place another baking sheet of the same dimensions under-neath (known as double-panning) to prevent the bottoms from burning.

3 · Bake the shortcakes in the center of the oven until the tops are brown and firm to the touch, about 15 to 18 minutes. Cool on racks.

4 · To serve, cut the warm or room temperature biscuits in half horizontally with a serrated knife. Place the lower portion of each biscuit on an individual serving plate and top with the prepared Grand Marnier Strawberries and chilled Crème Chantilly. Cover with the biscuit tops. Serve immediately.

Grand Marnier Strawberries and Crème Chantilly

If you would like a shortcake without liqueur, substitute an equal amount of orange juice or 2 to 3 teaspoons of good imported balsamic vinegar, to taste, on the berries (it is a remarkable combination) with a teaspoon of vanilla extract to flavor the whipped cream.

Makes enough topping for one batch of Old-Fashioned Shortcake Biscuits

3 to 4 pints ripe strawberries, washed, dried, and hulled
3 tablespoons orange liqueur, such as Grand Marnier, divided
5 tablespoons superfine sugar, divided
2 cups cold heavy cream

1 · To make the Grand Marnier Strawberries: In a large bowl, crush 1 pint of the strawberries. Mix in 2 tablespoons of the orange liqueur and 3 tablespoons of sugar. Slice or halve the remaining berries and add to the crushed berries. Set aside.

2 · To make the Crème Chantilly: In a chilled bowl using an electric mixer, whip the heavy cream with the remaining 2 tablespoons of sugar and 1 table-spoon of the orange liqueur until soft peaks form. Cover and chill until serving.

VARIATIONS:

Poppy Seed Shortcakes

Add 2 tablespoons fresh poppy seeds to the dry ingredients in Step 1. Continue to mix, shape, and bake as directed. These shortcakes are good with fresh plum slices.

Orange Shortcakes

Substitute 3 tablespoons frozen orange juice concentrate, thawed, for an equal amount of milk, buttermilk, or heavy cream in the liquid ingredients in Step 1. Continue to mix and shape as directed. Sprinkle the tops with 2 tablespoons of sugar mixed with the grated zest of 1 orange, and bake. These shortcakes are good with fresh peach slices.

Lavender Sugar Shortcakes

Substitute 2 tablespoons Homemade Lavender Sugar (recipe follows) for the plain sugar in the dry ingredients in Step 1. Continue to mix and shape as directed. Sprinkle the tops with an additional 2 tablespoons of the Homemade Lavender Sugar before baking. These shortcakes are good with fresh nectarine slices.

Homemade Lavender Sugar

Makes ½ cup flavored sugar

½ cup sugar
1 heaping tablespoon dried, unsprayed
  lavender flowers

In a food processor, combine the sugar and lavender flowers. Process until well combined. Store in an airtight canister.

Cinnamon and Caramelized Walnut Shortcakes

Add ⅓ cup chopped Caramelized Walnuts (recipe follows) and 1 tea-spoon ground cinnamon to the dry ingredients in Step 1. Continue to mix, shape, and bake as directed. These shortcakes are good with fresh raspberries.

Caramelized Walnuts

Makes ⅓ cup walnuts

15 walnut halves
15 bamboo skewers
½ cup sugar
¼ cup water

Skewer each walnut onto the end of a bamboo pick. In a small saucepan, combine the sugar and water over medium heat. Cover and cook for about 3 to 4 minutes without stirring until the syrup is a golden amber. Remove from the heat and dip each walnut into the syrup to completely coat the nut. Set the dipped nuts up against the rim of a plate to cool and harden. Remove each nut from its skewer and store in a covered container until needed, up to 1 week.

Amaretti Peach Shortcakes

From a small restaurant called Casa de Comida de Josie, on Water Street in Santa Fe, New Mexico, came the inspiration for these oversized squares of very tender shortcake that sandwich sweet mountain peaches. Josie wouldn't part with the treasured recipe, so until this re-creation, the recipe was lost when the café closed. The cream served at Josie's was hand-whipped just until very soft; it wouldn't even hold a peak. Almonds and almond extract pair naturally with a stone fruit like peaches. For added texture, these shortcakes contain crushed amaretti cookies, the Italian macaroons sold in the pretty red tins by Lazzaroni. The smell of both the dough and the finished biscuits is heavenly.

Makes 8 shortcakes

Peach Filling

3½ pounds very ripe but firm and good-
  flavored fresh peaches
½ to ¾ cup granulated sugar, or to taste
Juice of 1 large lemon
Chantilly Cream, following

5 pairs (½ ounce each) amaretti cookies
  (10 cookies)
1¼ cups white whole wheat flour or
  all-purpose flour
1 cup cake flour
3 tablespoons granulated sugar

1 tablespoon baking powder
1 teaspoon baking soda
1 teaspoon cream of tartar
1¼ teaspoons salt
½ cup (1 stick) cold unsalted butter
½ cup sour cream, measured in a dry
  measure, packed
1 teaspoon almond extract
About ¼ cup cold buttermilk
Milk or water, for brushing
⅓ cup sliced almonds, for sprinkling
¼ cup powdered sugar, for dusting

1 · Blanch the peaches in a large saucepan of boiling water for 10 to 15 seconds. With a slotted spoon, transfer the peaches to a bowl of ice water. Then place each peach on a layer of paper towel and slip off the skin with your fingers or a paring knife. Halve and pit the peaches. Cut them into ½-inch-thick slices and place in a large bowl (I use one that has a plastic lid). You will have about 7 cups. Sprinkle with the sugar and add the lemon juice. Stir the mixture together. Cover and refrigerate until needed, at least 2 hours. Make the Chantilly Cream (following).

2 · Preheat the oven to 450°F. Line a large baking sheet with parchment paper, preferably, or leave the baking sheet ungreased, or line it with foil. Place the amaretti in a small bowl and, using your thumb, coarsely crush the cookies. In the workbowl of a heavy-duty electric mixer, combine the crushed amaretti, the flours, sugar, baking powder, baking soda, cream of tartar, and salt on low speed.

3 · Cut the butter into 12 slices, then cut the sliced stick in half lengthwise. Distribute the pieces over the top of the flour mixture. With the mixer running on low, cut in the butter until the mixture resembles coarse crumbs laced with small chunks of butter, 2 to 3 minutes.

4 · Stop the mixer and add the sour cream. Combine the almond extract and the buttermilk in a small bowl or a 1-cup measure and pour in. Mix on low until the dough forms a sticky mass, about 30 seconds. Increase the speed to medium for about 25 seconds; the batter will form a moist, sticky clump on the paddle and clear the sides of the bowl. Do not overmix; you want to mix the dough only lightly.

5 · Sprinkle a smooth work surface with some cake flour. Scrape down the paddle and the sides and bottom of the bowl with a rubber spatula or plastic dough card, and add to the mass of dough. Sprinkle the top of the dough with some cake flour. With floured fingers, gently knead 8 to 10 strokes. Press and pat the dough into a rectangular cake about 7-by-8 inches and 1¼ to 1½ inches thick. With a sharp chef's knife, cut the cake into 8 squares. Place the squares 1 inch apart on the baking sheet. Brush the tops with some milk or water and sprinkle with the sliced almonds. Place another baking sheet of the same dimensions underneath the baking sheet (known as double-panning) to prevent the bottoms from burning.

6 · Reduce the oven temperature to 400°F. Bake the shortcake biscuits in the center of the oven until firm to the touch and the tops and bottoms are golden brown, about 15 to 18 minutes. Cool on the pan at least 20 minutes before splitting.

7 · To serve, warm the shortcakes slightly if they are at room temperature. Carefully separate the top from the bottom with your fingers. Place the lower portion of each biscuit on an individual dessert plate and, using an oversized spoon, spoon the peaches and their juices over the biscuit, using a scant cup of fruit for each shortcake. Spoon plenty of Chantilly Cream over the top of the peaches, letting it ooze down the sides, and cover with the biscuit tops. Dust the top of each biscuit with a coating of powdered sugar sifted through a mesh sieve. Serve immediately, passing a bowl of the extra Chantilly Cream.

Chantilly Cream

"Chantilly" describes whipped cream that is very softly whipped. It clings to the beater, yet it will move if the bowl is tilted. It is fluffy enough that it will create swirl patterns in the bowl when stirred with a spatula or beater. This is a good all-purpose whipped cream for shortcakes.

Makes about 4 cups topping

2 cups (1 pint) cold heavy cream
¼ cup sugar
2 teaspoons vanilla extract

Place the bowl and beater(s) in the freezer for at least 1 hour to chill thoroughly. Place the cream, sugar, and vanilla in the bowl. Whip on high speed with an electric mixer until soft peaks form, about 3 minutes. Cover and refrigerate until serving. Just before assembling the shortcakes, use a balloon whisk to hand-whip the cream, adjusting the consistency and integrating any separated liquid. Use no more than 10 vigorous strokes.

Chocolate Shortcakes with Stewed Rhubarb

This unusual shortcake is a memorable pairing of chocolate with ruby-colored rhubarb. A neglected summer fruit, rhubarb is often grown in old-fashioned backyard vegetable gardens. When stewed, it combines well with fresh strawberries or raspberries, so if you wish to, stir some in. Remember to use only the stalks, because the leaves contain a high concentration of oxalic acid, which is poisonous.

Makes 12 dropped shortcakes

2 cups unbleached all-purpose flour
½ cup unsweetened cocoa powder
½ cup sugar
2 teaspoons baking powder
1 teaspoon baking soda
¼ teaspoon salt

6 tablespoons (¾ stick) cold unsalted butter, cut into pieces
⅔ cup milk, buttermilk, or heavy cream, plus more if necessary
Stewed Rhubarb, following
Sweetened whipped cream, for topping

1 · Preheat the oven to 425°F. Line a baking sheet with parchment paper or leave it ungreased. In a mixing bowl, combine the flour, cocoa powder, sugar, baking powder, baking soda, and salt. Cut the butter pieces into the dry ingredients with a pastry blender or two knives until the mixture resembles coarse cornmeal laced with small chunks of butter. Add the milk, buttermilk, or heavy cream to the dry ingredients and stir just until moistened and a sticky dough is formed. If the mixture seems too dry, add additional milk, buttermilk, or heavy cream 1 tablespoon at a time.

2 · Drop the dough by big rounded tablespoonfuls, about 2 inches apart, onto the prepared baking sheet. It is important to mound the dough, as the biscuits spread during baking. Place another baking sheet of the same dimensions underneath (known as double-panning) to prevent the bottoms from burning.

3 · Bake in the center of the oven until the tops are brown and spring back when touched, about 15 to 17 minutes. Cool on racks. The biscuits will crisp slightly as they cool.

4 · To serve, cut the warm or room temperature biscuits in half horizontally with a serrated knife. Place the lower portion of each biscuit on an individual serving plate and top with Stewed Rhubarb and chilled sweetened whipped cream. Cover with the biscuit tops. Serve immediately.

Stewed Rhubarb

Makes about 3½ cups fruit

4 cups ½-inch-thick slices fresh rhubarb (3 to 4 stalks), or two 12-ounce packages frozen rhubarb, thawed

¾ cup orange dessert wine, such as Essencia, or other fruity wine, such as apricot or mead, divided

1½ cups sugar

2 tablespoons cornstarch

2 tablespoons unsalted butter

Combine the rhubarb, ½ cup of the wine, and the sugar in a heavy saucepan. Bring to a boil, reduce the heat to low, and simmer until tender, about 10 minutes. Combine the cornstarch and remaining ¼ cup of wine in a small bowl. Stir into the hot rhubarb mixture with a whisk. Cook until slightly thickened, about 1 minute. Remove from the heat and stir in the butter. Serve warm or chilled.

Pumpkin Shortcakes with Winter Fruit Compote

Although shortcakes are normally served with juicy fresh fruit, a compote that takes advantage of premium canned, dried, or frozen fruit is perfect for the winter months. If you are a wine harvest buff, in early fall use an available variety of fresh grapes such as Cabernet, Concord, or Zinfandel in place of the seedless grapes (but seed them first). I favor Bargetto fruit wines from Santa Cruz, California, for cooking and macerating the fruits for the compote. With their kaleidoscope of shiny, jewel-like colors, Pumpkin Shortcakes with Winter Fruit Compote are ideal for a cold-weather holiday brunch.

Makes 10 shortcakes

Yellow cornmeal, for sprinkling on baking
 pan
2½ cups unbleached all-purpose flour
½ cup packed light brown sugar
1 tablespoon baking powder
½ teaspoon fresh-ground nutmeg
¼ teaspoon salt
½ cup (1 stick) cold unsalted butter, cut
 into pieces

½ cup pumpkin puree, homemade (page
 351) or canned
¾ cup milk, buttermilk, or heavy cream,
 plus more if necessary
Winter Fruit Compote, following
Sweetened whipped cream or cold crème
 fraîche (page 339), for topping

1 · Preheat the oven to 375°F. Line a baking sheet with parchment paper or leave it ungreased; sprinkle the baking sheet with yellow cornmeal. In a mixing bowl, combine the flour, brown sugar, baking powder, nutmeg, and salt. Cut the butter pieces into the dry ingredients with a pastry blender or two knives until the mixture resembles coarse cornmeal laced with small chunks of butter. Add the pumpkin puree and the milk, buttermilk, or heavy cream to the dry ingredients and stir just until moistened, adding additional liquid 1 tablespoon at a time if the mixture seems too dry.

2 · Turn the dough out onto a clean work surface and gently knead a few times just until the dough comes together. The dough will not be totally smooth. Roll out to a thickness of 1 inch and cut into 3-inch circles, squares, or

hearts. Individual shortcakes can be made as small as 1½ inches (the dough can also be formed into 1 large biscuit for a shortcake that can be filled and cut into wedges to serve). Place the individual shortcakes about 1 inch apart on the prepared baking sheet. Place another baking sheet of the same dimensions underneath (known as double-panning) to prevent the bottoms from burning.

3 · Bake the shortcakes in the center of the oven until the tops are brown and firm to the touch, about 18 to 20 minutes. Cool on racks. Serve warm or at room temperature.

4 · To serve, cut the biscuits in half horizontally with a serrated knife. Place the lower portion of each biscuit on an individual dessert plate, and ladle with the Winter Fruit Compote and chilled sweetened whipped cream or crème fraîche. Cover with the biscuit tops. Serve immediately, passing more compote in the traditional footed serving dish, called a *compotier*.

Winter Fruit Compote

Makes about 4 cups fruit

½ pound dried apricots
1 cup apricot wine
¼ cup sugar
Juice and zest of 1 lemon
1 cup pitted whole dried prunes
One 8-ounce can pineapple chunks in unsweetened juice, undrained
One 16-ounce can sliced peaches, drained, or 2 cups unsweetened frozen peaches
One 11-ounce can mandarin oranges, undrained, or 2 fresh tangerines, seeded and sectioned
1 cup seedless green or red grapes
1 cup fresh or frozen whole unsweetened raspberries
⅓ cup slivered blanched almonds

2 tablespoons chopped candied ginger, candied orange peel, or candied lemon peel

Place the dried apricots, wine, sugar, and lemon juice and zest in a large saucepan. Bring to a boil, reduce heat, and simmer for 20 minutes, uncovered. Remove from the heat and add the prunes, pineapple, peaches, and orange sections. Let cool until warm and add the grapes, raspberries, almonds, and candied ginger, candied orange peel, or candied lemon peel. Serve slightly warm.

Tomato-Gorgonzola Shortcakes

Years ago I wrote a newspaper story in which I discussed how to use home garden vegetable surpluses by baking them into quick breads. Among the people I polled to write the article and those who read it, this was one of the most popular recipes. It has a unique combination of ingredients. Adapted from a recipe by the late Bert Greene, it is a luscious savory shortcake for the hot summer months. Serve with sliced cold ham, or with barbecued steak and chicken.

Makes 8 shortcakes

6 tablespoons (¾ stick) unsalted butter, at room temperature
3 ounces Gorgonzola cheese, at room temperature
4 or 5 large ripe tomatoes (about 2 pounds), seeded and coarsely chopped
3 tablespoons balsamic vinegar
2 cups unbleached all-purpose flour
2 teaspoons baking powder
½ teaspoon salt
¼ teaspoon fresh-ground nutmeg

¼ teaspoon fresh-ground white pepper
⅓ cup cold buttermilk, plus more if necessary
1 large egg
1 cup cold heavy cream, for whipping
1 tablespoon minced fresh basil
1 tablespoon minced fresh chives
Pinch of salt, or to taste
8 fresh basil leaves, or small sprigs, for garnish

1 · In a small bowl with an electric mixer or by hand, cream the butter and the Gorgonzola cheese until fluffy. Refrigerate for 1 to 2 hours to chill thoroughly. Sprinkle the tomatoes with the balsamic vinegar and chill for at least 1 hour.

2 · Preheat the oven to 425°F. Line a baking sheet with parchment paper or leave it ungreased. In a mixing bowl, combine the flour, baking powder, salt, nutmeg, and white pepper. Cut the butter-cheese mixture into the dry ingredients with a pastry blender or two knives until the mixture resembles coarse cornmeal laced with small chunks of butter and cheese. Combine the buttermilk and egg in a measuring cup or small bowl. Add to the dry ingredients and stir just until moistened, adding additional buttermilk 1 tablespoon at a time if the mixture seems too dry.

3 · Turn the dough out onto a clean work surface and gently knead a few times just until the dough comes together. The dough will not be totally smooth. Roll out to a 1-inch thickness and cut into 3-inch circles, squares, or hearts. Individual shortcakes can be made as small as 1½ inches across (the dough can also be formed into 1 large biscuit that can be filled and cut into wedges to serve). Place the individual shortcakes about 1 inch apart on the prepared baking sheet. Place another baking sheet of the same dimensions underneath (known as double-panning) to prevent the bottoms from burning.

4 · Bake in the center of the oven until the tops are brown and firm to the touch, about 12 to 15 minutes. Leave on the baking sheet or transfer to a wire rack to cool.

5 · Just before serving, in a chilled bowl using an electric mixer, whip the heavy cream with the herbs and with the salt to taste until soft peaks form. The herbed whipped cream can be covered and chilled for up to 4 hours before assembling the shortcakes.

6 · To serve, cut the warm or room-temperature biscuits in half horizontally with a serrated knife. Place the lower portion of each biscuit on an individual serving plate. Ladle the top with about ¼ cup of the chilled tomatoes, then top with a dollop of herbed whipped cream. Place a whole basil leaf atop the whipped cream to garnish, if desired. Cover with the biscuit tops. Serve immediately.

$\mathcal{P}$each Cobbler

It should be possible to make good summer desserts with ingredients that require little fuss: a pile of fragrant, ripe fresh fruit, and a few staples from the everyday pantry. After eating your fill of fresh fruit out of hand, use the rest to make a lightly sweetened stewed fruit filling and top it with a roughly shaped layer of plain old-fashioned biscuit dough; in other words, make a cobbler. Peach Cobbler probably is the most popular of the genre. Use firm-textured fruit from the yellow freestone and clingstone varieties. Peaches have velvety skins that will slip off when peeled with a paring knife, but for big jobs, lower the fruits into boiling water for 10 to 15 seconds, one at a time, using a large slotted spoon. Transfer the peaches to a bowl of ice water. Place each peach on a paper towel and slip off the skin with your fingers or a paring knife.

Cobblers probably get their name from the method of spoon-dropping biscuit dough over the fruit. The dough bakes up into a lumpy, cobbled-looking golden-brown, sugar-crusted shortcake. The dessert is deceptively simple, with a balance of sweet and tart flavors. Cobblers tend to be juicy, rather than thickened like a pie.

The following recipe is adapted from the Cooks' Round Table of Endorsed Recipes *(Better Homes and Gardens, 1949) and has stood the supreme test of time by being served to decades of food connoisseurs. It is still voted the best-tasting peach cobbler ever, possibly due to the dash of almond extract that accents the beautiful filling that heats in the oven and partially cooks the peaches before they are topped with the biscuit dough.*

Makes 6 servings

Peach Filling

6 cups fresh peaches (about 3 pounds),
  peeled, pitted, and thickly sliced
½ cup sugar
Grated zest of 2 lemons
2 tablespoons fresh lemon juice
2 teaspoons almond extract

Biscuit Dough

1½ cups unbleached all-purpose flour
1 tablespoon baking powder
1 tablespoon sugar
½ teaspoon salt
6 tablespoons (¾ stick) cold unsalted butter,
  cut into small pieces
½ cup cold milk, plus additional drops if
  necessary
1 large egg
2 tablespoons sugar, for sprinkling

1 · Preheat the oven to 400°F. Grease a shallow 13-by-9-inch rectangular baking dish or 10- to 12-inch oval ceramic gratin dish.

2 · To prepare the Peach Filling: Place the fruit in the prepared dish and toss it with the sugar, lemon zest, lemon juice, and almond extract. Place the fruit in the hot oven for 10 minutes while preparing the biscuit dough topping.

3 · To prepare the biscuit topping: Combine the flour, baking powder, sugar, and salt in a medium bowl or in a food processor. Cut in the cold butter with a fork or by pulsing the processor until the mixture resembles coarse meal. Make a well in the center and add the milk and egg, then mix or pulse until just evenly moistened, adding the extra drops of milk if necessary. Do not overmix.

4 · Remove the peaches from the oven. Working quickly, drop the dough by large tablespoons over the hot peaches so that the edges of the dough do not touch the sides of the dish. You do not want to cover the fruit layer completely with the dough (leave some spaces for the steam to evaporate). Sprinkle the top with the remaining 2 tablespoons of sugar. The dough will act as a lid during baking, creating the steam needed to cook the fruit in its own juices. Immediately return the dish to the oven and bake for 25 to 30 minutes, until the topping is golden brown and firm to the touch. Serve warm or at room temperature, with ice cream or with some cold heavy cream poured over.

Cherry Cobbler

Here is the second most popular cobbler that I make. The recipe came from my friend the home chef Rosemarie, and she scribbled "The best!" all over it. Whereas the peach cobbler has the biscuit batter dropped on top, this cobbler has little rolled-out biscuits laid over the top for an entirely different look. Serve it with the Rum Whipped Cream (following), which has some sour cream folded in to give it more substance. This cobbler can be made with fresh cherries in the summer and, conveniently, frozen pitted cherries in the winter. Serve it still warm if you can.

Makes 6 servings

Cherry Filling

½ cup sugar

2 tablespoons cornstarch

½ teaspoon ground cinnamon (or apple pie spice)

¼ teaspoon fresh-ground nutmeg

Grated zest of 1 lemon

6 cups pitted fresh tart cherries (about 2 pounds) or two 16-ounce bags frozen pitted cherries, thawed

2 tablespoons fresh lemon juice

3 tablespoons cold unsalted butter, cut into pieces

Biscuit Dough

1 cup unbleached all-purpose flour

3 tablespoons sugar

1½ teaspoons baking powder

½ teaspoon salt

2 tablespoons (¼ stick) cold unsalted butter, cut into small pieces

⅔ cup cold heavy cream or half-and-half, plus more if necessary

1½ tablespoons unsalted butter, melted, for brushing

2 tablespoons sugar, for sprinkling

Rum Whipped Cream (optional), following

1 · Preheat the oven to 400°F. Grease a shallow 9-inch square baking dish or 9-inch round ceramic baking dish.

2 · To prepare the Cherry Filling: In a small bowl, combine the sugar, cornstarch, spices, and lemon zest and stir. Place the fruit in the prepared pan. Toss the fruit with the lemon juice, then the sugar and spice mixture. Dot the top with the cold butter pieces.

3 · To make the biscuits: Combine the flour, sugar, baking powder, and salt in a medium bowl or in a food processor. Cut in the cold butter with a fork or by

pulsing the food processor until the mixture resembles coarse meal. Make a well in the center and add the cold cream or half-and-half. Mix until just evenly moistened, adding extra drops of cream or half-and-half as necessary. Do not overmix. Dough should be soft but not sticky, like soft biscuit dough. Turn out the dough onto a lightly floured work surface. With a rolling pin, roll out the dough into a 6-inch square, dusting the top as needed to keep the rolling pin from sticking. With a sharp knife, cut the dough into twelve 2-by-1½-inch rectangles.

4 · Arrange the little biscuits side by side on top of the cherries in the baking dish. It is okay if the biscuits are a bit uneven and there are small spaces between them (this lets the steam escape). Brush the tops of the biscuits with the melted butter and sprinkle with the 2 tablespoons of sugar. Bake for 25 to 30 minutes, until the biscuit top is golden brown, puffy, and firm to the touch. Serve warm or at room temperature with Rum Whipped Cream, if desired.

Rum Whipped Cream

Makes 2¼ cups topping

1 cup cold heavy cream
3 tablespoons packed light brown sugar
2 tablespoons golden rum
½ cup sour cream

Place the bowl and mixing beater(s) in the freezer for at least 1 hour to chill thoroughly. Place the cream, brown sugar, and rum in the bowl. Whip on high speed using an electric mixer until soft peaks form, about 3 minutes. Fold in the sour cream. Cover and refrigerate until serving.

Notes from the Kitchen

Ingredients, Techniques, and Basic Recipes

Almond Paste

Although good commercial brands of almond paste are available (such as from Solo), homemade almond paste is a good staple to have on hand for baking purposes. Tightly wrapped, it keeps indefinitely in the freezer. Bring to room temperature before using it in recipes.

Almond Paste

Makes about 4 cups of spread

- 1 pound blanched whole almonds
- 1 cup water plus 1 tablespoon, divided
- 2 cups sugar
- 3 tablespoons light corn syrup
- 2 teaspoons almond extract

1. Grind the almonds in the workbowl of a food processor, ½ cup at a time, with 1 tablespoon of water dribbled in to help keep the oil from separating, until the almonds are finely ground and pasty.

2. In a saucepan, combine the sugar, corn syrup, and 1 cup water to make a simple syrup. Bring to a boil, cover, and reduce heat to low. Cook for 4 minutes, or until the sugar is completely dissolved. Uncover and attach a candy thermometer to the pan. Continue cooking until the thermometer registers 240°F. Remove the syrup from the heat and let rest for about 1 minute. Add the almond extract.

3. Place the ground almonds in a bowl or in the workbowl of a food processor. While beating with a wooden spoon or electric mixer, or while the food processor is running, drizzle in the hot syrup and beat or process until the mixture is smooth and forms a ball. It will be soft initially, then stiffen as it cools. Use the almond paste immediately, refrigerate for up to 2 weeks, or freeze almost indefinitely.

Baking Powder

Baking powder is a versatile leavener that makes quick breads rise and creates a light texture. It starts a chemical reaction between two or more ingredients to create carbon dioxide and guarantees consistent baking results. The leavening is first mixed or sifted with the dry ingredients to evenly distribute it. It is then combined with the wet ingredients, which activates it immediately, giving off carbon dioxide gas in the form of bubbles of air.

During baking, the flour and egg proteins set with the heat and steam around the bubbles, forming texture. *Double-acting baking powder* is commonly available on supermarket shelves, a mixture of alkaline and acid ingredients: baking soda (sodium bicarbonate), cornstarch (a stabilizer and dryer), and monocalcium phosphate, sodium acid pyrophosphate, or sodium aluminum sulfate (some form of phosphate salt). Double-acting baking powder can be used in combination with all types of liquid ingredients. It reacts twice, once when moistened with liquid and again in the hot oven. Batters made with double-acting baking powder can sit in the refrigerator for a couple of days and still be light textured when baked. *Single-acting baking powder* is leavened with cream of tartar (crystals of tartaric acid, also known as potassium bitartrate) and reacts only once with the liquid ingredients. Single-acting baking powder is no longer commercially available because tartaric acid is expensive, but the instructions to bake batters immediately after mixing, a necessity with single-acting baking powder, has remained in many recipes. Many bakers find that single-acting baking powder yields a finer texture and higher volume, so they mix their own

(recipe follows) or use a small amount of cream of tartar (usually ½ teaspoon per 2 cups of flour) in recipes.

If you are on a sodium-restricted diet, seek out a special baking powder made for such diets. I recommend a brand of baking powder that does not contain aluminum, which has a bitter aftertaste. Rumford is aluminum-free and is sold in natural foods stores as well as supermarkets. Too much baking powder, especially those containing aluminum sulfate, can leave a bitter aftertaste in the baked good, so exact measures are important. Use the guideline of no more than 1½ teaspoons of baking powder to 1 cup of flour. When doubling or tripling a recipe, cut back the total amount of leavener by one quarter. For baking at altitudes over 3,500 feet, reduce the baking powder by half the amount to compensate for baking powder's ability to expand more quickly at higher altitudes. Baking powder has a shelf life of only 4 months before its effectiveness decreases. Most packages are dated. Test for freshness by placing a teaspoon in a small amount of hot water. If it is fresh, it will fizzle. Quick breads may have aerating leaveners added in addition to baking powder, such as whole eggs, egg whites, butter, lard, and solid vegetable fats, which, while adding moisture to the dough, will produce steam during baking and set the crumb.

Single-Acting Baking Powder

Combine 1 teaspoon baking soda (alkali) and 2 teaspoons cream of tartar (acid) to substitute for 1 tablespoon baking powder in a recipe's dry ingredients. Bake the batter immediately after mixing. This mixture will not store.

Baking Soda

Bicarbonate of soda, an alkali originally known as saleratus in the 1800s, is now made from trona, a natural mineral remaining in evaporated salt lakes, which is converted to sodium carbonate and refined to form the familiar $NaHCO_3$. It is an essential leavener needed to create carbon dioxide gas when acid ingredients such as buttermilk, yogurt, sour cream (lactic acids), citrus, molasses, maple syrup, vinegar (acetic acid), chocolate, cream of tartar, and acid fruits are used. Batters containing baking soda must be baked immediately after mixing for best results. Baking soda lends a distinctive flavor to traditional soda breads and darkens baked cocoa-infused batters to a ruddy red. It is often added to recipes just to neutralize the acids, as in sourdough batters. Too much baking soda gives quick breads a soapy flavor with an acidic odor. Modern baking soda is ground very fine and does not need to be dissolved in hot water before being added to the batter. Store your box of baking soda in a cool, dry place.

Blanching

Fruits or vegetables are immersed briefly in boiling water, usually for about 30 seconds to 1 minute, to set the color, remove the raw taste, or allow for easy removal of the peel from fruits such as tomatoes or peaches.

Blossoms and Leaves

Scented blossoms and leaves of edible homegrown (unsprayed) plants are a real blessing in baking. From decorating to flavoring, blossoms and leaves can lend recipes an artistic expression, as well as serve as a flavor enhancer. Use fresh violets, scented geraniums (Pelargoniums), rose or lilac blossoms, anise hyssop, cinnamon basil, a variety of mints, lavender, lemon thyme, sweet woodruff, lemon balm, and orange or lemon blossoms to delicately flavor compound butters and sugars to be used in recipes or sprinkled on top of your quick breads.

Blossom- and Leaf-Scented Sugars

Use only one type of flavoring per recipe of this sugar for the most distinctive, haunting flavors and scents.

Makes about 2 cups sugar

In an airtight container, create a bottom layer of about ½ cup of powdered or granulated sugar. Lay a few edible, unsprayed leaves or blossoms on top of the sugar. Continue to layer sugar and leaves or blossoms two more times, ending with a layer of sugar. Cover tightly and let stand at room temperature for 1 week to meld the flavors. Remove the blossoms or leaves before using. Flavored sugars keep for 3 months.

Brans

A protective outer layer covering the whole grain kernel before it is ground, bran is acknowledged to be very nutritious. It provides roughage in the form of soluble fiber and is a plentiful source of minerals. It is a by-product of the bolting process of refining flours, during which the bran and wheat germ are separated from the starchy center. Because brans are rather tasteless, they are used with flours to boost the nutrition and fiber content of quick breads, rather than used exclusively. Brans are high in natural oils, so refrigeration is recommended to retain freshness. *Wheat bran*, sometimes marketed as miller's bran or unprocessed wheat bran, is a favorite ingredient in quick breads and muffins. *Oat bran* is the outer coating of a hulled oat groat and is a favorite mild-flavored ingredient. *Rice bran* is a ground bran that is thought to be as effective as oat bran as a soluble fiber. *Corn bran* is a good addition to cornmeals made with degerminated meals or in combination with other brans. All brans are credited with lowering blood-cholesterol levels and are available in some grocery stores and natural foods stores.

Buckwheat

Buckwheat is a musky-flavored triangular-shaped grain that, when ground into flour, makes wonderful pancakes, blini (raised Russian-style pancakes), Japanese soba noodles, Brêton crêpes, earthy muffins, and quick loaves. The flour is available light or dark, the dark flour having a stronger flavor. I use light buckwheat flour the most. It is excellent in combination with oats. Order Pocono Buckwheat Flour from Birkett Mills, P. O. Box 440A, Penn Yan, New York 14527.

Butter

Butter tenderizes quick bread batters and doughs. Unsalted butter is recommended for the best results in baking. It has no added color or salt, a delicate flavor, a sweet aroma, and a lower percentage of moisture than salted butter. Whipped butter contains 40 percent air, so it is not recommended for baking unless you measure by weight instead of by volume. French *beurre* is known as an excellent flavorful addition to baked goods and differs from American butter because it is made with matured rather than sweet cream. These butters can be used interchangeably in recipes. Butter freezes well for up to 6 months. It can be substituted for margarine because it contains the same amount of fat.

Buttermilk and Buttermilk Powder

Buttermilk is a creamy, tangy, cultured lowfat milk product, no longer the by-product of butter making of yesteryear. It serves as a tenderizer in quick breads and is an excellent ingredient in biscuits and pancakes. Many of the recipes in this book use buttermilk as the primary liquid. If you need a substitution for buttermilk, mix 2 tablespoons of lemon juice or vinegar with 2 cups lowfat milk and allow the mixture to stand and thicken for 5 minutes. This substitution can be used in any recipe that calls for buttermilk. Dehydrated *buttermilk powder* is very delicious and perfect for use in baking. If you use it, mix the powder into the dry ingredients and add the corresponding amount of water to the liquid ingredients in the recipe. The powdered buttermilk is available in supermarkets. Refrigerate buttermilk powder after opening the package; it keeps for up to a year.

Caviar and Smoked Fish

Amber-colored American golden caviar is the roe from lake-bred whitefish. Mild-flavored and jewel-like in color, it is a real treat on hot buttermilk pancakes with dollops of homemade crème fraîche, for a special brunch or midnight supper. It is low in cost compared to imported varieties and freezes well. *Smoked salmon* from the Pacific Northwest or Maine is excellent, with a delicate, sweet flavor. It is cold-smoked over alder chips and worth seeking out for garnishing pancakes and biscuits. *Smoked trout* is a delicacy; it is hot-smoked with a bit of brown sugar.

Use it as an alternative to smoked salmon. Smoked fish is usually available vacuum-packed in grocery store meat departments and gourmet food stores. Some markets smoke their own, which will look darker and more rustic than commercial brands. Excellent smoked fish may be ordered from Ducktrap River Fish Farm, 57 Little River Drive, Belfast, Maine 04915.

Cheeses

Cheeses typically favored for cooking also lend themselves to baking. Cheddar, Swiss, Emmenthaler, Monterey Jack, goat cheese, Brie, blue, mozzarella, and Parmesan are among the most popular cheeses for baking into batters and doughs. Cheese blends well with other ingredients in a batter, which keeps it from separating or overheating. Soft curd cheeses, such as fresh cottage cheese, cream cheese, and ricotta, add distinctive flavor and moisture to quick breads. When buying cheese, remember that 4 ounces of cheese will measure 1 cup when grated.

Chestnuts

Chestnuts are edible once their hard husk and inner skin are removed after cooking. Although classified as a nut, they are very starchy, with a texture akin to that of sweet potatoes, and can be dried and ground into flour as well as candied, boiled, pureed, or roasted. Excellent Italian or French imported chestnuts are sold frozen, canned, or vacuum-packed. Chestnuts are available as *marron glacès*, whole sugar-glazed nuts, which can be chopped and added to batters with other fruits and nuts; in a sugar syrup; or as *crème de marrons*, a popular imported French paste of candied chestnut pieces with sugar, glucose, and vanilla. The flavor of chestnuts marries well with brandy and sherry. Chestnut puree is an excellent ingredient in batters or flavorful spreads.

How To Cook and Peel Fresh Chestnuts

With a sharp, pointed paring knife, press a slit or X into the flat side of each chestnut. Place the prepared chestnuts in a saucepan, cover with cold water, and bring to a boil. Reduce heat to a simmer and cook, uncovered, for 15 minutes. Remove from the heat. Remove a few chestnuts at a time from the hot water with a slotted spoon. Let cool enough to handle, about 20 minutes, and peel away the outer shell and inner skin with your fingers. Chestnuts can also be roasted in a 375°F oven in one layer on a baking sheet for 20 to 25 minutes, shaking occasionally to promote even roasting. After they are peeled, the nuts are then ready to be chopped or processed through a sieve to make a coarse puree. Use them plain in sweet or savory recipes. One pound of raw chestnuts yields about 12 ounces or 2½ cups shelled, peeled nuts.

Chestnut Puree

To prepare fresh chestnuts as a puree for use in quick breads, place peeled, plain chestnuts in a medium saucepan and cover with fresh cold water or a combination of half water and half milk. (One imported 15-ounce can of whole chestnuts may be substituted for each pound of the prepared fresh chestnuts.) Add 1 to 2 tablespoons of sugar, a piece of vanilla bean, and a tablespoon of butter per pound of chestnuts. Bring to a boil, reduce the heat, and simmer for about 40 minutes, or until the chestnuts are tender. Drain and cool before pureeing the flavored pieces. Makes about 1½ cups.

Chili Powder

Chili powder (chili with an i, not an e) is a spicy commercial blend of ancho chile powder, cumin, garlic, and sometimes salt, offered by all major spice companies. Chile powder composes 80 percent of the total volume of the blend. Each label has a slightly different recipe. This is not the same as ground chile pods, which are ground, then powdered. Pure ground chile powder (with an e, not an i) can be ground from many different types of chile pods, available extensively in the Southwest and Southern California.

Chili Powder

To make this very delicious spice mixture, use a pure chile powder to suit your taste, such as one ground from New Mexico, California, pasilla negro, ancho, or mulatto dried chiles, available in the ethnic section of supermarkets or acquired on your last trip to the Southwest. Or use several kinds of chile powders and blend them together to create your own unique mixture. If you grind your own from whole dried chiles, rinse off the dust and place the chiles on a baking sheet. Bake at 300°F for about 5 minutes, or until puffy. Break open, shake out the seeds, and pull out the vein. Grind to a powder in a blender or electric coffee grinder reserved just for chiles.

Makes about ⅓ cup

> ¼ cup ground dried chile powder (mild, medium, or hot, or a mixture to taste)
> 1 tablespoon ground cumin
> 1 teaspoon garlic powder
> 1 teaspoon dried Greek oregano
> ½ teaspoon ground cloves
> ½ teaspoon ground allspice
> ½ teaspoon Hungarian paprika

1. Place ground chile powder and cumin on a baking sheet. Toast lightly in a preheated 325°F oven for 3 to 4 minutes. Remove from the oven and let cool.

2. Combine the chile-cumin mixture and all other herbs and spices in a small bowl. Mix until all ingredients are evenly combined. Store indefinitely in a tightly covered container, away from heat and light.

Chocolate

Chocolate is an equatorial bean that is roasted and blended with sugar to form solid bars or powdered cocoa. *Unsweetened chocolate* is known as chocolate liquor and contains about 50 percent cocoa butter. It is sold in 8-ounce boxes, with each 1-ounce square conveniently individually wrapped. *Bittersweet and semisweet dark chocolate* contain 35 percent liquor and, depending on the manufacturer, a varying array of milk solids, butterfat, lecithin, and vanillin. American semisweet chocolate is the equivalent of European bittersweet chocolate. *Couverture* is a thin coating chocolate used especially for candy making, dipping fruits, and glazing, but couverture can be substituted for bittersweet and semisweet chocolates. It melts and spreads beautifully. When using this chocolate in a recipe, use less fat per recipe than for regular dark chocolates, as it contains 39 percent cocoa butter. Couverture is usually sold in blocks. *Sweet dark chocolate* contains 15 percent liquor plus more sugar and other ingredients than bittersweet and semisweet chocolates. *Milk chocolate* has 10 percent liquor and a high amount of butterfat and milk solids. It is very sensitive to heat. *White chocolate* is not a true chocolate, but a combination of sugar, cocoa butter, milk solids, lecithin, and vanilla flavoring. It is extremely sensitive to heat. Good-quality brands of white, dark, and milk chocolate are Lindt, Ghirardelli, Maillard, Callebaut, Tobler, Valrhôna, and Nestlé. Store your solid chocolates tightly wrapped in a cool, dry place for up to 6 months. If your solid chocolate develops a thin white surface, known as bloom, it has been stored at too warm a temperature. Bloom is harmless and the chocolate may be used as needed.

Unsweetened cocoa is chocolate liquor that has had some of its cocoa butter pressed out and is then ground to a fine powder. It is a good choice in baking for fat- and cholesterol-restricted diets. Dutch-process cocoa is alkaline-treated, and therefore darker in color, less bitter, and richer in flavor than nonalkalized cocoa. Quick bread recipes utilizing Dutch-process cocoa use slightly more baking powder to maintain the proper acid-alkaline balance. When using nonalkalized natural cocoa, such as Hershey's (in the brown can), baking soda is an important ingredient for balancing the natural acids. These types of cocoa can be substituted for each other in recipes, but the flavor and color of the finished baked good will be different. Good brands of Dutch-process cocoa are Dröste, Poulain, Baker's, van Houten, Hershey's European-style (in the silver can), and Ghirardelli. Cocoa keeps indefinitely in an airtight container. Do not substitute instant cocoa powder in recipes, since it is

precooked and sweetened. *To substitute unsweetened cocoa powder for unsweetened baking chocolate:* Substitute 3 tablespoons cocoa and 1 tablespoon vegetable oil or butter for every 1 ounce of unsweetened chocolate.

How to Melt Chocolate

The trick to melting chocolate successfully is to melt it slowly over low heat on the stovetop or briefly in the microwave (directions follow). Whatever method you use, first chop the chocolate coarsely for even melting. It burns very easily, so keep the temperature below 125°F. If overheated, chocolate will become grainy and taste scorched. The container in which the chocolate is melted must be dry. All types and brands of chocolate melt at different rates and have different consistencies. Semisweet and milk chocolates tend to hold their shape when melted and must be stirred with a whisk or rubber spatula to create a smooth consistency.

In a double boiler, place coarsely chopped chocolate over hot, just below simmering, water. Let stand until melted, stirring occasionally. Because milk and white chocolates are so heat-sensitive, remove the double boiler from the heat and let the chocolate stand until melted.

In a conventional oven, place the chocolate in a Pyrex or other oven-proof baking dish in a preheated 300°F to 350°F oven. Check the chocolate every 5 minutes until it is melted.

In a microwave oven, place coarsely chopped chocolate in a microwave-proof container and partially cover with plastic wrap. Microwave at 50 percent power for 2 to 4 minutes, depending on the volume, until the chocolate is shiny and slightly melted. Stir at 1-minute intervals throughout the melting process until completely melted. Milk and white chocolates take less time to melt than dark or unsweetened chocolates do.

Citrus Juices and Zests

For the best flavor, use fresh-squeezed lemon, lime, and orange juices in recipes. Commercial orange and tangerine juices are also very good. Lemons and limes miraculously yield more juice when heated in the microwave for 30 seconds or so before they are squeezed. Strained juices can be frozen for later use. An ice cube tray is a convenient way to do this. In a standard ice cube tray, each cube is about 2 tablespoons.

Zests are obtained from the outer part of the citrus peel, which contains the color and volatile oils. Zests give quick breads flavor without adding liquid. Remove the zest using a sharp knife, fine grater, zester (a tool that has a row of tiny holes to cut and curl fine slivers of zest), or vegetable peeler, taking care not to get any of the bitter white pith.

Coconut Milk

Coconuts are drupe fruits, a tropical member of the family including apricots, peaches, cherries, and plums. When unripe, coconut meat is soft, sweet, and jellylike and can be eaten with a spoon. In place of milk or water in quick breads, for a unique tropical flavor, use commercial unsweetened coconut meat juice, known as *nam katee* in Thai, which is available in Asian markets, or cream of coconut, available in supermarkets canned or frozen. If you plan to prepare your own coconut milk, choose a fresh coconut; shake it to make sure that you hear liquid inside. The inner liquid is really coconut water, a slightly fermented liquid that is very refreshing.

How To Open and
Prepare a Fresh Coconut

Hold the coconut at the top pole, wrap it in two layers of thick tea towels, and tap it with the blunt end of a large cleaver or hammer. Or bake it in a 350°F oven for 30 minutes first. (The baking makes it easier to hold the coconut in the towels and crack it with a hammer.) The coconut will crack open. Drain the liquid. Break the shell into smaller pieces. Insert a strong, small knife between the meat and the shell to remove chunks of meat. Use a vegetable peeler to scrape off the thin inner skin. Chop the meat into small pieces and process in a food processor or use a coconut scraper to shred the meat to the desired consistency.

Homemade Coconut Milk

Makes 3 cups milk

Combine 3 cups of scalded milk or hot water with 2 cups chopped or coarsely shredded fresh white coconut meat (which contains the fat). You can also substitute 3 cups unsweetened dried coconut for the fresh meat. Soak the mixture for ½ hour then puree in a blender for 3 minutes. Let stand at room temperature until completely cool. Strain through a colander lined with 3 layers of cheesecloth. Squeeze the cheesecloth to press out all of the liquid. If left to sit, the cream will rise to the top of the liquid. Stir the coconut milk before using it. Rich and creamy, coconut milk is an excellent liquid addition to quick breads in place of milk. The coconut milk should be used within 1 day.

Cooking Sprays

This is a grease-in-a-can product, such as Pam, also available with added flour or with a lecithin base, such as Baker's Joy. There is an olive oil–based spray that is good for savory baking. These vegetable oil–based sprays are invaluable for greasing intricate molds and muffin tins.

Cornmeal

White and *yellow cornmeals* come in a variety of grinds, from fine to coarse, and are used in cornbreads, biscuits, shortcakes, and muffins. Cornmeal has a unique flavor and texture, and there is no other grain to substitute for it. *Degerminated cornmeal* has had the germ removed for longer supermarket shelf-life, but for the best flavor, use fresh stone- and water-ground meals. Excellent yellow and white fine fresh-ground meals are available from Kenyon Cornmeal Company, 21 Glenn Rock Road, West Kingston, Rhode Island 02892; and Gray's Grist Mill, P. O. Box 422, Adamsville, Rhode Island 02801. White water-ground cornmeals and Southern-style grits are available from Woodson's Mill, P. O. Box 11005, Norfolk, Virginia 23517. *Blue cornmeal, maiz azul,* is slightly grainier and sweeter, with more corn flavor than other colored meals. It makes purple-pink to blue-green to lavender-tinged baked products depending on the type of liquid ingredients it is combined with. It is also known as Hopi blue corn. Muffins and biscuits made with blue cornmeal need a bit more fat per recipe, as this cornmeal contains about 7 percent less fat than other colored cornmeals. Like yellow and white cornmeals, blue meals come in a variety of grinds. *Harinilla* is a fine grade of blue corn flour, especially good in pancakes. *Harina de maiz azul* is a lime-treated, coarser grind used especially for tortilla making. It is also very good in cornbreads. Blue corn products are available from Casados Farms, P. O. Box 852, San Juan Pueblo, New Mexico 87566. *Polenta* is the Italian name for a very coarse-ground yellow cornmeal. It can also be bought mixed with wheat germ or buckwheat meal, and, occasionally, ground from white corn. Instant polenta is also available. These polentas may be substituted for yellow cornmeal in recipes, but the texture of the finished product will vary. *Masa harina* is a distinctly flavored, dehydrated yellow corn flour made from dried corn kernels treated with a lime solution (calcium hydroxide). It is used to make corn tortilla doughs. This cornmeal is ground much finer than regular yellow cornmeals. Blue cornmeal *masa harina* can also be ordered from Casados Farms. Store cornmeals, tightly covered, in a cool, dry place or refrigerate for up to 8 months.

Cornstarch

Ground from the endosperm, or germ, of the corn kernel, cornstarch is used to thicken liquids and is especially nice for thickening homemade syrups and sauces. Dissolve corn starch first in a small amount of cold water, or combine it with sugar to separate the granules. Cornstarch must be cooked for about a minute, until the liquid becomes thick and translucent in color, and stirred constantly to avoid burning and lumping. Cornstarch can also be added in a small amount to unbleached flour to lower the gluten, making a soft cake flour that results in more tender cakes, crêpes, or biscuits.

Corn Syrup

Light corn syrup is a translucent, sweet, but bland syrup made from cornstarch diluted with water. Dark corn syrup is more flavorful because refiner's syrup and a slight caramel flavoring are added to the light syrup. A homemade version of dark corn syrup can be made by combining 1 cup of light syrup with 1 tablespoon molasses. Both light and dark syrups are about half the sweetness of honey or granulated sugar. When measuring, use an oiled measuring cup for easier pouring.

Cream

Cream is classified by the percentage of milkfat, also known as butterfat, it contains. Sweet-tasting creams are available pasteurized or ultrapasteurized, a process that promotes a longer shelf life. Heavy cream, or heavy whipping cream, is 36 to 40 percent milkfat; it is the best cream for whipping. Whipping cream is 30 to 36 percent milkfat, light cream is 18 to 30 percent milkfat, and half-and-half, a mixture of milk and cream, is 10 to 18 percent milkfat. Ultrapasteurized cream is not recommended for whipping.

How to Whip Cream

When flavoring whipped cream, add about a tablespoon of liqueur or extract per cup of cream *just* as the

mixture starts to thicken, rather than at the beginning. Use fine-grained sugars, such as powdered or superfine, for sweetening whipped cream since granulated sugar can stay gritty. Good rules of thumb here are to make sure the bowl you use is very clean, make sure the bowl and the ingredients are well-chilled beforehand, and keep an eye on the mixture during the beating process so you do not overbeat.

Cream of Tartar

Cream of tartar is a naturally fermented leavener, like wild yeasts and sourdough starters, contained in the sediment scraped from the bottom of wine barrels. It is the main ingredient used with baking soda to make single-acting baking powder. Many bakers use a small amount of cream of tartar (usually ½ teaspoon per 2 cups of flour) in recipes made with double-acting baking powder, because it gives the baked good a finer texture and higher volume.

Creaming

When a recipe calls for creaming, room temperature butter or some type of solid fat is beaten with a wooden spoon, whisk, electric mixer, or food processor, alone or with sugar, until soft and light in texture or, in professional terms, until emulsified and aerated. Creaming is important for proper leavening in quick bread recipes.

Crème Fraîche, Sour Cream, Yogurt, and Other Cultured Dairy Products

In the United States, cultured milk products such as crème fraîche, sour cream, yogurt, buttermilk, ricotta, and cottage cheese are made from pasteurized cow milk, but in many countries they are also made from yak, goat, sheep, or water buffalo milk. The milk is fermented with a bacteria that transforms milk sugar (lactose) into lactic acid, and it curdles the milk naturally into a thick, creamy, and tangy product. Sour cream, crème fraîche, and yogurt can be used interchangeably in baking recipes, although the flavor and textures of the final product will vary. They are also excellent for use as toppings. *Sour cream* is thickened heavy sweet cream that, when added to quick breads, results in a dense, moist-textured bread owing to its lactic acid. It is a favorite luxurious addition to all types of quick breads. Lowfat sour cream may be substituted. *Crème fraîche* is made in the same manner but uses a different bacteria. Purchased crème fraîche is naturally low in calories and fat and contains no stabilizers or preservatives. The purchased or homemade crème fraîche can be drained in cheesecloth to make a *mascarpone* reminiscent of the authentic Italian cream cheese. It is a great topping for pancakes, drizzled with honey. *Yogurt* is also cultured from whole, lowfat, or nonfat milk, but it is thinner in consistency and more tart in flavor than sour cream and crème fraîche. *Yogurt cheese*, made simply by draining yogurt in cheesecloth, is a lowfat, tangy alternative to mascarpone and excellent as a spread on scones, drizzled with honey. It can be substituted with *kefir cheese*, a yogurt cheese, available in natural food stores, that has the beneficial acidophilus culture added. Do not freeze dairy products.

Crème Fraîche

Makes about 1 cup

1 cup pasteurized fresh heavy cream, 36 percent to 40 percent milkfat, without stabilizers (carrageen) or UHT treatment

¼ cup cultured sour cream or crème fraîche, commercially produced or from a previous batch

In a small saucepan, heat the cream to about 80°F. Gently whisk in the sour cream or crème fraîche until smooth. Pour the mixture into a clean jar or crock and cover loosely. Let stand at room temperature for 12 to 24 hours. Although crème fraîche tastes best fresh, it can be covered tightly and refrigerated for up to 2 weeks. If there is any separation, pour off the liquid.

Homemade Mascarpone

Place a colander or sieve lined with two layers of rinsed cheesecloth over a bowl to catch the whey. Spoon crème fraîche into the lined colander or sieve. Drain at room temperature for 2 to 4 hours, weighted with a large canned product wrapped in plastic, for a denser texture, if desired. Turn the cheese out onto a shallow plate and store covered with plastic wrap in the refrigerator until serving. Kefir cheese, available in natural foods stores, may be substituted for this cheese.

Yogurt Cheese

Makes about 1½ pounds yogurt cheese

On top of a bowl, place a mesh colander or sieve lined with two layers of rinsed cheesecloth large enough to hang over the sides of the colander. Spoon a quart of chilled yogurt that does not contain gelatin or agar agar as a stabilizer into the colander or sieve. Drain the yogurt at room temperature for 1 hour. Loosely tie the corners of the cheesecloth to form a bag and hang it from the kitchen faucet to drain overnight, 8 to 12 hours, or until the desired consistency is achieved. The longer the cheese hangs, the firmer the consistency. Turn the cheese into a bowl and season, if desired. To make a savory cheese, gently stir in such additions as salt, herbs, pimiento, roasted peppers, or capers. Or sweeten the cheese with chopped fresh fruits, macerated dried fruits, chopped lemon balm or cinnamon basil, spices, or nuts. Store, covered, in a decorative crock or formed into a mold, in the refrigerator for up to 2 weeks.

Dried Fruit

Sun- and air-dried fruits, such as golden and dark raisins, apricots, pears, peaches, papaya, dates, apples, prunes, pineapple, and currants, add nutrition, color, and lots of flavor to quick breads. New additions include dried blueberries, kiwi fruit, cranberries (one sweetened commercial brand is known as Crasins), and sweet and sour cherries. Most are available by mail order from American Spoon Foods, P. O. Box 566, Petoskey, Michigan 49770. Crystallized fruits, such as ginger, pineapple, angelica, and candied orange and lemon peel, are glistening, sweet alternatives, usually seen around the holidays. Choose plump, moist-looking fruits, because shriveled dried fruits will not become softer during baking. Dried fruits are an excellent alternative to commercial candied fruits in baking. Use sulphured or unsulphured fruits interchangeably, unless a recipe specifies otherwise. To cut dried fruits, sprinkle the fruit with a bit of flour from the recipe and chop it by hand with a chef's knife or snip with kitchen shears sprayed with a nonstick vegetable spray. Alternatively, pulse with a small amount of flour in a food processor. The light coating of flour will also help keep the fruit from sinking to the bottom of the batter. Before they are added to batters, dried fruits are plumped in hot water to reconstitute them and restore a softer texture.

How to Plump Dried Fruit

Dried fruit added to a batter of any kind will not soften further as it bakes, so it is often best to soak dried fruit in a warm liquid before adding it to a batter or dough. You can use water, wine, a liqueur, or a fruit juice to soften and add flavor to the dried fruit. The fruit should soak for at least 1 hour before it is added to a dough. If the fruit is very dry and hard, combine 1 cup of fruit with 1 cup of water or other liquid in a small saucepan and bring to a boil. Do not cover the pot while cooking or softening, so that the excess sulphur dioxide, used to preserve color and preserve freshness, will have a chance to evaporate. Simmer gently for about 10 minutes or until the fruit is soft. Let the fruit cool in the liquid. You can also soften fruit in a microwave: Combine the fruit and liquid in a microwave-proof bowl. Cover and microwave on high for 3 minutes. Stir the fruit; if it is still hard, cover it again and microwave for another minute. Let stand for 2 minutes before uncovering. Let cool and chop.

Eggs

Eggs add a wonderful golden color, rich flavor, and a tender cakelike texture to quick breads. Use large or extra-large A or AA grade eggs. One whole egg can be substi-tuted for two egg yolks and vice versa in baking recipes. Three small whole eggs can be substituted for two large eggs in recipes. One large egg equals ¼ cup liquid measure (about 2 ounces in weight); the white equals 3 tablespoons (about 1 ounce in weight), and the yolk is equal to 1 tablespoon. Two large whites equal ¼ cup, and 8 whites equal 1 cup. Egg whites can be frozen in ice cube trays for up to 6 months and defrosted to room temperature before using. The yolks cannot be frozen, since they are predominantly fat.

Ninety percent of the commercial egg market is white eggs from white leghorn chickens, but brown and blue eggs have a similar flavor and are laid by a variety of breeds. Use duck or quail eggs, if you should have an abundance, to vary color and flavor. All eggs should be at room temperature when added to quick breads.

Store eggs in the refrigerator in their carton for no longer than 4 weeks.

How to Separate an Egg

Crack the egg sharply on the edge of a small bowl. Break the shell into two sections. Lightly transfer the yolk, taking care not to break it, from one half to the other, letting the white drop through into the bowl beneath. If any yolk slips into the whites, scoop it out carefully using the jagged edge of the shell. Any yolk left behind will inhibit the whites from being beaten to their full volume.

How to Beat Egg Whites

It is very important that the bowl and beaters be dry and squeaky clean, free from any fat, which will inhibit the whites from reaching the proper consistency.

Extracts and Flavorings

For the best flavors, use only pure extracts and flavorings in your baked goods. Vanilla, almond, anise, and citrus are the most familiar distinctive extracts, with their essential flavors preserved in an alcohol solution. The best *vanilla* extracts come from Madagascar and Tahitian beans. For a more concentrated essence, split a quarter of a vanilla bean in half lengthwise, scoop out the grainy, black interior, and blend it with the batter ingredients. For a more subtle addition, use vanilla-flavored sugar. *Almond* extract is made from bitter almonds. Avoid imitation extracts, which will taste predominantly liks alcohol. *Citrus zests* are grated or slivered from the oil-rich rind of the peel from a variety of citrus fruits. Grate with a fine-textured grater or a metal zester, a tool that has a row of tiny holes to cut and curl fine slivers of zest. Take care not to grate the white pith beneath the skin, as it is bitter. Zests can be steeped in liquids to macerate for a few hours to create a delightfully fresh, mild-flavored addition to batters or doughs. *Orange- and rose-flower waters* are exotic, fragrant complements, distillations of bitter orange blossoms and rose petals. They originated in Middle Eastern cuisine and were introduced into European baking by the Crusades. Use only a very small amount of these flavored waters as their perfumed aromas are powerful enough to quickly dominate other flavors. For baked goods, the best *coffee flavor* is imparted by instant espresso powder.

Flour

Unbleached all-purpose flour is the type of wheat flour called for most in quick bread recipes, and it is the foundation of and main ingredient in American baking as we know it. I prefer unbleached flour, because it has been whitened by natural aging rather than through chemical bleaching and is therefore less processed. Unbleached all-purpose flour uses 80 percent hard-wheat flour and 20 percent soft-wheat flour. High-protein, hard-wheat bread flour is 14 percent gluten, and low-protein, soft-wheat cake flour is 6 percent to 8 percent gluten. This combination provides a tender crumb as well as the strength needed to support the quick rising brought about by chemical leaveners. Enriched flour has added B vitamins and iron. Some cooks recommend using two parts all-purpose flour and one part cake flour for the best-shaped muffins. Regional mills and large milling complexes all have different blending formulas and will often blend their all-purpose flours to meet the needs of their clients. Excellent unbleached flours can be mail-ordered from Walnut Acres, Penn Creek, Pennsylvania 17862; and The King Arthur Flour Baker's Catalogue, P.O. Box 876, Norwich, Vermont

05055. Southern soft wheat and self-rising flours for biscuit making can be ordered from White Lily Foods Company, P. O. Box 871, Knoxville, Tennessee 37901. Gold Medal, Pillsbury, and Arrowhead Mills are reliable national brands, and Stone-Buhr on the West Coast, Robin Hood in the Midwest, Martha White in the South, and King Arthur and Hodgson Mill on the East Coast are reliable regional brands.

Whole wheat flour is ground from the fiber-rich whole grain that includes the endosperm, bran, and germ. Each commercial brand is a different grind, each giving a slightly different texture to baked goods. Stone-ground flours are milled using slow millstones rather than huge steel rollers. With fine grinds, all the parts of the grain are equally ground; medium and coarse grinds have varying amounts of bran dispersed through the flour, lending baked goods a slightly more crumbly texture. Whole wheat flours are denser than white flour, and have a complex, nutty-sweet flavor. They also contain more fiber and overall nutrition than white flours. *White whole wheat flour* is milled from a strain of wheat with a white bran coating rather than the familiar rust color. It is lighter in taste than other whole wheat flours and may be substituted equally for darker whole wheat flours. *Graham flour* is a different grind of whole wheat that leaves the bran very coarse. Although it is easily substituted with whole wheat flour, it has a particularly rich, unique flavor not to be missed. *Whole wheat pastry flour* is ground from whole-grain soft wheat and is excellent in quick breads. It makes for a lighter product than regular whole wheat flours do. The "new" wheats, *kamut* and *spelt* (also known as *farro* or *emmer* in Italy and *dinkel* in Germany) were originally hardy ancient varieties cultivated for centuries in rural Europe. They are now grown domestically in Montana, and bakers will find these flours increasingly available. These flours can be used as an exact substitute for whole wheat flours in baking recipes, although the flavors will vary. Whole-grain flours contain a high percentage of oil and should be stored in the refrigerator to protect them against rancidity.

How to Measure Flour

Measure flour using the "dip and sweep" method. Dip the measuring cup into the flour, filling to overflowing. With a knife or spatula, sweep off the excess to level the top. One cup of unsifted all-purpose flour weighs 5 ounces. Store white flour in a cool, dry, dark place (I use a gallon plastic container with an airtight lid) for up to 6 months.

Folding

Folding is the technique used for combining dry ingredients with liquids or beaten egg whites to form a batter, without deflating the lighter mixture. The heavier ingredients should be on the bottom; then fold them with a large spatula to the top until no streaks are visible. Here is how: With a spatula, cut through the center of the batter down to the bottom. With a twist of the wrist, pull under the mixture and then pull over the top. Do this repeatedly, gently and quickly to maintain the batter's foamy consistency. This technique is used for pancake, waffle, and some muffin batters to lighten the texture or, as in the case of egg whites, to act as a secondary leavening agent.

Glazing

A glaze is a shiny, thin, flavorful or decorative layer poured onto quick breads, coffee cakes, or muffins. Glazing adds a counterpoint of flavor and texture to the finished product. Beaten eggs brushed on before cooking, melted chocolate, sugar syrups, melted jam, or thinned powdered sugar are favorite glazes.

Goat Cheese

Goat cheese, also known by its French name, *chèvre*, is cheese made from goat's milk. It is a rustic cheese that has found its place in the mass market and in the hearts of cheese lovers. It has an appealing acidy tang, is a smooth melter, combines well with other ingredients, and is tremendously versatile in cooking. It is sold fresh or aged, in creamy to hard textures, and in a variety of shapes, colors, and flavors. For all-purpose uses, choose Chabis or its French counterpart, Montrachet, for light taste and creamy texture. There are many excellent brands of domestic *chèvre* now available from cheesemakers such as Laura Chenel, Cypress Grove, Kendall Cheese Company, and Alpine Chèvre in California; Mozzarella Company, Coonridge, and Sierra Farms in the Southwest; Coach Farm and Little Rainbow in New York; Sheepscot Valley in Maine; and Mt. Capra Cheese in Washington State.

Herbs and Spices

Use the recently dried or fresh leaves of fragrant herbs for the best flavor in baking. My favorites are tarragon, oregano, basil, dill, rosemary, thyme, and sage. Spices from pungent barks, buds, and roots, such as cinnamon, ginger, nutmeg, mace, pepper, and allspice, are distinctive, exotic flavor additions to all quick breads. Many bakers grind their own spices in an electric coffee mill or by hand in a mortar. Replace dried herbs every 6 months and ground spices every year for the freshest essence. Store aromatics in a cool, dry place in airtight containers.

Honey

Honey is a thick, sweet liquid produced by nectar-gathering bees, and its flavor depends on the flowers from which it was gathered. Usually, light-colored honeys are mild in flavor and the darker honeys are more assertive. My favorites are raspberry, wild thistle, cherry, cactus, and French lavender, in addition to the familiar wildflower and clover. I also enjoy cinnamon-spiced honey and flavored creamed honeys (such as Oregon Apiaries' vanilla or blueberry honey *crèmes*) for spreading on biscuits, scones, and waffles. Always investigate your local shops or farmers' markets for a locally produced honey. Using an oiled measuring cup is the most efficient way to measure honey. For a more pourable consistency, gently warm honey on the stovetop or in a microwave oven for 20 to 30 seconds. Use liquefied honey in baking recipes rather than honeycomb or more solid, crystallized honeys, which are better for spreading.

Light Baking

All the recipes in this book use fresh ingredients, lots of different whole grains and stone-ground unbleached flours, high-fiber fresh fruits and vegetables, cold-pressed vegetable oils, and a minimal amount of sugar, but they can be further adapted for today's healthier lifestyles and special diets to contain less fat, sugar, and salt. Quick breads are naturally rich in fiber and complex carbohydrates; unbleached all-purpose flour contains about 9 to 13 grams of protein per cup. To lower cholesterol, for each whole egg in a recipe, substitute 2 egg whites or a commercial egg substitute equivalent to 1 egg. To increase fiber, substitute up to a few tablespoons of bran, oat, whole wheat, or other specialty flour for an equal amount of all-purpose flour. All-purpose flour can be substituted with exact measures of whole wheat pastry flour. Substitute reduced-calorie margarine for unsalted butter. Salt can be reduced by half or eliminated. Lowfat, low-calorie flavor enhancers include herbs, spices, and extracts. Eliminate any alcoholic spirit, if necessary, and substitute fruit juice. In many cases, high-fat dairy products can be substituted with non-fat yogurt, instant nonfat dry milk powder, nonfat or 1 percent buttermilk, evaporated skim milk, lowfat cottage cheese, Neufchatel cream cheese, part-skim ricotta cheese, and lowfat sour cream. Sugar can be cut back by one third the total amount in most recipes. Unsweetened fruit juices, apple or pineapple juice concentrate, pureed fruit, fructose, honey, and low-calorie syrups can also be used as alternative sweeteners. Experimenting is the key to finding the right flavors and textures to suit your tastes and needs.

Liqueurs and Other Alcoholic Spirits

Distilled spirits add a lavish flavor dimension to quick breads, either as an ingredient infused into a batter or in luscious glazes. The intensely per-fumed, fiery spirits should be used in small amounts to complement the other ingredients, such as nut liqueur, rum, or brandy in breads with nuts, for example. My favorite flavor combinations include maple and golden rum; nuts with Frangelico or amaretto; carrots or zucchini with brandy; apricots or peaches with Asti Spumante, an Italian sparkling wine; cream sherry with pumpkin; and chocolate- or cream-based liqueurs in glazes. Fruits combine well with corresponding crystal-clear fruit brandies (*eau-de-vie*) or fortified wines, such as raspberry. Two classics to have on hand in the kitchen for all-purpose uses are the imported bitter-orange Grand Marnier and a good brandy, cognac, or Armagnac. Also look for domestic brands of eau-de-vie, distilled fruit juices that are about 90 proof, such as St. George Spirits kiwi, cherry kirsch, or quince brandy; Creekside's apple brandy from Sebastapol; Clear Creek Distillery's Oregon Bartlett pear brandy (*Poire William*) or apple brandy. Bonny Doon Vineyards' Framboise is a delicious blend of macerated fresh raspberries in 17 proof neutral grape spirits. These spirits are good in sauces and for macerating. They enhance all baked goods, preserving their delicate fruit essences and flavor through the baking process.

Macerating

Macerating is a process whereby fruits are placed in a liquid to soften and absorb flavor, such as soaking dried fruit in an alcoholic spirit or fruit juice. Macerating is often confused with marinating, which refers to tenderizing and flavoring meats. See How to Plump Dried Fruit (page 340).

Maple Syrup

If you have never experienced the rich flavor of a pure fancy-grade maple syrup from the northeastern United States or Canada, prepare yourself for a treat. It is at once smoky-sweet, luxurious to the tongue, and a beautiful, earthy color. After tasting one cornmeal pancake breakfast drizzled with the real thing, you will *never* go back to imitation-flavored sugar syrups. Fancy (also known as Light Amber) is the first of the season, pale and delicate. Grade A and Grade B syrups (Medium and Dark Amber) are progressively darker and more potent in flavor. Grade A is perfect for all-purpose table use and in cooking. Grade B is quite robust in flavor, but less expensive, and it makes the best baked beans and baked goods.

The syrups are good for use as a sweetener in batters, as well as for making toppings, butters, poached fruits, and sweetened whipped cream. Refrigerate the syrup after opening it and store it for no longer than 3 months for the best flavor. *Maple sugar* can be bought in cakes and grated over sour cream or crème fraîche on hot pancakes and waffles. The pressed candies that come in the maple leaf form can also be crumbled or grated for use this way. *Granulated or powdered maple sugar* is free-flowing and can be substituted equally for regular granulated sugar. It can also be reconstituted to make maple syrup. *Maple butter cream* is maple syrup that has been reduced to the consistency of a thick spread that looks quite a bit like honey. Try it spread on toast, muffins, waffles, poured over ice cream, or as a frosting for white gingerbread. All maple products are available from The Vermont Country Store, RR1, Box 231, North Clarendon, Vermont 05759.

To substitute maple syrup for granulated sugar in a recipe: Use an equal amount of syrup for the sugar called for in the recipe. Add ¼ teaspoon baking soda for each cup of syrup used, and reduce the total liquid measurement by half.

Milk

Use fresh whole or lowfat milk for the best flavor in recipes. Ninety-five percent of the commercial brands of milk are from holstein-friesian cows. Excellent jersey and guernsey milks are regional favorites and have a slightly different taste. The milk source is usually marked on the carton. Nonfat milk and reconstituted nonfat dry milk can be used in place of whole milk. If you use the powder, it can also be mixed with the dry ingredients and the corresponding amount of water added to the wet ingredients.

Molasses

Molasses is manufactured from the juice of sun-ripened cane sugar, and it adds flavor, sweetness, and color to quick breads. Use unsulphured light molasses, known as Barbados molasses, for the best flavor. Dark and sulphured molasses are the by-products of the second boiling, and, compared to the light, they are much stronger in flavor. Most supermarkets carry a brand that falls between light and dark. Blackstrap is the most bitter, containing a high percentage of ash and a waste product of sugar refining, and it is not often used in cooking. *Malt syrups* are made from sprouted and fermented barley rice. *Dark Treacle* is a less bitter cane-sugar syrup that is popular in British baking. Malt syrups and dark treacle are mild substitutes for molasses and 25 percent less sweet than other sugars.

Nuts and Seeds

A recipe's flavor can be altered by the addition of raw or toasted nuts and seeds. My favorite nuts for baking are almonds, hazelnuts, pecans, walnuts, macadamias, pistachios, cashews, pine nuts, and Brazil nuts. Sesame, sunflower, and pumpkins seeds can also be used to add extra flavor, texture, and nutrition. Measure nuts in dry measuring cups or by weight.

How To Chop Nuts

Chop nuts by hand with a good chef's knife, in a nut grinder, or in a food processor, taking care not to overprocess or the nuts will become a paste. Always pay attention to the recipe instructions, as nuts may be chopped in sizes ranging from chunky to quite fine. Coarsely chopped nuts are slightly larger than a raisin, finely chopped nuts are about the size of a currant, coarsely ground nuts look rather like polenta, and finely ground nuts are a powder the consistency of coarse whole wheat flour. For the best results, grind nuts with a few table-spoons of flour from the recipe. Be sure to buy fresh nuts and store them in the refrigerator for no more than 9 months or in the freezer for no longer than 2 years to prevent rancidity.

How To Toast Nuts and Seeds

Place the nuts or seeds on an un-greased baking sheet in the center of a preheated 325°F to 350°F oven and bake until golden. Alternatively, shake the nuts in a dry skillet over medium heat until golden, a method that is especially good for toasting sesame seeds or rolled oats. The nuts or seeds will crisp as they cool. Do not bake nuts to the point that they are dark in color, as they will taste burnt. *To toast nuts in a microwave oven*, place the nuts in a single layer on a paper towel or a microwave-proof plate, uncovered. Microwave at full power for 1 to 4 minutes, stirring twice. The nuts will be golden brown.

Almonds can be purchased whole with skins, blanched, slivered, or sliced. They are the most important and widely used nut for baking purposes.

To toast whole almonds, bake them for 5 to 10 minutes; the sliced almonds cook the most rapidly. To blanch whole almonds, cover them with an inch of boiling water. Let stand 1 to 2 minutes. Drain, and squeeze each nut to pop off the skin. Dry and recrisp the nuts in a 200°F oven for 12 to 15 minutes. *Hazelnuts* are bought whole and may also be marketed as filberts. They have an exceptional flavor in quick breads. To remove the skins, bake the nuts for 10 to 14 minutes, or until lightly colored and the skins blister. Immediately wrap the nuts in a clean dish towel and let stand for 1 minute. Rub the nuts in the towel to remove the skins, and cool. *Pecans, cashews, macadamias* (also known as the Queensland nut), and *walnuts* are soft, buttery-flavored nuts. They can be bought in halves or pieces. Bake them for 5 to 8 minutes to toast. Macadamias are often hard to locate, but a good source is the Mauna Loa Macadamia Nut Corporation, 800-832-9993. *Pine nuts, sunflower seeds*, and *pumpkin seeds* bake in 7 to 10 minutes. *Pistachios*, which are naturally a pale green, need to be shelled, skinned, and oven dried if they are not bought already shelled. Buy salt-free pistachios for use in recipes. To remove the skins, place the shelled pistachios in a heatproof bowl, and pour boiling water over to cover. Let stand for 1 minute, then drain. Turn the nuts out onto a dish towel and rub off the skins. Place the nuts on an ungreased baking sheet and oven-dry at 300°F for 10 minutes. Cool before storing in an airtight container in the freezer for up to a year.

Oats

Use rolled and quick-cooking oat flakes interchangeably in recipes. They have a creamy consistency and a sweet, mild flavor, and they add lots of fiber to baked goods. The rolled flakes can be ground in the food processor to make a coarse flour. Rolled oats are good in combination with barley flakes.

Oils

To tenderize and preserve freshness in a loaf, for general baking purposes use a neutral-flavored cold-pressed vegetable or nut oil, such as sunflower, sesame, soy, or safflower, or a blend. For a more pronounced flavor, a recipe may specify a specific oil, such as corn or olive oil. *Olive oils* vary greatly in flavor depending on the method of extraction and where the olives were grown. Italian olive oils are the finest in the world, with a complex and sophisticated flavor. French oils are fruitier, Spanish oils are a bit harsher, Greek oils are very strong, and California oils are hearty. Pressings from unripe olives make an oil with a deep green color, while ripe black olives press into a golden oil. Virgin or pure olive oils are the best for use in the recipes presented in this book. Save the savory extra-virgin oils for salads and sautéing. *Walnut, hazelnut, and almond oils* have a nutty essence that also works well in quick breads. The cold-pressed domestic varieties are gentler in flavor than the imported ones made from toasted nuts. Since oils are 100 percent fat, they cannot be substituted exactly for butter. Replace ⅓ cup butter (or margarine or solid vegetable shortening) with ¼ cup oil in recipes.

Poppy Seeds

Poppy seeds are a crunchy addition to quick breads and can range in color from a clear slate blue to blue-black, with a corresponding wide range of sweetnesses. In specialty stores, look for Dutch blue poppy seeds, as they are the highest quality and very sweet. Store the seeds in the freezer to prevent rancidity since, like nuts, they have a high oil content.

Pumpkins

The American pumpkin is a member of the large family of winter squash that is ready to eat during the fall months. The meaty flesh is a bright orange and sweetish in flavor. The cooked and pureed meat is an excellent addition to quick breads. Other winter squash, such as Blue Hubbard, Blue Kuri, Delicata, Butternut, Turban, or Acorn, can be prepared in the same manner as the following Fresh Pumpkin Puree and substituted for it in recipes, although each type of squash has its own distinct flavor. Commercial canned pumpkin is actually part Hubbard squash, which has a distinct sweet flavor and a low percentage of moisture.

Fresh Pumpkin Puree

About 1 pound raw pumpkin will yield about 1 cup puree

Wash a medium-sized sugar or other cooking pumpkin and cut off the top. Cut in half and then into large cubes, leaving the skin intact. Scoop out the seeds and fibers. Place flesh-down in a baking dish filled with about 1 inch of water. Cover and bake at 350°F for 1 to 1½ hours, or until tender. Let cool. Peel off and discard the skin. Puree the pulp until smooth in a blender, food mill, or food processor. Cool, cover, and refrigerate for up to 5 days or freeze for up to 9 months.

Pureeing

To puree fruits and vegetables, use the old-fashioned hand-crank machine known as a food mill, fitted with interchangeable fine, medium, and coarse discs used for pureeing. The 5½ inch-diameter model is all-purpose. A food mill is a good tool for straining raspberries of their seeds. Foods can also be pureed in a blender or food processor, pushed through a conical sieve known as a *chinois*, or pressed through a mesh sieve with the back of a spoon. For pureeing whole garlic and pieces of onion or shallot, the other tool not to be without is a garlic press.

Roasted Garlic

How to Roast Garlic

Brush one or more heads of garlic lightly with some olive or corn oil and loosely wrap in heavy-duty aluminum foil. Roast in a 400°F oven for 50 to 60 minutes or until the tip of a sharp knife pierces a clove with no resistance. Unwrap and let cool to room temperature. Snip the root end of each clove and gently squeeze out the pulp into a small bowl. Mash or stir the pulp. Alternatively, puree the pulp through a food mill. Cover and store in the refrigerator, for no longer than 2 days, for use in savory recipes or as a spread on crusty bread.

Roasted Peppers

The flavor of roasted peppers is exceptional in quick loaves, pancakes, and scones, and worth the time invested. Roasted red peppers are also available canned, but the flavor is not quite as exciting as fresh roasted red peppers. Serve roasted peppers on their own as an appetizer, on salads, or as an ingredient in other recipes.

How to Roast Peppers

Using tongs, hold red, green, or yellow bell peppers over a gas burner, place on a charcoal grill, or place under a broiler until the skin blisters and blackens. Turn often with tongs to roast evenly. Remove to a clean plastic bag and close. Let stand until cool. Scrape off the skin with a sharp knife and rinse the peppers under running water. Seed the peppers. This method is also suitable for roasting fresh hot chile peppers, but handle them carefully with kitchen gloves to protect your skin and eyes from the extremely volatile oils.

Salt

Iodized rock table salt and fine sea salt can be used interchangeably in recipes. Salt is a flavor enhancer in quick breads, but it is optional.

Seasoning a Waffle Iron or Pancake Griddle

New, uncoated electric and range-top waffle irons or griddles and cast-iron skillets require seasoning to prevent batters from sticking during baking. New equipment will come with the manufacturer's instructions for the best results. In case yours doesn't come with instructions, or if you need to reseason an iron or griddle, follow these directions: Preheat the iron or griddle to medium-high. Brush the entire surface, coating all grids, with vegetable oil. Heat the griddle or close the iron and heat just until smoking. Remove the griddle from the heat, or open the iron, and let stand until completely cool. Wipe the griddle or iron clean with a soft cloth or paper towel. The griddle or waffle iron is now ready for use. Discard the first set of waffles baked. If the waffles stick, clean the grids carefully with a damp cloth and reseason.

Shallots

The French *éschalote* is a flavor cross between an onion and garlic, has a delightfully delicate flavor, and can be used in savory pancake batters and sauces.

Sifting

Flour, cornstarch, or powdered sugar is aerated, leaveners are evenly distributed, and lumps are removed when dry ingredients are sifted through a mesh sieve. Recipes will specify this step, if necessary.

Sugar

Most quick bread recipes call for regular *granulated cane sugar* (sucrose) for sweetening, which also makes for a brown crust and tender crumb. *Superfine sugar* is very finely granulated and can be either purchased or made by processing regular granulated sugar in a food processor for 10 seconds. It is known as castor sugar in British recipes. *Coarse sugar* is known as decorator's sugar and is used for toppings. Crushed rock sugar or sugar cubes can also be used to create a sweet-crusted top layer. *Powdered sugar*, also known as confectioners' sugar, is perfect for glazes, sweetening whipped cream, and decoratively dusting baked sweet loaves. It works best if sifted. To make homemade powdered sugar, combine 1 cup granulated sugar with 1½ teaspoons cornstarch in a food processor for 1 minute. This mixture cannot be ground fine enough in a blender. *Brown sugar* has a moist texture because it is a combination of granulated sugar and molasses. I prefer light brown sugar in my recipes. Dark brown sugar has more molasses added than light brown sugar does. It can be used as an exact substitute for granulated sugar or light brown sugar, but the flavor is more assertive. It is important that you pack brown sugar when measuring it, as it contains a lot of air. It is known as demerara sugar in British recipes. *Fructose* is granulated high-fructose corn syrup and is often used as an alternative to regular sugar. It is the sugar found in fruits and honey. Because it is easier to digest and absorbed more slowly into the bloodstream than sucrose, it is good for hypoglycemics and diabetics. Fructose is about 60 percent sweeter than granulated sugar, so adjust amounts downward when adding it to recipes as a substitute for granulated sugar.

Sun-Dried Tomatoes

Roma tomatoes are the variety used for imported and domestic sun-dried tomatoes, which are available dehydrated and marinated in oil. I find the imported brands more salty to the palate, but many people prefer them to the excellent domestic brands, such as Timber Crest Farms and Mezzetta. Drain oil-packed dried tomatoes before using them. The dry-pack tomato slices need to be reconstituted in hot water for about 1 hour, then drained, before using as directed in recipes. Sun-dried tomatoes are very concentrated in flavor, so a few go a long way. Order sun-dried tomatoes from Timber Crest Farms, 4791 Dry Creek Road, Healdsburg, California 95448. Timber Crest Farms also sells a large variety of top-quality dried fruits and nuts by mail.

Syrups

Without a doubt, pancakes and waffles are just not quite right served without a rich, sweet syrup. Besides the incomparable pure maple syrup, there are numerous commercial brands of peach, apricot, raspberry, blueberry, blackberry, and ollalaberry syrups from which to choose. Molasses-based syrups are also popular. Lyle's Golden Syrup, also known as light treacle, is pale yellow and thick, with a honeylike consistency and a unique taste that sings of British baking. Pure cane syrup, also known as golden refiner's syrup, is domestically available from C. S. Steen Syrup Mill, Inc., P. O. Box 339, Abbeville, Louisiana 70510. Many cottage industries specialize in fruit syrups, such as the superb honeyberry syrups from Oregon Apiaries, available in specialty foods stores. This book contains many recipes for outstanding homemade syrups, including whole blueberry and apple cider, that you will find indispensable.

Fruit Syrup

In contrast to commercial brands, homemade fruit syrup is less sweet and the fruit flavor more pronounced, as with homemade jams. The process is very easy and is not messy. Enjoy favorite fruit combinations such as boysenberry-raspberry, kumquat-cranberry, fig-orange, apricot-pineapple, or peach-plum. The addition of the pectin is important in this recipe to retain a bright, clear fruit color after cooking.

Makes about 1 quart syrup

3½ to 4 cups fresh fruit pieces, such as strawberries, blueberries, or raspberries; peeled, pitted, and chopped apricots, peaches, Santa Rosa plums, purple prune-plums, or mangoes; 1 pound kumquats (discard the seeds and end pieces; the skin is edible); 1 pound cherries, pitted; or 25 fresh figs
½ cup fresh lemon juice
One 1.75- or 2-ounce package powdered pectin
1 cup water
1 cup light corn syrup
1 to 1½ cups sugar, or to taste

In a food processor, puree the fruit and lemon juice until smooth. Place in a glass or ceramic bowl and stir in the pectin. Let stand at room temperature for 30 minutes. Place in a deep non-aluminum saucepan and add the water, corn syrup, and sugar to taste, stirring with a large whisk. Place over medium-high heat and bring to a boil. Reduce heat slightly and cook until the sugar is dissolved and a candy thermometer reaches 160°F to 170°F. The mixture will come to a very low boil and a thin layer of foam will coat the surface. Skim off the foam. Cool the syrup to lukewarm and pour into a clean glass storage jar. The syrup will thicken slightly when cooled and

chilled. Store, covered tightly, in the refrigerator for up to 4 months.

Unmolding

To prevent sogginess, baked quick breads must be turned out of their hot pans to cool on racks. If a quick bread sticks, run a knife around the edges to loosen, or avoid the problem by lining pans with pieces of parchment paper before baking or by greasing and flouring the pans.

Whipping

Whipping is the process of incorporating air into a mixture by beating in a vigorous circular motion with a whisk or an electric mixer until fluffy. But if ingredients such as cream are overbeaten, the protein walls will break down, making butter and whey out of the cream.

Wild Rice

Delicious by itself or in combination with other rices, wild rice has a strong woodsy flavor and a chewy texture. Wild rice is an excellent addition to quick breads, scones, muffins, and pancakes. It is not really a rice, but the seed of an aquatic grass native to the Great Lakes region. Wild rice is known as the "gourmet grain," and each brand of wild rice has its own particular taste, so if you have experienced a brand that was too husky for your palate, experiment with others. For a milder taste, look for varieties labeled as hand-harvested on the package. They are a tell-tale gray-green in color and are known for their delicate flavor. Although some wild rice is still harvested by hand by Native Americans in the traditional manner, most is now cultivated in man-made paddies, with California being the biggest producer. Clearlake and Sutter County, California, produce good brands known by their dark, shiny kernels. They are readily available in supermarkets. Teals Super Valu, P.O. Box 660, Cass Lake, Minnesota 56633, is a good source for traditional hand-harvested wild rice, and Gibbs Wild Rice, P.O. Box 277, Dear River, Minnesota 56636, is a good source for excellent, mild-flavored, paddy-grown wild rice.

How To Cook Wild Rice

The ideal texture of cooked rice is a personal preference, so adjust the following cooking directions to suit your taste. For a crunchy rice, cook for less time, until the kernels just start to open. For a tender, fluffy version with the kernels popped open, cook a bit longer with about ¼ to ½ cup more water.

Makes 1½ to 2 cups cooked rice

In a medium saucepan, bring 1½ cups water to a rolling boil over high heat. Add ¾ cup wild rice. Return to a rolling boil. Cover tightly and reduce heat to low. Cook paddy-cultivated rice for 55 minutes, and hand-harvested rice for 30 minutes, or until the rice is tender and all the liquid has been absorbed. Set aside to cool. The cooked rice can be refrigerated for up to 3 days or frozen for up to 6 months.

Kitchen Equipment

Bakeware

Always use the best-quality bakeware for baking quick breads. Quality bakeware is a satisfying lifetime investment. The best bakeware is made of heavy-duty aluminum, which makes a big difference in absorbing, retaining, and distributing heat during baking. I also use the disposable/reusable aluminum loaf pans that are available in the supermarket with excellent success. Chicago Metallic is the stalwart commercial brand of the restaurant industry. If you have a large oven, Chicago Metallic's popover frames with 20 cups, mini-loaf frames with 12 sections, bread pan straps in sets of four muffin and cluster roll frames with 24 sections, and Mary Ann frames with 12 or 24 sections are top of the line. One of my favorite brands of nonstick pans is Kaiser, a German brand featuring a silicon coating. I especially like Kaiser's fluted *kugelhopf* (also known as *gupelhopf* in Britain or *gugelhupf* in Germany), the scalloped turk's cap molds with sloping, patterned sides and a center tunnel for even baking; the 11-by-4-inch braided loaf pan; the 8-inch square pan with deep handles; and the springform pans. Many springform pans come with an interchangeable section that transforms it into an attractive fluted ring mold. Half-loaf pans, sold in pairs, bake unique, ridged, half-moon-shaped loaves. Other unusual baking pans for your quick breads are miniature loaf pans, heart-shaped terra cotta loaf pans, king-sized crown muffin pans, cast-iron loaf pans, baby Bundtlette pans, 1- and 2-quart fluted tin molds with clip lids for making steamed breads, and borosilica glass pans that can be used in recipes calling for 1-pound or 2-pound coffee cans (all available from the King Arthur Baker's Catalogue).

Different sizes and shapes give quick breads their unique characters. For the best results, always use the pan size indicated in a recipe, to avoid flat tops or overflowing batters. Fill pans no more than half to two-thirds full, leaving room for expansion. If you are substituting another shape, be certain the pan holds the same volume of batter. Smaller pans need less baking time, so adjust the baking time accordingly. Pans with dark finishes and Pyrex pans brown breads faster, so reduce the oven temperature by 25°F when using them. Glass, lightweight, or burned bakeware conduct heat in an uneven manner. Excellent mail-order sources for specialty bakeware are Sweet Celebrations, P. O. Box 39426, Edina, Minnesota 55439; and the King Arthur Flour Baker's Catalogue, P. O. Box 876, Norwich, Vermont 05055.

The following chart gives the amount of batter that will fill each pan, rather than the total volume of the pan.

Round Cake and Springform Pans (2½ inches deep)

- 6-inch pan holds 2 cups batter
- 8-inch pan holds 4 cups batter
- 9-inch pan holds 5 cups batter
- 10-inch pan holds 7½ cups batter
- 12-inch pan holds 9 cups batter
- 14-inch pan (deep pizza pan) holds 14 cups batter
- 11-by-1½-inch scalloped Swiss rosette pan holds 4 cups batter
- 11-by-2½-inch pleated celebration pan holds 8 cups batter
- Two 8-inch or 9-inch round pans will fill one 13-by-9½-by-2-inch or 15½-by-10½-by-1-inch rectangular pan

Square and Rectangular Pans (2½ Inches Deep)

- 8-inch pan holds 3½ cups batter

- 9-inch pan holds 4 cups batter
- 10-inch pan holds 6 cups batter
- 12-inch pan holds 9 cups batter
- 13-by-9½-inch pan holds 9 cups batter

Loaf Pans

- 4-by-2½-by-2-inch loaf pan holds ¾ cup batter
- 6-by-3-by-3-inch loaf pan holds 1½ cups batter
- 7½-by-3½-by-3-inch loaf pan holds 2½ cups batter
- 8½-by-4½-by-2½-inch loaf pan holds 3 cups batter
- 9½-by-5¼-by-3-inch loaf pan holds 4 cups batter
- 11-by-4-by-3-inch braided loaf pan holds 5½ cups batter
- One 9½-by-5¼-by-3-inch loaf pan will fill one 9-inch square pan or one 6-inch charlotte mold
- One 8½-by-4½-by-2½-inch loaf pan will fill one 8-inch square pan

Half-Loaf Pans

- 8-by-4½-by-2-inch half-loaf pan holds 2½ cups batter
- 12-by-4½-by-2-inch half-loaf pan holds 4 cups batter

Heart-Shaped Pans
(2½ Inches Deep)
- 3½-inch individual heart mold holds ⅓ cup batter
- 6½-inch heart pan holds 2¾ cups batter
- 9-inch heart pan holds 4¾ cups batter
- 12-inch heart pan holds 9 cups batter

Muffin Tins
- 1⅝- to 2-by-¾-inch miniature muffin cup holds 2 tablespoons batter
- 2¾-by-1¼-inch standard muffin cup holds ⅓ cup batter
- 3¼-by-l-inch oversized muffin cup holds ½ cup batter

Charlotte Molds
- 6¼-inch round mold (size 16) holds 4 cups batter
- 7-inch round mold (size 18) holds 6 cups batter

Brioche Molds
- 3-inch individual brioche mold holds 3 tablespoons batter
- 5-inch brioche mold holds ⅔ cup batter
- 7-inch brioche mold holds 2½ cups batter

Tube Pans
- 3¼-inch individual *savarin* ring mold holds 3 tablespoons batter
- 4-inch fluted Bundtlette pan holds ¾ cup batter
- 6-by-1½-inch fluted tube pan holds 1½ cups batter
- 6½-inch fluted *kugelhopf* mold holds 3½ cups batter
- 7-by-6½-inch pannetone tube mold holds 8 cups batter
- 8-inch fluted Bundt pan holds 3 cups batter
- 8-inch plain tube pan holds 5 cups batter
- 8¾-inch fluted *kugelhopf* mold holds 6 cups batter
- 10-inch plain tube pan holds 10 cups batter
- 10-inch fluted Bundt pan (12-cup mold) holds 9 cups batter
- 10-inch fluted *kugelhopf* mold holds 9 cups batter
- 12-inch tube pan holds 16 cups batter
- Two 9½-by-5¼-by-3-inch loaf pans or one 13-by-9½-by-2-inch pan fills one 10-inch tube pan

Baking Sheets
An important piece of equipment for baking scones, biscuits, and any free-form quick bread, a standard-size,

good-quality aluminum baking sheet is 15 by 10 inches with a ¾- to 1-inch-high rim. Half-sheet cake pans are 18 by 12 inches and are available in restaurant supply stores. Chicago Metallic and Leyse Toro are the best brands of professional heavy-weight aluminum baking sheets and pans. Baking sheets are also available in air-cushioned and nonstick types. Baking sheets are not the same as a jelly-roll pan, which must be 15 by 10 by 1 inches, preferably with a nonstick surface.

Cake Tester

A cake tester is a straight, firm wire with a looped end for grasping that is inserted into the center of a loaf or muffin to test for doneness. If the tester pulls out clean, the quick bread or cake is done baking. If it has batter or some crumbs attached, bake the bread or cake for another 5 to 10 minutes and then retest with a clean tester. Toothpicks, thin knives, and bamboo skewers can be used in the same manner.

Cheesecloth

Cheesecloth is an inexpensive, porous, lightweight, finely woven natural cotton gauze designed for wrapping foods to maintain their shape, or for straining liquids. It is an essential piece of equip-ment in a well-stocked baker's kitchen: It drains homemade cheeses, molds multilayered cheese tortas, wraps mulling spices and herb bouquets, and slowly soaks fruitcakes and quick breads in spirited essences. Cheesecloth is available in supermarkets and cook-ware stores.

Cooling Racks

Wire or wood cooling racks come in a variety of sizes and in round, square, or large rectangular shapes. They are used to slightly elevate hot baked goods to allow for even circulation of air around them during cooling, preventing sogginess.

Danish Dough Whisk

The Danish dough whisk, a *brofpisker*, is a 15-inch-long hand-mixing utensil specifically designed for the delicate mixing of quick batters, especially quick loaves, cornbreads, muffins, and pancake batters. With its sturdy wooden handle, it looks like a cross between a large wooden spoon and a flat wire whisk. The thick wire loop pattern mixes as well as cleans the sides of the bowl efficiently. Imported exclusively by the King Arthur Flour Baker's Catalogue, this tool is indespensible if you make a lot of quick breads.

Electric Mixers

All quick breads can be made with the aid of a heavy-duty electric mixer, as they are powerful and efficient machines. They come with an aluminum mixing bowl, a whisk for whipping, a flat paddle for general beating, and a dough hook for yeast breads. I use a Kitchen Aid stationary model K45. Small hand-held or old-fashioned stand mixers are not strong enough for mixing most quick bread doughs and may quickly overheat. Use them for small jobs, such as whipping cream or egg whites.

Food Processor

The food processor is a very efficient kitchen tool, especially for grating, grinding, and pureeing foods. It has a plastic workbowl that holds 4, 7, or 10 cups of dry ingredients, and is fitted with a sharp steel blade. The speed of the blade is controlled by pulsing or a quick whirl. The blade should be handled with care and never be touched or disassembled until the machine is at a full stop. The problem with most food processors is that overprocessing can occur very quickly, creating a very fine puree or powder. However, when used properly, this is a machine the baker will greatly appreciate. I use a Robot Coupe, which is made by the French company that originally manufactured Cuisinart and the KitchenAid ultra power KFP600. If you do not own a food processor, the mandoline is the traditional hand tool that does many of the same shredding jobs.

Measuring Cups

In the United States, the standardized measures for calibrated nested dry-ingredient measuring cups are ¼-, ⅓-, ½-, and 1-cup capacities. These cups are the most accurate for dry measuring of flour and sugar. They are available in stainless steel or plastic. Measuring cups for liquid ingredients have a lip for easy pouring and graduated amounts marked on the cup. They are available in glass or plastic. Please use the dry measures for dry ingredients and the liquid measures for liquids, as they are not interchangeable.

Ovens

It is essential that your oven thermostat be calibrated to the proper temperature. Also, for some reason, a clean oven bakes best. Whatever pans you are using, especially when you're using baking sheets, there should always be a minimum of 1 inch of space around the pans to allow for heat circulation around all sides for even baking. Stagger baking sheets on separate racks when more than one is in use, with the bottom pan doubled to protect the bottom of the baked goods from browning too quickly. Rearrange pans halfway through baking, if necessary. Always preheat the oven for 15 minutes before baking, since batters will react poorly in cool ovens (some popover recipes are the exception to this). Use an auxiliary oven thermometer to be sure your thermostat is accurate. Use heavy-duty insulated oven mitts for secure handling of hot pans. I especially like larger mitts designed for barbecue cookery, because they provide the best protection of the wrists and lower arms. Many bakers prefer *convection ovens* for baking, which circulate the heat with a fan, providing an even temperature throughout the oven, unlike standard ovens, which can have hot spots. Convection ovens are popular in professional bakeries, but the professional models bake differently than the home models do—they tend to bake much more evenly. If you bake in a convection oven, quick breads are apt to bake more quickly and dry out, so reduce the oven temperature by 25°F to 50°F

and reduce baking times by 10 to 15 minutes. Please consult the manufacturer's literature accompanying your oven for precise directions. Bread will rise, but not brown, when baked in a *microwave oven*, so it is not advisable to bake bread in a microwave oven. You may heat breads in a microwave oven; the heating times will vary according to the power of the oven.

Pancake Griddles

If you make pancakes regularly, consider investing in a griddle specifically designed for the job. Griddles are also good for cooking tortillas, eggs, French toast, blintzes, and homemade English muffins. *Electric griddles* as well as waffle irons with a reversible grill/grid are very popular as backups to stovetop cooking. Many professional ranges used in home kitchens come with an optional family-sized steel griddle attachment built into the top of the stove. *Stovetop griddles* are usually thick and flat, round or square with a shallow rim, and from 9 to 14 inches wide. For making larger quantities, there are long, rectangular or oval griddles that fit over two burners, often made of heavy black cast aluminum or soapstone. *Soapstone griddles* are made of nonporous, acid-resistant greyish stone that retains heat and needs no greasing. They are aesthetically rimmed in a thin band of copper and have small handles. They are available in 10- and 12-inch rounds and 13-by-9-inch or 20-by-10-inch oval shapes from Vermont Soapstone Company, Box 168, Perkinsville, Vermont 05151. They are a lifetime investment and cost no more than a good saucepan. For directions on how to season your pancake griddle, see Seasoning a Waffle Iron or Pancake Griddle (page 352). *Specialized pans used to create uncommon pancakes* include individual 4-inch blini pans; crêpe pans with flat bottoms of seasoned rolled steel in sizes from 5 to 8½ inches; shallow 11- to 15-inch-diameter Breton crêpe pans for thin buckwheat crêpes; and the cast-iron plett for making seven 3-inch, thin-battered Swedish pancakes or blini at the same time. Nonstick coated skillets or sauté pans need to be used with care as some cannot withstand the high heat needed for making pancakes, and the nonstick coating can disintegrate over time.

Parchment Paper

Parchment paper is a nonporous, silicone-treated paper used for lining pans and preventing baked goods from sticking. Baking pans do not need to be greased if parchment paper is used. It is available in rolls in most supermarkets. It is not the same as waxed paper, which is coated with paraffin and is highly flammable.

Pastry Brushes

Flat or round pastry brushes with soft natural bristles are available in a variety of sizes from ½ to 3 inches wide. They are indispensable for applying glazes, greasing pans, and dusting doughs.

Pastry Scraper

The all-purpose pastry scraper is made of metal or flexible plastic. It is a rectangular blade with a wood or plastic handle, and it is used for scraping work surfaces clean, as a straightedge for cutting dough, or as a spatula, bowl scraper, or spreader. I label it a hand extension, because it does many jobs the outer edge of the hand can perform.

Pastry Wheel and Dough Cutters

A pastry wheel, made of metal with a wooden handle, is used for cutting dough. The pastry wheel is rolled along the dough as it rests on a work surface. Hand-held metal dough cutters come in various simple shapes with a raised handle. They are made in the shapes of the playing card suits, as well as hearts, rounds, squares, and triangles, and are used to form quick dough breads, such as biscuits and scones, into individual decorative shapes. Also look for special shapes, such as a half-moon. Pastry wheels and metal cutters both come with smooth or zigzag edges.

Rolling Pins

I use a heavy 28-inch ball bearing–loaded hardwood rolling pin made by Rowoco for its smooth, even rolling action. Since a rolling pin is perhaps one of the most personal staples in a cook's *batterie de cuisine*, choose one that feels right for you. They are available in a variety of shapes and sizes. I never use marble or ceramic models, as I find their qualities are overrated and they are not wide enough or long enough.

Ruler

For general pastry and quick bread making, keep a flat metal ruler or retractable tape measure in the utility drawer for measuring doughs when cutting and shaping, as well as for checking pan sizes.

Serrated Knife

A serrated knife is a long knife with a sawtooth edge that makes a clean cut through delicate breads and pastries without tearing or squashing. Use one with an 8-inch blade, and always use an easy back-and-forth sawing motion when slicing breads. A fiddle-bow bread knife is a serrated blade set into a fiddle bow–shaped frame, which acts as a guide for uniform slicing. Handmade cherry-wood fiddle bows for left- or right-handed slicers are available from The Wooden Spoon, P. O. Box 931, Clinton, Connecticut 06413 or the King Arthur Flour Baker's Catalogue.

Spatulas

Spatulas are another indispensable kitchen tool, used for scraping and mixing doughs. Made of flexible rubber and plastic, they come in a variety of shapes. The large, oversized spatulas, used extensively by professional bakers, are a wonderful tool. Hard plastic spatulas are made especially for use with the food processor. Metal icing spatulas are for frosting but are also excellent for spreading doughs evenly. Wide metal or heat-proof plastic spatulas are useful for removing pieces of coffee cake or loosening baked goods and transferring them to serving dishes.

Timer

A kitchen timer to remind you that there is something in the oven is invaluable, even for the most seasoned baker. They are available in good kitchen and hardware emporiums.

Waffle Irons

Modern electric waffle irons are designed to cook both honeycombed sides of a waffle simultaneously, fast and evenly. Different models form waffles in the shapes of rectangles (which break into two 6-by-5-inch waffles), rounds (a 6½-inch round that breaks into four sections), squares (which break into four 3½- to 4½-inch small squares), or lobed rounds (a 6¼-inch round that breaks into five individual hearts). Waffle irons are usually made from cast aluminum with plain or nonstick grids in regular and exaggerated Belgian styles. Stovetop nonelectric models with heatproof handles make four 3½-inch squares for both waffle styles. The plain grids need to be seasoned before use, but the nonstick, easy-release surfaces are so efficient, they eliminate the need for seasoning. It is important to grease both grid types before pouring in the batter to save yourself from the ordeal of prying the waffle out of the maker and the subsequent messy cleanup. On electric models, built-in thermostats signal when the iron is hot, usually about 7 minutes after turning it on, as well as when the waffle is done, after about 4 minutes of cooking. Many models have the grids permanently set into their frames, but others snap out for easy washing and reverse to form a flat griddle for grilling sandwiches and making pancakes or a *pizelle* Italian cookie mold. All models carry 1- to 3-year warranties and are readily available in hardware, department, and cookware stores. Good brands include Black and Decker, Rowenta, Toastmaster, Oster, Nordic Ware, and Vitantonio. For information about how to season your waffle iron, see Techniques, page 352.

Whisks and Other Utensils

Whisks are an important part of a properly equipped kitchen. They range in dimension from finger-sized, for beating one egg yolk, to 12-inch balloon, for beating liquid batters and egg whites. Use stainless steel with a metal or wooden handle for the most agility. Wooden spoons, metal spoons, heatproof plastic spoons, zesters, graters, ladles, a pizza cutter, biscuit cutters in a variety of sizes, and a good pair of kitchen shears are also good basic elements in a well-equipped kitchen.

Index

$17.95

*"A truly wonderful collection
of quick and easy recipes.
Breads and muffins and
cakes—yes. But also a great
variety. These recipes will keep
you happy for a long time."*

—**MAIDA HEATTER**
author of *Maida Heatter's
Book of Great Desserts* and
Maida Heatter's Cakes

With *The Best Quick Breads*, a busy schedule no longer stands in the way of fresh baked goods. Most of the recipes can be prepared in a hurry—in less time than it takes to run to the corner bakery. This new collection of recipes from Beth Hensperger, 100 of them from her much-loved *The Art of Quick Breads* (now out-of-print) plus 50 brand-new creations, has favorite fare for breakfast on the run, lazy Sunday morning repasts, and elegant holiday brunches. A delightful array of savory recipes brings quick breads into all the meals of the day. Beyond the 150 breads, there are recipes for flavored syrups, sweet and savory sauces, and fresh jams and curds to add extra elegance when the occasion calls for it.

*"Beth Hensperger brings us a collection of delightfully simple
quick breads. Here are scores of recipes, both sweet and
savory, that are easy enough to make on a weekday and delicious enough to serve at any meal, from a casual family breakfast to a have-friends-in Sunday supper. This is the kind of
book that earns a permanent place on the kitchen bookshelf."*

—**DORIE GREENSPAN**
author of *Baking with Julia* and *Waffles*

*"Just when you thought it had all been said and done,
Beth Hensperger comes along with a collection of quick
breads that looks utterly enticing, fresh, and new,
yet happily familiar."*

—**DEBORAH MADISON**
author of *Vegetarian Cooking for Everyone* and *The Savory Way*

*"Not only is Beth's book packed with delectable recipes,
but it provides useful information on timing, techniques,
and baking pans. With this book you will never run out
of ideas for delicious goodies."*

—**AMY SCHERBER**
author of *Amy's Breads* and owner of Amy's Breads,
New York City

Beth Hensperger is the author of *The Bread Lover's Bread Machine Cookbook* and the James Beard Book Award–winning *The Bread Bible*, as well as eight other books on baking bread. She writes the column "Baking with the Seasons" for the *San Jose Mercury News*.

Easy and quick...

Lemon–Poppy Seed Bread

Fresh Apple Coffee Cake

Banana Waffles

Buttermilk Cherry Scones

Oat Scones

Orange–Chocolate Chip Muffins

Black Olive and
Goat Cheese Muffins

Skillet Cornbread with Walnuts

Mushroom Oven Pancake
with Chive Sauce

Classic Crêpes

Butternut Squash Gnocchi
with Sage Butter

Chocolate Gingerbread with
Bittersweet Glaze

*...piping hot
and delicious!*

Harvard Common Press
*535 Albany Street
Boston, Massachusetts 02118*

www.harvardcommonpress.com

Distributed by
National Book Network
*4720 Boston Way
Lanham, Maryland 20706*

Cover design by Night & Day Design · Cover photographs by Joyce Oudkerk Pool

ISBN 1-55832-171-3